Rich Dad's
ADVISORS ™□

My poor dad often said, "What you know is important." My rich dad said, "If you want to be rich, *who* you know is more important than *what* you know." Rich dad explained further, saying, "Business and investing is a team sport. The average investor or small-business person loses financially because they do not have a team. Instead of a team, they act as individuals who are trampled by very smart teams." That is why the Rich Dad's Advisors book series was born. Rich Dad's Advisors will guide you to help you know who to look for and what questions to ask so you can go out and gather your own great team of advisors.

Robert T. Kiyosaki

Author of the *New York Times* Bestsellers
Rich Dad Poor Dad™
Rich Dad's CASHFLOW Quadrant™
Rich Dad's Guide to Investing™
and *Rich Dad's Rich Kid Smart Kid*™

Rich Dad's™ Classics

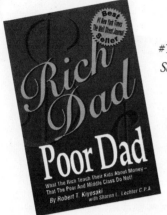

#1 *New York Times,* #1 *Wall Street Journal,*
#1 *Business Week,* #1 *Publishers Weekly,* as well as a
San Francisco Chronicle and *USA Today* bestseller.
Also featured on the bestseller lists of
Amazon.com, Amazon.com UK and Germany,
E-trade.com, *Sydney Morning Herald* (Australia),
Sun Herald (Australia), *Business Review Weekly*
(Australia), Borders Books and Music (U.S. and
Singapore), and Barnes & Noble.com.

Wall Street Journal, New York Times
business, and *Business Week* bestseller.
Also featured on the bestseller lists of the
Sydney Morning Herald (Australia), *Sun
Herald* (Australia), *Business Review Weekly*
(Australia), and Amazon.com, Barnes &
Noble.com, Borders Books and Music
(U.S. and Singapore).

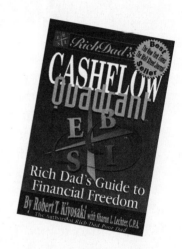

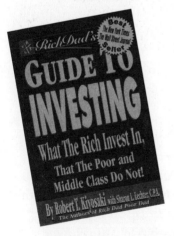

*USA Today, Wall Street Journal, New York
Times* business, *Business Week,* and
Publishers Weekly bestseller.

Wall Street Journal, New York Times,
and *USA Today* bestseller.

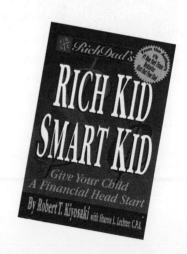

Rich Dad's Advisors™ Series

Rich Dad said,
"Business and Investing is a team sport."

Each of us has a million-dollar idea in our head. The first step in turning your idea into millions, maybe even billions of dollars, is to protect that idea. Michael Lechter is an internationally known intellectual property attorney who is Robert Kiyosaki's legal advisor on all his intellectual property matters. His book is simply written and is an important addition to any businessperson's library.

Loopholes of the Rich is for the aspiring as well as the advanced business owner who is looking for better and smarter ways to legally pay less tax and protect his or her assets. It gives real solutions that will be easy to apply to your unique situation. Diane Kennedy offers over twenty years of experience in research, application, and creation of innovative tax solutions and is Robert Kiyosaki's personal and corporate tax strategist.

Your most important skill in business is your ability to communicate and sell! SalesDogs™ is a highly educational, inspirational, and somewhat "irreverent" look at the world of sales, communications, and the different characters that occupy that world. All of us sell in one way or another. It is important for you to find your own unique style. Blair Singer is respected internationally as an extraordinary trainer, speaker, and consultant in the fields of sales, communication, and management.

Rich Dad's
ADVISORS™

Protecting Your

#1 Asset

Creating Fortunes from Your Ideas
An Intellectual Property Handbook

MICHAEL A. LECHTER, ESQ.
INTELLECTUAL PROPERTY ATTORNEY

WARNER
BUSINESS
BOOKS™

Published by Warner Books

An AOL Time Warner Company

Warner Books Edition

Copyright © 1994, 2001 by Michael A. Lechter, Esq.
Portions of this book were previously published as *The Intellectual Property Handbook* by Techpress, Inc., in 1994.
All rights reserved.

Published by Warner Books in association with CASHFLOW Technologies, Inc., and BI Capital, Inc.

CASHFLOW, Rich Dad, and Rich Dad's Advisors are trademarks of CASHFLOW Technologies, Inc.

 is a trademark of
CASHFLOW Technologies, Inc.

"From Ideas to Assets" and "Building Forts and Fighting Pirates" are service marks of Michael A. Lechter.

 Warner Business Books are published by Warner Books, Inc.,
1271 Avenue of the Americas, New York, NY 10020
The Warner Business Book logo is a trademark of Warner Books, Inc.

Visit our Web site at www.twbookmark.com.

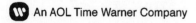 An AOL Time Warner Company

Printed in the United States of America

First Printing: June 2001
10 9 8 7 6 5 4

Library of Congress Card Number: 2001089567
ISBN: 0-446-67831-7

Designed by imagesupport.com, llc

Acknowledgments

I gratefully acknowledge the support and assistance of my lovely and dynamic wife, Sharon Lechter, without whom this book would not have come together, and my good friend Robert Kiyosaki for his suggestions and the foreword to this book. I also acknowledge the folks at Warner Books for making the process of publishing this book an enjoyable experience, in particular: Larry Kirshbaum for his abiding interest in intellectual property, Rick Wolff and Maureen Egen for their valued support and guidance, Carol Ross for her patience with my often hectic schedule, and Mari Okuda for putting up with my grammatical idiosyncrasies.

Contents

Foreword

In 1975 I began building a company to manufacture and market the first nylon-and-Velcro surfer wallets. I did not listen to my rich dad's advice. I did not protect my company's ideas.

In 1977 I designed the "Shoe Pocket," which was a tiny nylon wallet that attached to the laces of a runner's shoes. Again, I did not listen to my rich dad's advice. I did not protect my ideas.

Early in 1978 my little "Shoe Pocket" took the sporting goods market by storm. This little product was featured in *Runner's World* magazine, *Gentleman's Quarterly,* even *Playboy.* Orders poured in from all over the United States and the world. We were soon taking in millions of dollars in orders for our product.

Late in 1978, at the Sporting Goods Trade Show in Los Angeles, all my *competitors* were selling my Shoe Pockets as well as my wallets. They flooded the market with my products. I was out of business in 1979. That was the price of not listening to my rich dad's advice.

In 1994, after designing my board game CASHFLOW 101, the first person I contacted was Michael Lechter, the author of this book. Before telling anyone else about my ideas, I finally followed my rich dad's advice and *first* found a patent attorney who could protect my ideas.

Today Michael Lechter is my friend; my legal advisor; the husband of my business partner and co-author of my books, Sharon Lechter; and the protector of my company's ideas.

Learning from My Mistakes

Today people are often shocked to hear me say "Losing my first big business was the best experience of my life." The reason it was a great experience was because I learned so much about myself and how much I did not know. I often say "Failure is part of success. People who avoid failure also avoid success." There were many things I learned from my first big failure . . . and one of the things I learned was the importance of protecting my ideas.

Life is an interesting event. When I look back on my first big business loss, the loss may have been avoided *if* I had listened to my rich dad's advice. Yet I think losing that business was part of my destiny. Not listening to rich dad way back then taught me a priceless lesson: the value of our ideas. If not for that financial disaster, I would never have fully appreciated how rich each and every one of us really is. We are all rich because we are all blessed with a mind—a mind full of ideas. If not for that business failure, I would never have come to realize that my number one asset is *not* my home, my money, or my investments. I now know that my number one asset is my mind and the ideas that come from my mind. I now know to respect my ideas and to protect them. I believe that each and every one of us has an idea that has the potential to make you and your family wealthier beyond your wildest dreams. But before that wealth can happen, you must protect your idea. As rich dad said to me, I now say to you, "Protect your number one asset. Protect your ideas."

Einstein Was Right

Rich dad loved Albert Einstein's statement:

"Imagination is more important than knowledge."

Rich dad loved that statement for many reasons. One reason was because he never finished school. For a while he felt inferior to those people who did complete school. After reading Einstein's statement on imagination, rich dad realized that he had become wealthier than many highly educated people simply because many educated people had knowledge but very little imagination. Another reason rich dad loved Einstein's thought was because he realized that *knowledge was limited* and *imagination was infinite.* Many times when rich dad got in trouble financially, he would say to his son and me, "When I get into tough financial binds, I call on my imagination to get me out of the mess I am in. It is the use of my imagination that makes me rich and enriches my life."

Protect Your #1 Asset

I am honored to have Michael Lechter allow his book to be a part of the Rich Dad's Advisors series of books. In 1994 I sought him out because of his reputation as one of the most respected attorneys in America on the subject of intellectual property.

For those of you who may not be familiar with the term "intellectual property," please take a moment to study the two words. Notice the word "property." One of the reasons I had trouble listening to rich dad's advice years ago was because to me the word "property" meant something *tangible*—something like a house or car or my TV. Back then I understood protecting my tangible property but I did not understand the importance of protecting my ideas—my intellectual property. In other words, back in the 1970s I did not think my ideas were valuable, I did not think of my ideas as my property, and that is why I did not listen to my rich dad's advice and protect them.

Today I know better. I have always known that it is important to lock my house and lock my car to protect my *tangible properties* from being stolen. After losing a multimillion-dollar business, today I now know that it is as important, if not *more* important, to also protect my *intellectual property.*

We are now in the Information Age and in the Information Age your ideas are even more valuable. So use this book as a guide to protect your #1 asset and alway keep rich dad's advice in mind.

**"YOUR FORTUNES WILL COME FROM YOUR IDEAS.
SO PROTECT YOUR IDEAS."**

ROBERT KIYOSAKI

AUDIO DOWNLOAD

In each of our books we like to provide an audio interview as a bonus with additional insights. As a thank-you to you for reading this book, you may go to the Web site www.richdad.com/advisors.

Thank you for your interest in your financial education.

Introduction

You are a creative person. You have great ideas. You find solutions to problems and come up with better ways of doing things. You put a lot of thought and effort into building a business and work hard to develop a reputation for quality and good service in the minds of your customers. You have created a lot of potentially valuable "intellectual property." So how can you use this to your advantage? How can you take your thoughts and efforts from mind to money?

What is "intellectual property"? It is a term much bandied about in these days of the Internet and the new economy. It is something that every successful business, whether they know it or not, builds and accumulates. This is true whether the business is part of the new economy or a traditional business, and whether the business is high-tech or low-tech. Intellectual property is something that every business should consciously protect.

Two Basic IP Issues
- Maximize return on investment
  —Identify, create, and preserve potentially exploitable IP assets
  —Erect sustainable barriers to completion
- Minimize risk of third-party claims

The term "intellectual property" covers a broad gamut of intangible assets. These assets are widely recognized to include patents, copyrights, mask works, and trademarks. Intellectual property, however, also comprises such things as trade dress, goodwill, and reputation, as well as expertise, data, know-how, and other information regarding technology and business subjects (such as management and operations, marketing and sales). It can be the collective knowledge and expertise of a company, or that of individual employees.

Creating and maintaining rights in such intellectual property, and avoiding infringement of the intellectual property rights of others, are becoming increasingly important aspects of any business. This is particularly true with small and emerging businesses. To survive in the marketplace you have to be able to deal with a spectrum of different types of competition. In particular, you must contend with three types of competition that I refer to as "Big Boys," "Spoilers," and "Pirates."

The Big Boys are competitors with market power. Typically they have vast economic resources, and can call on marketing departments, R&D budgets, and sales forces. They can take advantage of the economy of scale, and often have cheap labor available. They typically have established distribution channels, relationships, and customer goodwill. While the Big Boys will be very careful not to infringe your legitimate intellectual property rights, they will take advantage of any weakness in those rights, and will try to crush you with their money and market power.

The "Spoilers" are competitors who introduce less expensive, lower-quality versions of your product into the marketplace. They can erode your prices and, sometimes, where the quality of their product is particularly low, destroy the market. A Spoiler will tend to put on blinders with respect to your intellectual property rights, but will respect legitimate intellectual property rights when confronted.

Then there are the "Pirates." These are the unscrupulous folks who will disregard your intellectual property rights and consciously copy your product and/or create confusion in the marketplace, palming off their products as yours or making consumers think that the Pirate is somehow associated with or sponsored or endorsed by you. They will tend to appropriate your investment in your product and goodwill until you force them to stop.

Of course, in the real world, your competitors will probably not fit cleanly into any of these categories. There are typically a few "pure" Big Boys and "pure" Spoilers in most markets. Luckily, there are relatively few "pure" Pirates; many more businesses are legitimate than not, and most will respect the legitimate rights of others. For the most part, you will face competition that exhibits a mix of Big Boy, Spoiler, and Pirate characteristics. For example, a competitor who is primarily a Spoiler in that they are more concerned with low cost than quality, may have a Big Boy marketplace advantage, such as the availability of cheap labor or established distribution channels. Likewise, a market giant may not have any compunction at all about copying the unique aspects of your product and attempting to capitalize on your goodwill if they perceive any weakness in your intellectual property protection.

How can a small business realistically compete head-to-head in the marketplace with the Big Boys? It can be done. For example, a small business can successfully compete by having a unique or better product or some specific special expertise or know-how. A competitor's market power can also be counteracted by having a better (more economical or faster) way of doing things or perhaps by having a good reputation and establishing strong customer goodwill. All of these things have something in common—intellectual property.

Intellectual property is to the world of business what the Colt .45 was to the dime-novel Old West: the great equalizer. It is often the only thing that permits an emerging business to compete successfully against larger, established competitors with vastly more marketing power. In other words, if you are going to compete against the Big Boys, you will typically have to do so through the creation and use of intellectual property.

The only way that you can sustain head-to-head competition against the Big Boys over time is to maintain and protect your intellectual property. There is a reason why the Big Boys are where they are in the marketplace. If they see a competitor beating them, they will try to determine the "how and why"—and, once they have figured it out, they will adapt and, to the extent that they can without legal repercussions, "adopt." And then they will apply their market power with a vengeance. You want to make sure that it is not "legal" to "adopt"—to make sure that you have secured and maintained enforceable rights that will prevent them from adopting (taking/using/appropriating) the intellectual property that lets you beat them in the marketplace.

You will hear stories about large companies riding roughshod over smaller competitors, ignoring patents, upon the assumption that their victim will not have the resources to enforce its rights. This is, for the most part, myth. There are relatively few Big Boys that are also outright Pirates. There are, undoubtedly, isolated instances where market giants have knowingly ignored a smaller business's intellectual property rights. However, this is very much the exception. In the first place, the Big Boys can rely on their market power—they typically don't have to resort to piracy. There are also provisions in the law to punish someone who infringes someone else's intellectual property rights willfully, and the Big Boys are very much aware of those provisions. Generally, cases where the Big Boys are aware of a smaller competitor's patent and yet still proceed with apparent disregard for the patent can be attributed to a weakness in the patent itself. Often, when such a patent application was prepared and negotiated through the Patent and Trademark Office, the emphasis was on expediency—having it done cheap, as opposed to having it done right. But that is a different story, and we will deal with it later in the book.

True Pirates will tend to ignore your intellectual property rights and will oblige you to enforce them. However, unless you have maintained enforceable intellectual property rights, you will have no defense against these unscrupulous competitors. They will be able to copy your products and trade with impunity on the market that you create.

A properly laid foundation of enforceable intellectual property rights is also the most effective barrier against the Spoilers. For example, a strong trademark can clearly differentiate your products from the lower-quality products of the Spoilers, thus preventing them from polluting the marketplace. A strong patent may be able to preclude them from the marketplace altogether.

Let's look at an example from history. Many people believe that one of the primary factors in the advent of the age of the personal computer was a particular spreadsheet program. This spreadsheet program was the first on the market. Perhaps it even created the market. In many circles, it was considered revolutionary. However, once the investment and risks had been taken, and the market had been established, other companies began to place conceptually identical spreadsheet programs in the marketplace. The newcomers not only had the benefit of the publicly available information regarding the original spreadsheet program, and the market acceptance created by that program, but arguably had greater resources (and perhaps more marketing and/or technical talent), and the market-making spreadsheet program was ultimately supplanted by the competing programs. Much later, one of the developers of the original spreadsheet program was reportedly asked at an interview if it made a difference that his company had not pursued patent protection for its product. He responded, "Only several hundreds of millions of dollars."

My good friend Robert Kiyosaki has his own similar story. I first met Robert when he came to my office to discuss engaging me as his attorney. Robert had invented a board game to teach the basic concepts of personal finance. The design of the game (now known as CASHFLOW 101) represented a substantial investment; it was the result of a great deal of thought, research, and testing, not to mention expense. Yet, unless the appropriate protections were put in place, once the game was made public, it would be a simple matter for a competitor to copy its most valuable aspects with little investment or cost. This would place the competitor at a distinct advantage: it would have a product on the market without being obliged to spend the time and money for all the research, development, and testing that Robert had put in to actually create the product. Robert recognized this. He had been through it before and wanted to make sure that history did not repeat itself.

Years ago, in connection with his first company, Robert developed what is now known as a "surfer wallet"—a trifold wallet made of brightly colored nylon and Velcro. He also invented the "shoe pocket," a miniature wallet, also made of nylon and Velcro, that attaches to the laces of running shoes. Robert is now a self-proclaimed evangelist for laying a proper legal foundation for a business. However, back then, he did not believe that intellectual property protection warranted the expense of patent attorney fees, and did not take any steps to protect his intellectual property.

The initial success of Robert's first company was phenomenal. The jogging craze was at its height, and Robert had soon created a market for his nylon-and-Velcro products. There was a huge demand. He soon began receiving orders for more products than he had the capacity to manufacture. However, raw materials cost money, and the expansion of production facilities costs even more. Robert did not have the money at hand, the necessary capital, to immediately meet the market demand. This meant that he was forced to go out and raise money—to find investors or take out loans—for his company.

Given time, Robert may have been able to raise the necessary capital.

However, he wasn't given that time. The market does not stand still. In any event, it's not clear that even having the funds to meet demand would have helped. The Spoilers pounced.

Foreign competition (including his own manufacturer) flooded the market with cheap imitations, some at retail prices below what it cost Robert to have his products made. Not only was his company no longer attractive to investors, but it just plain could not compete. The result was downsizing, and ultimately the rethinking of his entire business strategy. Because Robert had not taken the necessary steps to protect his intellectual property in his products, he had lost control of the situation.

Robert learned from experience. This time, before he introduced his new game to the public he wanted to be sure that his rights were properly protected. He sought out patent counsel. That's where I came into the picture.

A good patent attorney can help you develop and implement a strategy for building intellectual property and using intellectual property rights to protect your business. The relationship should be interactive: you and the attorney should "think tank," considering the applicability of all of the various forms of protection to the different aspects of your business, how to lay a proper foundation to maximize the effectiveness of the different protection mechanisms, and how to use each of the protection mechanisms to maximum effect. Good IP advice is not cheap, but it's worth every penny. Intellectual property rights can not only be a barrier to competition, but also a source of income, and an alternative to raising outside capital.

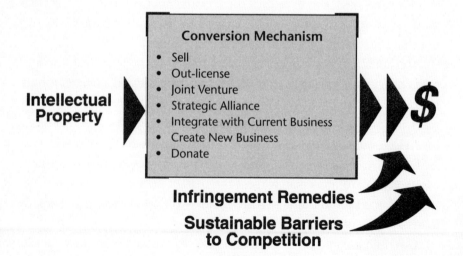

This book is designed to familiarize you with the basic mechanisms for protecting your rights in technology and other intellectual property. The characteristics and relative advantages of each protection mechanism will be discussed, as will the basic procedures for obtaining, maintaining, and exploiting rights through these mechanisms.

At the outset, however, it must be stressed that this handbook is *not* intended to be an exhaustive treatise on the subject. There are many subtleties involved in establishing and protecting rights in intellectual property that are totally beyond the scope of this handbook. *This handbook will not turn you into an "instant attorney."* What it will do is alert you to the pitfalls that can strip the rights from the unwary.

Horror Stories—
Tales of the Unwary

To illustrate some of the pitfalls, I pose the following hypotheticals (based very, very loosely upon actual situations).

Horror Story 1

Ackman developed a new video game conceptually different from all previous video games. In addition, this game's program employed radically new data manipulation techniques, which permitted the generation of amazingly lifelike images on conventional displays. Ackman began marketing the game software in both ROM "cartridge" and disk form. Each article sold was dutifully marked with a copyright notice.

The game was an instant success and the programming technique was proclaimed a major breakthrough. Within a matter of months, competing games, conceptually the same as Ackman's but employing different audiovisual effects and minor functional differences, began to appear. Ackman sued for copyright infringement. He lost.

Ackman also learned that a number of companies were employing his display programming techniques in other products and games. His attorney advised him that his copyright provided no recourse and that he should have obtained patent protection on his program. Ackman learned the hard way that a copyright provides only a very limited form of protection.

Horror Story 2

After years of R&D, Z-Corp develops a revolutionary new microcomputer that takes the market by storm. Only a little more than a year after its introduction, Z-Corp's product has literally become the premium micro on the market. Then, suddenly, sales begin to drop. Z-Corp learns that its archcompetitor, CopyCo, has purchased, then copied a Z-Corp unit and is now marketing a competing product. The CopyCo unit differs from the Z-Corp product only in the details of the casing and the unmistakable "CopyCo" decal on the front of the unit. However, since CopyCo has essentially no research-and-development costs to recoup, its unit is being sold at a substantially lower price. At this point, Z-Corp for the first time seeks legal advice on how to protect its R&D investment. Z-Corp is out of luck.

Horror Story 3

Dr. A is employed by Y-Corp in its R&D section and has developed a new semiconductor device with phenomenal frequency characteristics. Anxious to receive credit for developing the new device, Dr. A immediately publishes a technical paper. Within the next few months, Y-Corp perceives that the primary market for the new device is in Japan and Germany, and attempts to protect its rights in the device there. But Y-Corp is too late for patent protection in those countries.

Horror Story 4

Mr. D had an idea for a new product. He approached his employer, Ms. E, to see if she was interested in manufacturing it. Ms. E immediately saw great potential for the product, and agreed to pay Mr. D a substantial sum for rights to it, but only if they were successful in obtaining a patent—showing Ms. E as the inventor, even though both knew Ms. E had no part in making the invention. Mr. D agreed, and a patent application was immediately filed in Ms. E's name. The Patent and Trademark Office determined that the product was indeed patentable. However, because Mr. D and Ms. E intentionally misidentified the inventors, the patent was vulnerable to invalidation.

Horror Story 5

Ms. B had an idea for a new system architecture, and jotted down notes and a diagram on a piece of scrap paper, without signing or dating the paper. A few months later, Ms. B approached her employers to see if they were interested in manufacturing a system using her architecture. Her employers immediately saw great potential for the architecture, and agreed to pay Ms. B a substantial sum for rights to it, if they were successful in obtaining a patent. A patent application was immediately filed in Ms. B's name, and the Patent and Trademark Office determined that the architecture was indeed patentable. However, a third party had also developed a similar architecture, and had also filed a patent application. An "interference proceeding" was instituted in the Patent and Trademark Office to determine who was entitled to claim the invention of the system architecture. It soon became evident to Ms. B that the third party did not come up with the idea until just before she disclosed the idea to her employers—thus she was the first to have the idea by a matter of months. Unfortunately, she had no way of proving it, and the third party was awarded the patent.

Horror Story 6

Mr. X is president of X-Corp, a service company that lays out and manufactures custom PC boards. X-Corp has developed a new computer-aided technique and software that permits it to substantially increase the density of components per unit area on a PC board as compared to the products of its closest competitor. In attempting to obtain a substantial order from a potential customer, Mr. X explains the new technique and software in detail to the potential customer without reservation. Later, after it appears that X-Corp cannot meet all of the customer's demands, the customer places a second order with one of X-Corp's fiercest competitors, and, in the course of doing so, explains the X-Corp technique and software to the competitor. The competitor thereafter begins using X-Corp techniques in all of its work. X-Corp loses its edge over the competition.

Horror Story 7

OK-Corp was in the private-branded widget business. It had been very successful in developing a number of extremely large accounts, supplying them widgets bearing the customers' trademarks. To take advantage of the low cost of foreign labor, OK-Corp outsourced the manufacture of its widgets offshore. The widgets were drop-shipped from the foreign manufacturer's facility directly to OK-Corp's customers. Then one day, to OK-Corp's dismay, the orders from its large accounts abruptly ceased. When it called to investigate, it was told that the customers were now buying directly from OK-Corp's offshore supplier. OK-Corp had no patents on the widgets. OK-Corp was anything but okay.

Horror Story 8

Z-Corp spared no expense in rolling out its newest product in December 1989, and blanketed the market with advertising prominently featuring a catchy trademark. A great deal of thought and expense had gone into the choice of the trademark, and Z-Corp was certain that no one was using it. Unfortunately, Z-Corp had not thought to do a search of the Patent and Trademark Office files; just days before Z-Corp's rollout, Agresso Corp had filed an application for federal registration based upon an intent to use the identical mark. The notice of trademark infringement caught Z-Corp completely by surprise.

Horror Story 9

H-Co was in the construction business. It discovered that substance X, an ordinary, commonly available product, was phenomenally effective as an insect repellent when mixed with cement. The material was well-known, and had been sold in bulk for years for use as a fertilizer, but no one had discovered its insect-repelling properties. In an initial testing, H-Co brought bags of the material to a construction site and manually mixed it with the concrete used in the footings and floor of a building in progress at a location known to be infested by termites. Over the next eighteen months H-Co monitored the site and ultimately established to the inventor's satisfaction that the structure was effectively termite-proof. After determining that the additive was effective against termites, H-Co began to perform tests on its effectiveness against other types of insects, such as ants, wasps, Africanized bees, and roaches. The H-Co inventors were relatively sure that the additive would repel the other insects, but were not positive, and felt that the tests were necessary. They also suspected, although it was far from a sure thing, that the additive would work when mixed with other types of building materials, such as plaster, gypsum, stucco, or textured water-based paints.

H-Co had a sense that a patent could be valuable both as a barrier to competition and as a marketing tool. At the very least, they wanted to be able to mark their product "patent pending" to aid in marketing. If they were actually successful in obtaining a patent, that would be a bonus. However, they were just getting their business started, their funds were limited, and they did not want to spend any more money than they absolutely had to on obtaining a patent.

One of the inventors had a neighbor who was a patent attorney. The neighborhood patent attorney practiced on his own and specialized in preparing inexpensive patent applications for small businesses. He and his secretary worked out of a small office located in a nearby strip mall. The H-Co inventors visited the patent attorney's office, and spent an hour or two with him describing their discovery. H-Co emphasized that they were on a very tight budget and wanted to minimize attorneys' fees. Based on the description provided by H-Co at the meeting, and without requiring any further input from the company, the attorney prepared a patent application.

The application described the use of the material as a termite repellent, and the specific manner in which H-Co had mixed the material with the cement as it was poured in H-Co's initial tests. It did not explain why the material acted as a termite repellent. (There was no way that it could; at that time H-Co did not know why the substance worked.) There was no discussion of the use of any substance in the additive other than the specific substance used by H-Co in its initial test, nor any mention of substances that might be used as an alternative to substance X in the additive. There was no mention of insects other than termites.

The patent application included three claims. The first claim was extremely broad: "1. A product for repelling insects comprising substance X." The second claim depended from claim 1 (that is, incorporated claim 1 by reference) but specified that the insects were termites. The third claim was an independent method claim describing in exacting detail the particular method by which H-Co had mixed substance X with the cement as it was poured in H-Co's initial tests. The application was filed without a declaration in order to obtain the earliest possible filing date. After the application was filed, a copy was sent to the inventors at H-Co for their review, together with the required declaration for execution. The inventors were very busy. They gave the application only a cursory review before they signed the declaration and returned it to the attorney for filing with the patent office.

It was well over a year before H-Co had any further word from their patent attorney. During that time, H-Co had determined that selling cement premixed with substance X not only resulted in far better quality control, but was far more profitable than selling substance X alone as an additive for mixing with cement on-site. By the time H-Co heard from their patent attorney, they had also determined why substance X was so effective as an insect repellent, and had identified other substances with the same property that might be used as an alternative to substance X. In fact, H-Co found an equivalent substance Y that was nearly as effective as substance X but was considerably less expensive. They also discovered that adding a small percentage of an additional substance Z made the additive even more effective, particularly if substance Y was employed rather than substance X, resulting in a far less expensive but more effective product. H-Co's tests proved the effectiveness of the additive against other types of insects, such as ants, wasps, Africanized bees, and roaches, and that it would work when mixed with other types of building materials, such as plaster, gypsum, stucco, or textured water-based paints. The Y-Z additive was surprisingly effective against wasps and bees when mixed with textured paint, and particularly effective against roaches when mixed with gypsum.

When a letter from the patent attorney finally came, H-Co was estatic. The letter read, "I am happy to report that the patent office has allowed claims in the application. A copy of the office action by the patent office is enclosed, along with a proposed response that will place the application in condition for allowance. Unless I hear from you to the contrary, I plan to file the response this Friday."

The H-Co inventors glanced through the PTO office action and the proposed response. In the office action, the examiner had allowed claim 3 (including the details of mixing the additive with cement), but had rejected the broad claim 1 as indefinite, and had objected to claim 2 as "depending from a rejected claim." However, he did state that claim 2 "would be allowable if placed in independent form including all of the limitations of claim 1." The proposed response took a straightforward and simple approach.

The attorney did not contest the rejection; instead, he simply amended claim 1 to substitute the term "termites" for "insects," and canceled claim 2. The inventors didn't understand why the patent examiner thought original claim 1 was indefinite; it seemed perfectly understandable to them, and they could not see how using the term "termites" instead of "insects" made it any more understandable. However, they figured the attorney knew what he was doing and deferred to him. The proposed response was filed as the attorney proposed, and, sure enough, H-Co's patent was granted with the amended claims.

For the next few years, things couldn't have been better for H-Co. They became a leader in the cement market. Then one of their employees left, and took a position with one of the cement industry giants. And when they went to enforce the patent against the competitor, they discovered its weaknesses. They discovered the hard way that, where patents are concerned, you really do get what you pay for.

Horror Story 10

B. Hindthetimes brought his newest product to market in record time to meet the competition—but he did it without considering his competitor's patent position. He almost immediately received notice from his primary competitor that the new product infringed the competitor's patent. In B. Hindthetimes's opinion, this was not true. In any event, someone had once told him that patents were rarely successfully enforced in the courts. He opted not to consult an attorney and continued to market the product. B. Hindthetimes was soon in court and found himself faced with an injunction and a judgment for treble damages plus attorneys' fees. B. Hindthetimes learned the hard way that patents, if properly prepared, are now very enforceable in the courts, and that he would have been well served to consult a patent attorney before he went to market.

Horror Story 11

Salco was very proud of its new customer tracking software; the software was custom developed for the company by a consultant, and had cost it in excess of $500,000 in fees to the consultant, not to mention all the time and effort that had been devoted to providing the consultant all the data and feedback necessary to develop the software. That is, Salco was very proud of its software until it learned that after the software had been developed, the consultant had licensed substantially the same software to Salco's fiercest competitor. To add insult to injury, since Salco had already paid for the development costs, the competitor paid only a fraction of the fees Salco had paid to the consultant.

Horror Story 12

A number of years ago, Mr. D had an idea for a new interface circuit, but he came to the conclusion that it was too expensive to manufacture. He decided it was not worth pursuing and put it aside. A number of years after the fact, lo and behold, Mr. D finds out that P Company is about to come out with a line of hardware using precisely the interface circuit that he conceived years before. Mr. D goes directly to his patent attorney and requests that an application be filed. It is determined that Mr. D, in fact, developed the interface before P Company, and that the application could be filed within one year of any "printed publication," "public use," or "on-sale" bars. Just the same, Mr. D is barred from obtaining a patent because he "abandoned" the invention.

These hypotheticals are typical examples of how valuable rights in intellectual property are unwittingly lost by seemingly innocent courses of action, and how failing to consider third-party rights can lead to disaster.

The Basic Categories of Intellectual Property

You should be familiar with the various types of intellectual property if you plan to succeed in today's business environment. The major categories of intellectual property include information, data, and know-how; inventions; industrial designs; patents; utility models; copyrights; mask works; trademarks, reputation, and goodwill; character trademarks and sponsorship; and trade dress.* The nature, applicability, and scope of legal protection mechanisms for the different types of intellectual properties will be noted here, but will be discussed in more detail later.

> **Types of Intellectual Property**
> - Information, Data, and Know-How
> - Inventions
> - Industrial Designs
> - Patents
> - Utility Models (Petty Patents)
> - Copyrights
> - Mask works
> - Trademarks, Reputation, and Goodwill
> - Character Trademarks and Sponsorship
> - Trade Dress

*As will be discussed in the next section, the terms trade secrets, patents, copyrights, mask works, and trademarks have come to denote both a type of intellectual property asset and a legal mechanism for protecting the underlying assets.

Information, Data, and Know-How

What you (and your employees) know can be valuable. Accumulated information, data, and know-how are perhaps the most overlooked or undervalued intellectual property assets.

There is no universally accepted term that describes these assets, nor is there a universally accepted definition of the term "know-how." For the purposes of this book, however, know-how will be used as a generic term, generally defined as accumulated practical skill, expertise, data, and information relating to a business and its operations, or to the performance of any form of industrial procedure or process. Examples of business know-how include such things as strategic business plans, marketing plans, internal procedures, sales techniques, and client lists. Examples of technological know-how may include manufacturing processes, vendor and parts lists, inventions, technical developments, and skill and expertise in operating equipment and instrumentation.

Know-how may be either proprietary or nonproprietary. Nonproprietary know-how is information that is generally known in an industry, or basic skills or practices employed in an industry. A typical example would be the skills and knowledge acquired by an employee resulting from being trained in the operation of a commercially available machine (as opposed to learning a trade secret process). There is clearly an investment by the company in training the employee; even this nonproprietary know-how can be an asset, as will be discussed.

Proprietary know-how, sometimes referred to as a "trade secret" or "confidential information," is know-how that is not readily ascertainable from publicly available information. It preferably cannot be obtained other than from its owner. Or, if it can somehow be obtained from somewhere other than the owner, it requires a substantial effort and expenditure of time and money.

A trade secret may be information developed through experimentation or experience. For example, you might discover that certain desirable properties can be obtained in a composition by adding a specific amount of substance A at a specific temperature before adding substance B, or that waste can be minimized by performing a step that would otherwise be thought redundant or merely adding expense in a manufacturing process. Perhaps the most famous example of a trade secret is the formula of Coca-Cola.

As will be discussed, to be subject to an enforceable trade secret right, your know-how must meet certain requirements. It must not be generally known in the industry. It must be subject to appropriate measures to maintain its secrecy. And it may not be disclosed to any entity that is not obligated to maintain the know-how in confidence.

Know-how can be embodied in many forms. It can be business or technical documents such as strategic plans, customer lists and files, specifications, manuals, blueprints, and the like. It can also reside in your personal knowledge and expertise and that of your employees.

How can you protect the nonproprietary know-how of your business? The best way is by retaining employees, and by establishing procedures for "institutionalizing" the know-how (ensuring that it is possessed by a number of people within your business) and "memorializing" it (ensuring that it is documented or recorded). Establishing procedures for recording the details of processes, methods, techniques, and data used by skilled employees, and for retaining possession of those records, also accords a modicum of protection; at least the know-how would not be entirely lost should the employee leave. As will be discussed, you can sometimes use noncompetition provisions to prevent competitors from appropriating your investment in employee training. However, such agreements with employees are often difficult to enforce.

As will be discussed in more detail, rights in proprietary know-how are typically maintained through physical security procedures and by imposing a contractual obligation of confidentiality on all parties permitted access to the know-how. The obligation of confidentiality is typically imposed through appropriate provisions in confidentiality, employment, development, supply/vendor, manufacturing, foundry, and license agreements. Noncompetition agreements are also sometimes used to prevent inevitable disclosure of trade secrets by former employees.

Inventions

In general, "inventions" are new technological developments or discoveries produced or created through the exercise of independent creative thought, investigation, or experimentation. Inventions may constitute know-how (typically trade secrets) and be protected as such, or they may be the subject of patents granted by the governments of various countries.

Industrial Designs

The term "industrial design" tends to mean different things from country to country. In general, however, it typically refers to the appearance and non-functional aspects of a product. The scope of protection granted with respect to industrial design varies from country to country. In the United States, design patents typically protect industrial designs.

Patents

A patent is the grant by a sovereign government of some privilege or authority, typically the exclusive right to make, use, or sell with respect to an invention (that is, to exclude others from making, using, or selling the invention). Patents are territorial in nature; they are enforceable only within the territory of the government granting them. Typically, patents are granted on a country-by-country basis. Various international conventions and treaties, however, accord varying rights in the respective signatory countries to an applicant for a patent in any one of the signatory countries. For example, the International Convention for the Protection of Intellectual Property (Paris Convention) permits the applicant for a patent in one member country to file an application within any other member country within twelve months of the date of the original filing (or within six months of filing for a design patent), and to obtain the priority of the original filing date with respect to the subsequent filing. The Patent Cooperation Treaty (PCT) permits a single application to be filed in a designated receiving office, and provides for an international search. The application is then forwarded to respective designated individual countries, and is processed according to that country's procedures and laws. The European Patent Convention (EPC) established the European Patent Office (EPO), and permits a single application to be filed in the EPO, designating various member countries (limited to European countries) where the patent will apply. The application is examined by the EPO, and is ultimately granted or refused in accordance with the law of the treaty. The laws of each individual country govern the rights and enforcement of European patents in the various designated countries, but the law of the treaty governs their validity. The patents of the various countries differ widely in scope and effect.

Utility Models (Petty Patents)

Some countries grant "petty patents" (sometimes referred to as utility models) on functional elements of a product or process of minor importance, which may not meet minimum requirements for a patent. There is no provision for utility models in the United States.

Copyrights

A copyright is a statutory right provided to the author of a literary or artistic work. The scope and effect of a copyright varies from country to country. However, a number of international conventions and treaties pertain to copyrights, most notably the Pan American Convention of Literary and Artistic Property (Buenos Aires Convention) (subscribed to by numerous countries in the Western Hemisphere), the Berne Convention, and the Universal Copyright Convention. In general, a copyright precludes unauthorized copying of artistic or literary aspects of the copyrighted work.

Mask Works

A mask work is a "series of related images, however fixed or enclosed," that represents three-dimensional patterns in the layers of a semiconductor chip. The Semiconductor Chip Protection Act has created a statutory protection in the United States for mask works (basically a registration system that incorporates a "not commonplace" threshold). Registration precludes the reproduction, importation, or distribution of chips embodying a registered mask work. In essence, registration prevents the use of reproductions of mask works in the manufacture of competing chips. Similar protection has been implemented in a number of other countries.

Trademarks, Reputation, and Goodwill

A trademark (or service mark) is a word or symbol (or anything that is nonfunctional) used to distinguish the goods or services of one company from those of another. The mark identifies the source of the product or service and, in effect, connects the goodwill and reputation of the company to its products and services.

Under the laws of most countries, a competitor is prevented from capitalizing on your reputation and goodwill by using your mark (or a similar mark) and attempting to pass off its goods as those made or sponsored by you. In this way, a trademark protects the market value of your reputation and goodwill, and protects investments in advertising and other promotional activities used to develop goodwill.

In some countries, exclusive rights to use a trademark in a given geographical market can be acquired without registering the mark with the government. (In the United States, rights can be established by being the first to actually or constructively use the mark. Federal registration can constitute constructive use, effectively expand the geographic scope of the rights, and provide additional remedies.) Other countries, however, require registration, and in some cases various other formalities, as a prerequisite to any exclusive right in the trademark. In fact, a few countries require that a mark be registered with the government before it is used in that country.

Character Trademarks and Sponsorship

Sometimes a product is associated with or sponsored or endorsed by a celebrity, such as a famous actor or athlete, or a character such as Mickey Mouse, Snoopy, or Indiana Jones. The manifestation of this association, or sponsorship, is actually a form of trademark, sometimes referred to as a character or personality trademark. Some states have also enacted additional statutes specifically directed to the use of a personality's image or voice. A character or celebrity name cannot be associated with a product without permission of the celebrity or owner of the character.

Trade Dress

Trade dress, in general terms, is the appearance and packaging of a product. Where trade dress is sufficiently distinctive, and begins to identify the source, origin, or sponsorship of a product, it can, under the laws of some countries (like the U.S.), take on trademark significance and be protected as such.

An Overview of the Basic Protection Mechanisms

There are six basic legal mechanisms available for protecting your rights in intellectual property: trade secrets, patents, design patents, copyrights, mask work protection, and trademarks. Each mechanism is designed to protect a different type or aspect of intellectual property:

- **Trade secret protection,** as the name implies, entails keeping technology and business information secret to prevent your competition from copying the technology.
- **Patent protection** is available for inventive concepts embodied in a product, and prevents others from making, using, or selling any product embodying the patented concepts.

Legal Tools
• Utility Patent
• Design Patent
• Copyright
• Trade Secret
• Trademark
• Mask Work Protection

- **Design patent protection** is available for the ornamental (nonfunctional) appearance of a product.
- **Copyright protection** is available for the form of expression of an idea (as opposed to the idea itself).

- **Mask work protection** is available for works embodied in semiconductor chips (masks) and prevents others from reproducing, importing, or distributing chips embodying the work.
- **Trademark protection** prevents your competition from attempting to trade on your company's reputation.

> **Worth Protecting?**
> - Does it provide an advantage in the marketplace?
> - Do you care if the competition appropriates it?
> - How much was invested in developing it?

There are many different aspects of a product embodying technology. For example, with respect to a microprocessor-based product, there are system, component, hardware, and software aspects. The software itself has many aspects: functionality (what the software does), the context of the software in the overall system, the software architecture, algorithms and implementation techniques employed in the software, the code implementing the software, databases operated upon by the software, and documentation. Each of the different aspects may be valuable and worthy of protection in its own right.

> **Technical/Competitive Advantage**
> - New function
> - Improved performance or efficiency
> - Lower cost
> - Easier service or maintenance
> - Reduced size or weight
> - Easier installation

Each protection mechanism has distinct advantages and disadvantages and provides a varying scope of protection as applied to the different aspects of a product. Combinations of different types of protection can be used to protect different aspects of a product. The particular approach to protecting a given product must be tailored to the specific characteristics and form of the product, and to the particular marketing approach and distribution scheme adopted for the product. An intellectual property protection strategy should be a major component of every business plan.

Putting It in Perspective

It was the crack of dawn on a Monday morning, and I had actually forced myself to get into the office. I had been on the East Coast for the last week, and was trying to work my way through an accumulation of mail more than a foot thick. The phone rang. I had been hoping that things would hold off until I made it through the mail—I had come in early specifically to beat the phone. I answered anyway.

"Hey Mike, it's Frank." Frank is a longtime friend and sometime client, in-house general counsel for a large corporation.

"Frank—it's good to hear from you. How's the family?"

"All is well out this way. Hey, I've only got a couple of minutes—I'm due in a meeting—but I wanted to give you a call. I've got a friend that's gotten himself into a situation, and I suggested he give you a call. I wanted to fill you in beforehand."

"Talk to me."

"My friend's name is Joe Theoretico. He's the president of Theoretico Software Incorporated . . . TSI."

"I've heard of them. They've made quite a splash in the personal computer industry. They put out the Hi-Bird 3-D graphics product . . ."

"That's them. Anyway, Joe called me last night to get my opinion on how he should handle a problem that he has with one of his former distributors, an outfit called Piraco in Texas. As I understand it, Piraco is about to introduce what Joe characterizes as a copy of the Hi-Bird product. Joe wants to make sure that it doesn't happen.

"I should warn you, Joe is a bit of a character. He hasn't had much experience with intellectual property . . . and doesn't have much use for attorneys. It took Joe a while before he finally decided that it was necessary to consult with an attorney. Then, before he called me, he apparently met with some personal injury attorney—Joe had seen his advertisement on television."

"Oh, great."

"Yup. According to his ads he specializes in 'injury cases and divorce,' but he assured Joe that he was more than capable of 'handling a computer law case.' He is a very experienced litigator, you see, and Joe couldn't find better representation. Joe told me the guy wants to bring a trade secret action against the distributor."

"Super." At this point I had no idea whether or not a trade secret action was appropriate (as it turned out, it was not). But, as I guess you can tell, I (and Frank) had real doubts about the ability of the personal injury attorney to competently handle the matter.

"Well, at least Joe called me for a second opinion—he called it a reality check. I told Joe that he needed to go to a bona fide intellectual property attorney—a patent attorney. I told him to call you."

Why a patent attorney? Why not an "experienced litigator" like the personal injury attorney? Well, it's not just a matter of conceit or ego. Law, like everything else these days, is very specialized—and intellectual property is one of the more esoteric specialties. There is a big difference between a PI (personal injury) attorney and an IP (intellectual property) attorney. Not every attorney is an intellectual property attorney, much less a patent attorney. In fact, not every attorney calling themselves an IP attorney (or a computer law specialist) is a patent attorney.

As a general proposition, there are few controls with respect to attorneys holding themselves out as "intellectual property" or "computer law" specialists. With a very few exceptions, there are no certification procedures relating to intellectual property in general or computer law. Patent attorneys, however, are different. They are specially licensed by the Patent and Trademark Office. They are required to take an additional bar exam—the "patent bar"—to obtain that license. As a prerequisite even to taking that exam, they have to establish that they have a technology or science background. That typically means having a degree in engineering or a "hard" science.

The courts will let non–patent attorneys litigate intellectual property cases in the courtroom. But most general litigators will not be able to counsel you with respect to your intellectual property issues. In fact, most non–patent attorneys simply won't be able to counsel you on patent matters, let alone actually do nonlitigation patent work. Even more significantly, a lot of the time, non–patent attorneys (even those practicing other aspects of intellectual property law) simply don't fully understand the patent law. Patent protection may or may not be the solution, but it clearly should be considered as part of an overall strategy for protecting your IP assets. Developing a strategy for protecting your intellectual property assets should be a thorough and analytical process. There are a number of tools available to protect intellectual property, and you want to be sure that each is used to maximum effect. To do that, you sometimes need to lay a foundation in advance. Non–patent attorneys are typically just not sensitized to all of the traps or opportunities.

Most attorneys will admit it when they recognize that they're not competent to take on a matter. But some will tend, albeit unconsciously, to try to "force-fit" the matter into the legal cubbyholes that they are competent to handle, ignoring the potential application of aspects of intellectual property law with which they are less familiar. Going to a non–patent attorney on an IP issue is like hiring a carpenter who has a saw but no hammer. On the other hand, not all patent attorneys (and particularly not those catering to individual inventors) are capable of handling complex litigation, business law issues, or, typically more importantly, the nonpatent aspects of your intellectual property needs, or of ensuring that your intellectual property is used to best meet your business goals.

So you need to go to a good patent attorney, preferably someone who also has some commercial law and litigation experience, or is a member of a firm with other attorneys with that experience who work cooperatively with the patent attorney on a regular basis. There's a catch, though—a good patent attorney is not necessarily the least expensive, and doing it right takes time and effort, both on your part and that of your attorney (which in turn means additional expense). Too many patent attorneys (particularly those catering to individual inventors) are more concerned with "doing it cheap" than doing it right. The last thing you want to do is to be penny-wise but dollar-foolish in protecting your intellectual property.

Where IP protection is concerned, you typically get what you pay for. Intellectual property protection, by its nature, will be scrutinized by adverse, and sometimes outright hostile, third parties looking for a chink in your IP armor. This is particularly true with respect to patent protection. Developing an IP protection strategy, and in particular preparing a patent application, should be a cooperative and extremely interactive process between you and your patent attorney. That's the only way to ensure that a patent, when you get it, is valid and furthers your business strategy.

But that's another story that we will get to later. Unfortunately, many businesspeople do not appreciate the need for a coordinated strategy for IP protection, or the role a patent attorney could play in developing and implementing that strategy. By the time they come to appreciate it, it's often too late. Intellectual property protection is to a business what a foundation is to a house. If you do not lay a proper foundation before you build the structure, the house will have a tendency to collapse—and it is very difficult to come back after the fact and fix an inadequate foundation. The same is true with respect to intellectual property. If you do not take proper and timely steps to protect your intellectual property, your rights are at risk.

"Got to go. Keep me posted," Frank said.

"Will do. Thanks for the referral."

"Who else would I send an IP case to? You're the best. Got to go. Ciao."

He hung up. I don't know if I'm the best, but it's always nice to pretend that your peers are serious when they say so. I initiated a conflicts check— to make sure that taking on the representation of TSI would not create any conflict of interest (as would occur, for example, if one of the other lawyers in my firm was representing some third party in a matter adverse to TSI, or was representing Piraco in some matter)—then went back to my pile of mail, hoping to finish before Frank's friend called. I didn't; he phoned precisely thirty minutes later.

"Mr. Lechter?"

"Yes."

"Hello. My name is Joe Theoretico of TSI."

"Yes, Joe. Please call me Mike. Frank told me to expect your call. I understand you have an issue with a former distributor."

"That's right—a major issue. The slimebag is stealing our technology!" Joe barked, clearly exasperated by the subject. "How much do you know about TSI?"

"A little bit," I replied. "But let's assume I know nothing—that way we can be sure that I am not operating under any misapprehensions."

"Okay. TSI developed the 'Hi-Bird' 3-D graphics display system. It generates real 3-D images on a conventional color monitor. It is absolutely revolutionary—and the number-one-selling graphics system on the market." The pride in Joe's voice was unmistakable . . . and justified. I recalled reading some of the press on the Hi-Bird system. He was not exaggerating—it had revolutionized the market.

"Piraco was our exclusive distributor in the Southwest. Now I find out that they've come out with their own version of Hi-Bird. They are going to introduce it this Wednesday at the Display-Dex show. I want to stop them! Can you help me?"

"Possibly. Let's talk about it. I'll need to see your agreement with

Piraco—and your other distributor agreements if they are different—and the end user agreements that you are using with the Hi-Bird product."

"Uhhhh . . ." Joe hesitated for a moment. "I'll get you what we have." I realized that I had made an assumption—that there were such agreements. It turned out that my assumption was only partially correct.

"Okay. Do you have any patents?"

"No."

"Copyright registrations?"

"We put a copyright notice on the start-up screen."

"But have you actually registered any copyright?"

"I don't know what you mean."

"Okay. Do you have any trademark registrations?"

"Yes. That we do have—on TSI, Hi-Bird and our Logo . . ." Joe hesitated again for a moment, then continued. "Uhh . . . I guess I should tell you . . . Before I talked to Frank, I spoke to another attorney . . . a very experienced litigator . . . and he told me that I should sue them for theft of trade secrets. So what do you think?"

"Hard to say without knowing more. How did you leave it with him?"

"I told him to hold off unless I got back to him. I've got to be candid with you—the guy made me a little nervous. He talked a real good game—was real gung ho—but he kept mixing up some basic terminology, like he couldn't seem to keep 'software' and 'peripheral' straight, and kept referring to the system 'CPA.' That's why I called Frank, and he told me to call you. Frank said that you are an electrical engineer." The inflection of his voice made the last statement a question.

"Used to be. I have an electrical engineering degree. But I've been doing more lawyering than engineering for quite a while now."

Joe started asking me technical questions—testing my knowledge of computers and software. I could answer most of them, and when I didn't know the answer to a question I just told him so. I guess I did okay—I had passed the test—because Joe set up an appointment to see me later that morning. I asked him to bring copies of the documents we had discussed.

"Uhhh . . . one more question," Joe blurted out as we got ready to hang up. He seemed much less tense then he had at the beginning of our conversation. "You any relation to Hannibal Lecter? You know, Hannibal the Cannibal. *Silence of the Lambs.*" He laughed.

I had only heard that one a million times before. I responded in kind: "Yeah, I think we are cousins or something. You know that Lechter is not a very common name. Although most people don't really see the resemblance except when I'm dealing with clients who don't pay their bills."

Joe really thought that was funny. I could hear him laughing as he hung up the phone. The thing was, I was only kidding about the cousin part.

Before long, Joe was sitting across from me at my conference table. We started out with a few moments of small talk, just getting acquainted, and Joe regaled me with a few dozen of his favorite lawyer jokes. (Actually, some of them were pretty funny.) Then we got down to business.

"Okay, Joe, so tell me more about TSI."

"Okay. TSI is in the computer industry. The bulk of our business is sales of turnkey systems, and associated aftermarket and peripheral product lines. Like I mentioned over the phone, our flagship product is the Hi-Bird 3-D graphics display system. It is absolutely revolutionary—it generates real 3-D images on a conventional color monitor. We introduced it less than a year ago, and it is already the number-one-selling graphics system on the market. We typically sell turnkey systems, the whole package: the computer, the monitor, the printer, and other peripherals—add-on hardware—together with our software. The software will work with pretty much any modern PC system, but works best with specific combinations of hardware. By providing complete systems we are able to optimize—to make sure that the customers are using hardware that works well with the Hi-Bird software and is configured properly. We also make sure that the hardware is compatible with our specialized peripheral and other software products.

"We sell through independent distributors. We give the distributors extensive technical training, documentation, and a master disk of the code—including the source code for the products—so they can customize the system for individual customers. Then they go out and solicit orders from customers, and submit them to us.

"We ship the hardware to the distributor—or directly to the customer, if the distributor asks us to. The distributor does whatever customization on the software that's necessary, sets up and configures the hardware, and installs the customized software in object code on a hard disk in the hardware. The distributor pays us a discounted price, and keeps whatever's actually received from the customer—for the system, and installation and customization services. That's the way a lot of companies are doing it."

Joe became very animated, accompanying each statement with a gesture as he continued. "Those crooks took all our training courses, got all our materials, got our code. Then they tell us they're no longer going to distribute our products. And now I find out that they've come out with their own version of Hi-Bird. It looks like they're using the same basic hardware setup as Hi-Bird, but they're getting the components from different manufacturers than we use. And they're using our software. There's no way they could have developed the software on their own in a couple of months. They knew squat when they started our training course.

"Here's the thing. We make about eighty percent of our sales at the Display-Dex show. It's beginning Wednesday in Phoenix. We've got to stop Piraco from pitching their new system at the show. We were going to sell out of Piraco's booth. It's a prime booth. We don't have any other booths—they were our exclusive distributor, for cripes sake! They'll take all our business!

"And it's more than just lost sales of Hi-Bird. If customers buy the Piraco hardware instead of ours, we'll lose the customers for not only Hi-Bird, but also for our aftermarket and peripheral product lines."

He paused briefly to take a breath, and seemed to calm down a little. "I'm supposed to be the keynote speaker at the technical program. But I'm supposed to give a technical presentation on our newest technology. We've got a brand-new product coming out. We call it the Big-Bird. It's an educational aid system for children. It's totally different from the Hi-Bird system. That's what I'm supposed to talk about. It won't help with the sales of Hi-Bird.

"So here's what I want. I want to stop those buzzards from even displaying their product at the show—and I want to stop them from marketing a competing system, period."

Then it was my turn to play inquisitor. We spoke at length, and my questions elicited a number of facts Joe hadn't thought to mention on his own:

- The Hi-Bird system was first introduced at the Display-Dex trade show last year. TSI began offering copies for sale not long thereafter.
- Hi-Bird uses TSI hardware and TSI proprietary software. The software is revolutionary, and, while all of the individual components are com-

mercially available, the specific combination of hardware components used in the system is novel.

- There were no explicit obligations of confidentiality imposed on Piraco with respect to the master disk or source code in the distributorship agreement. In fact, TSI has never actually requested return of the materials.
- TSI has not employed any sort of end-user agreements with respect to the software, or even any proprietary legends in the software or user documentation. They simply sell the system outright.
- The software displays a log-on screen that includes a Hi-Bird logo and what purports to be a copyright notice:

© 2010 TSI software.

The date on the screen is indeed 2010—even though when Joe and I were meeting it was still in the year 2001. Joe told me he used next decade's date in the screen because TSI wanted the user to know that Hi-Bird "was a really new product—the cutting edge."

- No copyrights have actually been registered with respect to the software.
- TSI does not hold any patents, nor had any patent applications been filed.
- The system does not employ any custom integrated circuits that might be subject to mask work protection, but—
- TSI does have federal and Arizona state trademark registrations on its name, its logo, and the word "Hi-Bird," all of which appear prominently in the start-up screens of the Hi-Bird program. For various reasons, Piraco is clearly aware of those registrations.

Joe had faxed a demand to Piraco that it cease and desist. Piraco however, had less than respectfully declined. Piraco admitted that it was using the Hi-Bird software, but contended:

- That the software has become public domain, and in any event it's only using the Hi-Bird software until it completes development of its own improved version;
- That the brand of the hardware is clearly marked so no one will think that it is a TSI product; and

- That Piraco advises all of its customers that it is no longer associated with TSI and that Piraco will have a sign to that effect prominently displayed at its booth at the show.

After I had finished questioning Joe, he looked me in the eyes. "Okay, Counselor, what do we do?"

"Okay, Joe. First of all I need to point out to you that there are a number of issues here. Piraco is not your only problem. Did the attorney you spoke to earlier talk to you about getting patent protection on Hi-Bird or your new children's product?"

"No."

"Did he talk to you about using the name 'Big Bird' for your children's product?"

"Yeah. He thought it was really catchy. You know, 'Hi-Bird,' 'Big-Bird' . . . kind of go together, don't you think?"

"Maybe, but I suggest that you consider a name other than 'Big-Bird' for your new product. The 'Big-Bird' educational aid system for children? I don't know if you are aware of Sesame Workshop? *Sesame Street*? Big Bird from *Sesame Street*?"

"Of course I've heard of *Sesame Street.* That's why I picked the name. I thought it was a great play on words. Hi-Bird. Big Bird for Kids . . ."

"Joe, if you use Big-Bird on an educational aid for children, you're just asking to be sued. And you'll get hammered—probably would end up paying Sesame's attorneys' fees. We can come back to this later. There are some other issues we need to address.

"Let me just touch on one thing so I don't forget. If you are interested in patent protection outside of the U.S. on the educational system, we should have an application on file before your talk next week. Unfortunately, it's too late for patents on Hi-Bird in most foreign countries. I'll explain later.

"With respect to Piraco, there is a possibility that we can effectively shut them down at the show. We may be able to prevent them from running your software by pursuing a trademark infringement claim, since the software displays your registered Hi-Bird trademark.

"Long-term, though, the only thing that might be able to prevent them from developing their own analogous product is a patent on some strategic aspect of Hi-Bird."

Joe was a little puzzled. "Well, what about suing them for stealing my trade secrets?"

I took a deep breath and replied. "Joe, based on what you've told me they didn't steal any trade secrets from you. Unfortunately, it looks like you gave them away."

"Huh?"

"Joe, if we could show that Piraco had misappropriated a valid trade secret, we would have a pretty formidable arsenal of remedies available to us—injunctive relief, damages, unjust enrichment, and, if the misappropriation could be shown to be willful, punitive damages and reasonable attorneys' fees.

"The problem is that you have to take reasonable measures to maintain confidentiality in order to have trade secret status. With respect to the object code, you haven't taken any. You don't have any enforceable trade secret rights in Hi-Bird.

"You can enforce trade secret rights only against an entity that is subject to an obligation of confidentiality and/or that obtained the trade secret knowing that it was coming to them through improper channels. Piraco could easily have been made subject to an obligation of confidentiality in a distributorship or other agreement, or perhaps even by implication, if there had been agreements imposing confidentiality on end users—but there were none.

"The bottom line is that the Hi-Bird object code has, in effect, been published, and trade secret protection simply is not applicable to published material or anything that is readily ascertainable from it."

One of Joe's oxen had just been gored. "But what about Piraco's use of my source code? Could that be misappropriation of a trade secret?"

I shook my head. "Frankly, based on what you told me, it's extremely doubtful that under these circumstances the source code could be established as a trade secret. You released the source code to the distributors without any obligation of confidentiality, and on top of that, in view of the commercial availability of decompilers that will generate source code from object code—in effect, translate the object code—the publication of the object code may well be enough to destroy any trade secret rights in the source code."

"Okay, I guess a trade secret action is out. Well, I've still got my copyrights—right?"

"Sort of. It would be great if you do . . . and it's applicable. If a case of copyright infringement can be made out, we can get injunctive relief—stop Piraco from selling its system. Depending on the circumstances, we could also get impoundment—actual damages and profits or statutory damages; and discretionary costs and attorneys' fees.

"But there are a couple of problems. There may be a problem with the copyright notice. The date in the notice is improper. It is supposed to be the date of actual publication. The fact that you intentionally used the wrong date could cause some problems. Over and above any effect it may have on your copyright, it could conceivably be the basis for a false advertising claim. You need to change that, by the way . . . but let's ignore that issue for now. The real problem is that, even assuming you have a valid copyright, it is not registered—and registration of the copyright is a prerequisite to an infringement suit."

"Okay," said Joe. "We can just register the copyright now, can't we?"

"Sure. Preparing a copyright application involves filling out the appropriate copyright office form and filing it, together with deposit materials and a fee, at the copyright office. So, assuming we have appropriate listings and copies of the program for use as deposit materials, we could probably have the application on file with the Copyright Office in a day or so."

"Okay. Then file the application."

"Well, we can get it on file, but then the ball is in the copyright office's court. Registration is not instantaneous. You can request special handling by the copyright office—I think they're charging about five hundred dollars or so—but the earliest you can realistically expect to get the registration in hand is probably sometime next week—it typically takes five working days, and they won't even guarentee that. We might be able to do better than that if someone actually hand-carries the application through the copyright office, but I would not want to depend on it. We will want to pursue copyright registration, but it won't help for Display-Dex."

"Could we get away with filing a copyright suit before obtaining the registration, based on having made the application?"

"Maybe, but probably not. Anyway, I am not comfortable with it and strongly advise against it. Most courts require a certificate of registration, or copyright office denial of registration, as a threshold of jurisdiction, and if the issue arises, the suit would be dismissed.

"This is a typical problem encountered with respect to copyright protection of software. The practice of delaying registration of a copyright until an infringement situation arises is prevalent in the software industry, primarily as an attempt to avoid questions as to the trade secret status of the software. This tends to delay filing of copyright actions. And more importantly it limits the available remedies. Attorneys' fees and statutory damages are generally not available if infringement commences prior to registration."

"Okay—it looks like my copyrights won't stop Piraco from displaying at the show, but can we use them to stop Piraco long-term?"

"You're asking how effective a copyright will be against the Piraco-developed version of the software, presupposing that TSI has a valid, registered copyright? The answer is: it depends. It depends on just what aspects of the Hi-Bird program are reflected in the Piraco program.

"We would have to prove actionable copying. This is typically done by showing access and substantial similarities to copyrightable aspects of your program. That is not an issue with respect to Piraco's initial system—they admit that they are using an outright copy of your code. That is clearly a copyright infringement.

"The real issue is whether the 'improved' software that Piraco develops will be an infringement. Here's the thing: a copyright is intended to protect artistic expression—it protects the expression of an idea, not the idea itself. So if the only similarity between the respective programs is that they perform the same functions, there would be no copyright infringement. On the other hand, if Piraco lifts substantial blocks of code from Hi-Bird for its 'improved' software, it probably would be a copyright infringement.

"Infringement might be shown if the structure, code sequence, and organization of the respective programs were the same—but that's a huge question mark.

"What is clear, though, is that Piraco could get around any claim of copyright infringement by proving it employed a clean room scheme to develop its program. A first set of programmers dissect Hi-Bird and provide a functional specification to a second group of programmers who have never had direct access to the Hi-Bird software. The second group of programmers then develops the Piraco program from the functional specification.

"If this can be credibly shown, notwithstanding any similarities between the programs, a copyright infringement claim would be defeated. So, depending upon the extent to which the ultimate Piraco program incorporates aspects or portions of Hi-Bird, there may or may not be a copyright infringement."

Joe was beginning to get queasy; his understanding of software protection was being severely shaken. "Geez . . . what are we going to do? If you can get around copyrights that easily . . ."

"Easy, amigo. Copyrights are only one of the tools available. There are a number of different legal mechanisms available to protect intellectual property. They are part of a logical system—each mechanism is designed to protect a different type of intellectual property. Copyrights are only intended to protect artistic expression and works of authorship. There are other mechanisms available to protect other types of intellectual property. We talked about trade secret protection. It is intended to protect secrets. Trademarks protect reputation and goodwill. You have mask work protection for semiconductor chip layouts. There is design patent protection for nonfunctional appearance, and utility patent protection for invention."

Joe raised his eyebrows in consternation. "There is more than one type of patent protection?" he asked.

"Yeah. Generally, when someone says 'patent,' they are referring to a utility patent—when I say patent I generally mean utility patent—but there is also a design patent for protecting ornamental—nonfunctional—appearance.

"Let's assume that some of the aspects of Hi-Bird that make it work are patentable. We don't know that, but based on what you said it's probably a safe bet. Again, we don't know, but it's my guess that we could get a patent that covered the functions of the Hi-Bird program. Copying is not a requisite for patent infringement—a patent can protect against independent development of competing software by others. So Piraco couldn't avoid patent infringement by setting up a clean room.

"If we prove patent infringement, injunctive relief is available, and lost profits may be obtainable—based not only on sales of the Hi-Bird program, but also on convoyed sales of the hardware, and aftermarket and peripheral products. Given the equities here and the strong presumption of validity that now attaches to patents, if there is an enforceable patent, preliminary relief might be a possibility with respect to the Piraco product that actually uses the Hi-Bird software." I took another deep breath. "The thing is, you told me that you don't have any applicable patents. That rules out patent protection as a way of stopping Piraco at Display-Dex. But, long-term, patents are probably your only viable protection."

"I didn't think you could patent software," Joe said.

"You can, in the U.S. and many other countries, as long as the software doesn't merely implement some mathematical algorithm—$x + y = 2$. By and large, patent protection is available for software just like anything else. According to the Supreme Court, patent protection is available for 'anything made by man'—anything that doesn't occur naturally in nature, and is not a law of nature or abstract information—as long as it meets the other requisites for patentability."

"But is Hi-Bird patentable?"

"I am not in a position to say for sure. To do that I'd have to investigate what else is already out there. For an aspect of the program to be patentable, the aspect has to be 'novel' and 'unobvious.' From what you said, and what I have heard from others, the Hi-Bird program is revolutionary—it does something that no previous product has ever done. It's clearly not obvious—"

"So," Joe piped in, "that means it's patentable, right?" He was starting to perk up again.

I couldn't help but smile. "Well, it's not quite that simple. Novelty is defined by statute, 35 U.S.C., section 102. Under a portion of that statute, you can lose rights by prematurely publishing or exploiting an invention. Basically, in the United States you're given a one-year grace period to file an application. The one-year clock starts with the first publication describing the invention, or the first public use or offer for sale in the U.S. of a product employing the invention. After that year the patent is barred.

"You told me the Hi-Bird system was introduced almost a year ago. Sometimes products are offered for sale before there is an actual rollout of the product. We need to determine whether there were any offers for sale more than a year ago"

"There weren't. Can a patent application still be filed?"

"Yes, in the U.S. The Hi-Bird system is still within the one-year grace period. I need to point out, though, that most foreign countries have no grace period. That's why it's too late for patent protection in most, if not all, foreign countries other than NAFTA countries—Canada and Mexico."

Now Joe was enthused. "So what do you think? Can you throw together a patent application and get it on file before Wednesday?"

I chuckled. "Maybe, but it would take a heroic effort. A patent application is not a matter of merely filling out forms. It's really in the nature of a proposed patent. You have to include a description that's sufficiently detailed to permit someone to actually make and use the invention—in this case, to develop software that would perform the functions performed by Hi-Bird. But it could be done as long as you can get me the information that I would need, and the inventors are available to work with me. And we're talking an around-the-clock proposition here.

"Okay, Joe, but let's take a step back Exactly what will getting the application on file before Display-Dex buy us? Well, if it's not filed by then, you will be barred from filing because the one-year grace period will clearly have run. So if you want to pursue a patent we have to get an application on file. But just filing the application isn't going to stop Piraco at Display-Dex. You don't get any enforceable rights until the patent is actually granted, and on average, that takes on the order of two years from the date of filing. Once the patent is filed, a patent pending notice can be placed on the software, and this does have an *ad terrorem* effect on potential copiers, but it doesn't create any enforceable right."

Joe just shook his head. "Okay. It looks like patent protection provides no help with respect to stopping the display at Display-Dex, but may well be the long-term answer for preventing Piraco from developing a competing product."

I nodded affirmatively.

Joe squinted his eyes and looked up at the ceiling for a moment. I could see the wheels turning. "Hey! What about filing a provisional patent?" Joe asked.

"I'm sorry?" I wasn't sure that I had heard Joe correctly; based on our conversation, I wasn't expecting a question regarding provisional patent applications.

"A provisional patent," Joe repeated. "What about filing for a provisional patent? A friend told me that provisional patents were the way to go. He said that they could be done quickly—you just file them. The patent office doesn't even look at them, and they are a whole lot less expensive than a regular patent. In fact, he told me he did his himself. Maybe I could throw something together this evening. We could get it into the patent office tomorrow morning, then sue Piraco tomorrow afternoon—"

I'm always amazed at some of the myths that are out there, and I interrupted him. "It doesn't work quite that way, Joe. There actually is no such thing as a provisional patent. We can file something called a provisional patent application—an application that isn't subject to some of the formal requirements for a regular patent application—but it is just a stopgap measure. You don't get any enforceable rights by merely filing a provisional application, any more than you do from filing a regular patent application, and you have to file a regular application—and, for that matter, any corresponding foreign applications—within a year of filing the provisional application. A provisional application is a tool that has its uses. In fact, given the time constraints we are working under, we may well file provisional applications with respect to Hi-Bird and your new children's product. But generally I only recommend filing a provisional application when there is a real time crunch, when it's advantageous to 'timeshift' the term of the patent, or in a couple of other very special circumstances."

"I'm not sure I follow," Joe responded.

I paused for a moment, trying to determine the best way to explain the strategic use of provisional applications. "Okay. Let's take a step back. You can think of a patent as an agreement between the inventor and the government. It's a mechanism for providing an incentive for people to bring inventions to market—make them public instead of keep them secret. The inventor teaches the public to make and use the invention, and in return for that is given the right to keep them from using the invention for a certain period of time—under the present law, twenty years from the date a regular patent application is filed. A patent application is, in effect, a proposed patent. If things go well in the patent office the patent will correspond essentially word-for-word to the application. There are three primary parts of a patent application: a drawing, a written description, and claims. The drawing and written description—and the details in the initially filed claims—provide the teaching that the inventor gives the public, and the claims define the scope of the inventor's exclusive rights.

"There are basically two requirements with respect to the written description. The first requirement, referred to as the enablement requirement, is that the description has to include sufficient detail—and be sufficiently clear—to enable the typical person practicing in the relevant technology to actually make and use the invention. The second requirement, the best mode requirement, basically means that the disclosure has to describe the best version of the invention—the inventor can't hold back details about the best way to practice the invention.

"The claims are essentially a one-sentence definition of the invention. Of course, some claims are relatively lengthy, and you see some really creative use of indentation and punctuation so that you can make sense of them. Each claim is considered individually. Something infringes a claim if it has the equivalent of each and every element included in the claim. Okay. So the written description has to provide a certain level of detail with respect to each element of the claim.

"Patentability of a claim is measured against what we refer to as 'the prior art.' This includes information that was known to the public either before you made your invention, or more than one year prior to the effective filing date of the claim. It also includes some other things that are defined by the novelty statute that I mentioned before—but we don't need to go into that now. Anyway, a claim is entitled to an effective filing date of an application only if the application includes the required detail with respect to each element of that claim. A provisional application does not require formal patent claims, or various other formalities typically required in a regular application. Filing a provisional application lets you establish an early effective filing date for a patent claim—as long as you follow up with a regular application within a year, and as long as the provisional application includes the required level of detail for the elements of the claim. So you need the same level of detail in a provisional application as you do in a regular application.

"Okay, so if you need the same detail in a provisional application that you need in a regular application, why not just file a regular application? Well, you are required to include at least one claim in a regular application, and there is no requirement for claims in a provisional application. This is not really much of an advantage. You may need at least one claim in the provisional application to get the benefit of filing the provisional application in countries other than the United States, and, frankly, you can get by with a makeshift claim for the purposes of getting a regular application on file. The real difference between the requirements for a regular application and a provisional application is that you arguably have more flexibility with respect to the manner in which the information—the required detail—is presented in a provisional application than you do with a regular application.

"So if there just plain isn't the time to draft a regular patent applica-tion—like when someone comes to his patent attorney two days before an application has to be filed—you can file what is basically an information dump as a provisional application, and hope that your bases are covered. It's better than nothing. The danger is that some necessary detail may not be in-cluded or described with sufficient clarity. The more different the provisional application is from the ultimate regular application, the more likely that suf-ficiency of disclosure will become an issue.

"There are a couple of other reasons for filing a provisional application. For example, you can shift the effective term of the patent in time by filing a provisional application. In general, the term of the patent is twenty years from the filing date of the application. However, the pendency of the provi-sional application does not count toward the term of the patent. So if you need a filing date, but the market for the product is not mature, you can file a provisional application—with all the detail of a regular application. That way, you can obtain the desired filing but still delay filing of the regular ap-plication for up to a year. Delaying the regular application effectively shifts the term of the patent. The delay in filing the regular application typically will delay the grant of the patent—so the ability to enforce rights will be de-layed, but will extend later in time. Another thing: once a provisional appli-cation has been filed, you are permitted to mark products including the invention described in the application with 'patent pending.' Like I said, this doesn't give you an enforceable right, but it does tend to scare away poten-tial copiers."

Joe was perplexed. "So where are we with respect to the show? What I hear you telling me is that a trade secret action is out—we didn't do what we had to for the software to qualify as a trade secret. The likelihood of obtain-ing timely relief based on copyrights is pretty dismal. A patent action is out. So what can we do?"

"We sue for trademark infringement and request a TRO—a temporary re-straining order—against Piraco displaying at the show. Essentially, anything that's capable of indicating the source of the software can be a trademark, and exclusive rights are acquired immediately through use. In this case, Hi-Bird displays registered trademarks on the screens of the software. Use of a mark that is likely to cause confusion as to source, affiliation, or sponsorship is a trademark infringement under the common law, and under the Lanham Act.

"If we can show trademark, under these circumstances we can get injunctive relief, as well as destruction orders, defendant's profits plus damages and costs, and, in exceptional cases, reasonable attorneys' fees—and more if it's an instance of counterfeiting.

"The primary drawback of trademark protection is that infringement does require a showing of likelihood of confusion. So trademarks are not the proper tool for preventing Piraco from ultimately developing its own version of the Hi-Bird system. The technology of the software can be appropriated without trademark infringement by merely adopting a different mark and excising the original mark from the software. But in the initial product, Piraco didn't do that—it's using unauthorized copies of the Hi-Bird software, which displays the screens featuring TSI's trademarks.

"The only issue is whether, under the circumstances, use of the unauthorized copies displaying the trademarks will create a likelihood of confusion as to source, affiliation, or sponsorship."

"Wait a minute!" Joe blurted out. "They've got a disclaimer. How can anyone be confused? How can consumers be confused if Piraco tells them that Piraco is not affiliated with TSI, and we didn't make the copy of the software, they did?"

I grinned. "There can be confusion based on what happens after the sale. Aftermarket confusion—post-sale confusion—comes into play. Confusion doesn't have to occur at the point of sale—a likelihood of aftermarket or post-sale confusion is actionable. There have been a number of cases like this that have involved Levi's jeans and Rolex watches.

"In those cases, point-of-sale disclaimers, packaging, or both, precluded any confusion on the part of the initial purchaser, but the courts nonetheless found trademark infringement based on the potential for post-sale confusion.

"You see, potential purchasers that observe the counterfeits in use will not necessarily be privy to the disclaimers or packaging, and they may well tend to associate any observed defects or problems in the counterfeit with the genuine goods. If there is a potential that the use of the unauthorized copies will be observed by individuals who were not advised that the copy is unauthorized, a likelihood exists that those potential consumers would believe that the software was an authorized copy. And this could, in fact, have an adverse impact on TSI's reputation.

"Look, let me give you an example. Let's say you pay five dollars for a 'copy watch'—a counterfeit Rolex. It bears the Rolex trademark, and superficially looks like a Rolex. But you know darn well that it's not a real Rolex—you don't get real Rolex watches for five dollars. Let's say that the seller made no bones about it; he came right out and told you that it was fake. He made a complete and unequivocal disclaimer. So it's clear that you were not confused when you made the purchase.

"Okay. But let's say you wear the 'copy watch' for a few weeks, and it begins to turn your wrist green. Your neighbor knows nothing about the history of the watch—as far as he knows it is what it purports to be, as far as he knows it's a real Rolex. And he says to himself, 'Boy, I'm sure not ever going to buy a Rolex. Look at that, it's turning Joe's wrist green.' So Rolex got tagged with the problems caused by the counterfeit. And that's what trademark infringement is all about.

"The same thing is true with respect to the unauthorized copy of software. For example, the unauthorized copy might not have been updated with a program fix, and the observer would be exposed to an apparent bug in the program, which had actually been cured. Or the observer may be exposed to an operator having difficulties that would be cured by a quick call to TSI's support services if an authorized copy had been involved.

"So there is clearly an actionable likelihood of confusion. The use by Piraco of the Hi-Bird marks in the screens displayed by the unauthorized copies presents a potential trademark action. In fact, the infringement arguably comes within the anticounterfeiting provisions of the Lanham Act—the trademark statute. In any event, it's entirely feasible that a TRO—a temporary restraining order—could be obtained, preventing Piraco from displaying Hi-Bird at the show.

"On top of that, assuming that we bring suit in Arizona—and we should be able to do that since the show is in Phoenix—we can include a count under the state trademark statute. The Arizona state trademark statute creates an irrebuttable presumption of actionable customer confusion in instances of knowing distribution or use of unauthorized copies of software displaying trademarks registered in Arizona." I couldn't help bragging a little. "I helped draft that legislation.

"So the bottom line is this. Nothing is guaranteed, but we've got a shot at a TRO to stop Piraco at the show. Hopefully that will take care of the short-term problem. To stop Piraco from developing its own analogous software, it looks like we should get a patent application on file with respect to Hi-Bird, posthaste. If we get that patent, and the claims are broad enough, that will take care of the U.S. We should also go ahead and register the copyright on Hi-Bird software. At this point it doesn't look like there is any chance of establishing trade secret status for the software, so there is no reason to delay. Unfortunately, it looks like it's too late for patent protection on Hi-Bird in most countries outside of the U.S. And, if you are going to want to patent your new technology outside of the U.S., we'll have to get an application file on it by the day you give your speech. Either that or cancel or change the subject of the talk. I'm also counseling you to choose something other than 'Big-Bird' to call the new product. If you use 'Big-Bird' you're just going to end up paying me a bunch of money and still get hammered. Speaking of money, we really should talk about what it's going to cost you to have me do all this work . . ."

Now Joe really began to feel nervous.

So, in our hypothetical, the good guys ultimately prevail. More importantly, however, the hypothetical illustrates that the different protection mechanisms will be applicable to a greater or lesser degree depending upon the circumstances.

In the following sections, we will explore in somewhat more depth the different legal mechanisms for protecting intellectual property. The principles discussed later are generally applicable. However, we will also look at special considerations that arise when a software, firmware, or semiconductor chip product is at issue.

Trade Secret Protection

Everybody has secrets. Keeping things secret is probably the most ancient form of intellectual property protection. Any proprietary information that you can keep out of the public domain can be a "trade secret." Maintaining technology as a trade secret protects it in the sense that, if the competition doesn't know about the technology, it can't copy it.

In the United States, trade secret rights that are affirmatively enforceable against others are provided under the laws of the various individual states. Unlike patents, copyrights, mask works, and trademarks, there is no federal law directly pertaining to trade secret actions other than by the government.[1] Accordingly, trade secret rights tend to vary from state to state. However, the existence of the federal patent and copyright statutes has been found to "preempt" the states from enacting statutes that overlap or conflict with the federal law.[2] This has tended to force state trade secret statutes to require the "classical" common-law elements for trade secret protection, effectively engendering some commonality in the state laws. Historically, state trade secret laws have differed primarily with respect to treatment of nontechnological information, such as customer lists, and with respect to the extent to which the subject matter at issue had to be unknown to others in order to qualify for the protection. More recently, widespread acceptance of a model trade secret statute, the Uniform Trade Secrets Act, has brought an additional element of consistency to the trade secret laws of the various states. Some form of the Uniform Trade Secrets Act has presently been adopted in forty-three states and the District of Columbia.[3]

Uniform Trade Secrets Act

Requisites for Trade Secret Status:

- Derives independent economic value . . . from not being generally known . . . and not being readily ascertainable by proper means . . .
- Is the subject of efforts that are reasonable under the circumstances to maintain its secrecy

In essentially every jurisdiction, however, in order to qualify for protection, the subject matter of the trade secret right must meet certain prerequisites: it must be confidential (not generally known or readily ascertainable from publicly available information); it must be subject to reasonable efforts to maintain its secrecy (e.g., restricted access, disclosed only under confidentiality agreements, etc.); and it must derive some value from being kept secret.

Scope of Protection

You can protect technology as a trade secret for a potentially infinite period. The technology is "protected" as long as it is not accessible to competitors.

However, a trade secret can be very fragile. Once it becomes generally known, irrespective of how it becomes known, as a practical matter, trade secret protection is lost. The primary disadvantage of trade secret protection is that it provides you absolutely no protection what-

Trade Secret PROs

- Available for anything that gives a competitive edge as long as it can be kept secret
- Protects as long as it can be kept secret—potentially infinite

Trade Secrets CONs

- No protection against:
  —independent development
  —reverse engineering from publicly available information
- As a practical matter, trade secret protection is simply not applicable to technology in any product that is sold to the public

soever against someone else independently developing the technology. Moreover, it is conceivable that the person who later independently develops the technology could obtain a patent on it and foreclose you from further use of it.[4]

It should also be appreciated that some types of technology are totally unsuited for trade secret protection. Any technology embodied in a product that is sold to the public and can be reverse-engineered simply cannot effectively be maintained as a trade secret. *In general, absent an express or implied contractual obligation, you (and everyone else) are at liberty to use and copy any unpatented, uncopyrighted technology that comes into your (their) possession legally, as long as there is no likelihood that the public would be deceived or confused as to the source of a product or sponsorship or affiliation between different entities.*

Procedure for Maintaining a Trade Secret

The procedure for maintaining a trade secret is relatively simple. All technology considered proprietary should be clearly defined as such. As a basic proposition, all printouts, flowcharts, schematics, layouts, blueprints, technical data, test results, and so forth that contain confidential information should be marked with a proprietary legend.

It is important, however, that you not be overzealous in categorizing information as confidential, or in the use of nondisclosure and noncompetition agreements. The indiscriminate use of proprietary legends can dilute the significance of a legend when it is used on something that is truly confidential. It can also cause evidentiary problems. Consider the situation of the company that marks a widely distributed manual "Confidential," then years later must prove that a competitor had access to the manual.

You should maintain tight security and restrict entry and view into the area in which the trade secret is practiced or kept. Access to and knowledge of the trade secret should be permitted only on a need-to-know basis. Records should be kept as to all persons given access to any portion of the trade secret. All copies of printouts should be accounted for. For example, it is difficult to assert that a program is a valuable trade secret when it can be shown that the programmer's children took printouts to school to use as scratch paper. Ideally, except for an archive printout of each version of the program, all printouts of trade secret programs and data should be destroyed (shredded, incinerated, etc.).

Confidentiality agreements should be executed with all parties who are given access to any part of the trade secret technology. In this regard, it is especially important for you to be sure that any potential customer, vendor, or contractor who is permitted access to any aspect of the proprietary technology signs a confidentiality agreement. Moreover, each principal and/or employee of a company who has access to any aspect of the technology should sign an appropriate employee's invention and confidentiality agreement. Generally, such agreements should be entered into with employees at or prior to their hiring. While it is not necessary in all states,[5] if the individual entering into the agreement is already an employee, it is prudent to give some additional form of consideration (money, promotion, or the like) for signing the agreement. It also may be prudent for a business to adopt a policy of interviewing all exiting employees to remind them of the confidentiality agreement.

Absent some express or implied contractual obligation to the contrary, there is no obligation to maintain information received or obtained in confidence. While an obligation can often be implied as a matter of law or from the surrounding circumstances, a maxim of general applicability that is particularly apropos to trade secrets is: "A verbal agreement is not worth the paper it's written on."

To put the issue in perspective, recall Horror Story 6 (p. 3). If X-Corp had obtained a confidentiality agreement from the customer before divulging the X-Corp technique, the customer could possibly have been prevented from disclosing the X-Corp program to the competition, or made liable for the damage resulting from the disclosure. However, as a practical matter, even if the customer disclosed the program to the competition in violation of an express confidentiality agreement, under many circumstances it would be impossible to prevent the competition from using the technique after the disclosure.

In some instances, where employees have access to trade secret information and leave the company to take a similar position with a competitor, disclosure or use of the former employer's confidential information may be inevitable, notwithstanding any agreement to the contrary. Where this is the case, a noncompetition agreement with the employee should be considered as a mechanism for ensuring that the confidential information is not disclosed. However, such agreements are disfavored and strictly construed by the courts. To ensure enforceability, the noncompetition agreement should be carefully crafted so that geographic scope, duration, and scope of prohibited employment are restricted to the minimum necessary to protect the proprietary rights of the former employer; if any of the aspects of the agreement are deemed to be overly broad or overreaching, a court is likely to find the agreement unenforceable.[6] For example, a noncompetition agreement that precludes employment by a competitor irrespective of capacity (such as one that would preclude a former employee from taking a position as the janitor for a competitor) would likely be deemed overly broad, and hence unenforceable by the courts. The same is true for a noncompetition provision of infinite duration. The provision of (or failure to provide) special compensation to the employee for accepting the noncompetition obligation may also be a factor in the enforceability of the agreement.

It is important that noncompetition agreements be used judiciously. The use of noncompetition agreements with employees who do not have access to confidential information tends to detract from the viability of noncompetition agreements in situations where a noncompetition agreement may be the only effective mechanism for preventing disclosure or use of confidential information.

Exploiting Trade Secrets

You typically exploit trade secrets (make money from use by others) through a licensing program. Basically, you permit a third party to use the trade secret under a license agreement that expressly obligates them not to disclose the trade secret and to take various precautions to ensure that it is not inadvertently disclosed to others. The license agreement should be very explicit as to exactly what information is provided to the licensee. However,

> **Legal Fiction of Secrecy**
>
> Contractually impose obligation of confidentiality on everyone with access to the information

as a practical matter, it is often difficult to police and enforce trade secret licenses, particularly when there are a substantial number of licensees. License agreements will be more fully discussed in the section titled "Overview and Comparison of Agreements Affecting Intellectual Property Rights and Liabilities" later in this book.

Special Considerations with Respect to Software Developments

Trade secret protection for software that is distributed to others (distributed software) is typically effected by licensing others to use the software and/or through various technological mechanisms built into the program that tend to prevent copying.

Technological mechanisms such as encryption, nonstandard formats, a requirement for special interface hardware, or, in the case of firmware, encapsulation and/or nonstandard packaging or pin-spacing are often used in an attempt to prevent copying. Other security mechanisms are typically used in conjunction with a license, such as techniques for identifying the source of unauthorized copies of a program. For example, serial numbers, digital watermarks, or other identification are often included in the body of each copy of the program to help identify the source of unauthorized copies. A program may also be "keyed" to a particular hardware system, or may include encrypted destruct mechanisms that erase or disable the pro-

**Issues with
Technological Security**

- Potential product liability
- Potential violation of computer crime statute

There is ALWAYS someone out there who CAN break it

gram unless periodically "defused" or reset by the licensor. However, potentially serious product liability problems are inherent in the use of some types of physical security mechanisms. Reliability is a major concern. Any physical security mechanism must be capable of *reliably* discriminating between authorized and unauthorized uses. The failure of a security mechanism, which prevents someone rightfully in possession of a software product from using it, or which destroys a rightful user's database, may result in large damage claims.

In addition, the use of a physical security mechanism without adequate warning to the user may well give rise to criminal liability under the "computer crimes" statutes in various states. All of the states, with the exception of Arkansas, Maine, Vermont, and West Virginia (and the District of Columbia), have enacted "Computer Crime Statutes" that prohibit individuals from tampering with computers, or from accessing unauthorized computer records. The Arizona statute is typical:

§13-2316. Computer fraud; classification

A. A person commits computer fraud in the first degree by accessing, altering, damaging or destroying without authorization or exceeding authorization of use of any computer, computer system, computer network, or any part of such computer, system or network, with the intent to devise or execute any scheme or artifice to defraud or deceive, or control property or services by means of false or fraudulent pretenses, representations or promises.

B. A person commits computer fraud in the second degree by intentionally and without authorization or by exceeding authorization accessing, altering, damaging or destroying any computer, computer system or computer network or any computer software, program or data contained in such computer, computer system or computer network.

C. Computer fraud in the first degree is a class 3 felony. Computer fraud in the second degree is a class 5 felony.

Software licenses are often based on trade secret rights—contracts between the licensor (typically the proprietor of the software) and the end user. A typical software license[7] contains an acknowledgment of the secret or confidential nature of the software and requires the licensee to maintain the software in confidence. For example, the licensee agrees not to show or provide the software to anyone outside of the licensed company without the permission of the licensor. The license often also contains provisions restricting the use of the licensed software, for example, to a designated central processing unit (CPU), or to "internal use only." Under a typical license, the software remains the property of the licensor, and the licensor has the right to terminate the license and demand the return of the licensed software if the licensee breaches the license agreement. The license also typically includes "warranty" or "warranty disclaimer" provisions, precisely defining the obligations and liability of the licensor if the program does not operate as expected. The programmer/licensor generally attempts to disclaim all warranties (and thus all liability) including warranties of "merchantability" and "fitness for a particular purpose" often implied by law. From the perspective of the licensee, however, it is desirable to obtain a warranty that the program will operate in the manner represented, that is, as described in the user's manual.

Trade secret protection of software has a distinct advantage in that, through a license, items that are not necessarily patentable or copyrightable can be protected. However, where high-volume products are involved, particularly where intermediaries such as distributors and retailers are involved in marketing the software to the end user, the requirement of affirmative acceptance is a formidable obstacle to a trade secret licensing program. In order for a license to be valid, the requirements for a valid contract must be met. There must be an offer setting forth the terms of the agreement, and an affirmative acceptance of those terms. Generally, when ongoing obligations are imposed, acceptance of the terms of an agreement is manifested by signing the agreement. However, it is typically impracticable to obtain signed agreements from each end user of a mass-marketed product.

Mass Marketing of Software

The software industry has attempted to create contracts through a number of different mechanisms that do not require the actual execution (signing) of a written agreement: the "shrink-wrap" or "package" license, and the "web-wrap" or "click" license. There are three primary practices now generically referred to as shrink-wrap licenses:

- *Box-top license.* A complete agreement is printed on the package exterior (or visible under the shrink-wrap) with a legend to the effect that opening the package indicates acceptance of the terms of the agreement. The agreement is visible prior to opening the package. This approach was the original exterior shrink-wrap license, but soon came into conflict with marketing concerns. The visible exterior "real estate" on the packaging was considered particularly valuable for marketing purposes; it could be used to send a sales message to the purchasing public. Marketing concerns prevailed and box-top licenses became a rarity.

- *"In-the-box surprise license."* An "agreement" is included inside the package, the existence of which is not apparent until after the software is purchased and the package is opened. On an envelope inside the box containing the disks or CDs, a legend is provided to the effect that opening the envelope indicates acceptance of the terms of the agreement, and/or a legend appears during the installation process to the effect that use of the software indicates acceptance. The legend is not ascertainable until after the package is opened. The no-notice, terms-hidden-in-the-box license is, in effect, the converse of the box-top license. Marketing, as opposed to legal, concerns were predominant.

- *"Exterior notice, terms-hidden-in-the-box license."* This approach is an intermediate form. The actual terms of the agreement are not apparent until the package is opened, but a legend noting the existence of a "license agreement" is provided on the packaging.[8] While this type of license is becoming more prevalent, relatively few software publishers presently include any manner of "subject to license" notice on the exterior packaging of their products.

The "click" or "web-wrap" license involves requiring a potential user to click on a button indicating the acceptance of the terms of a license (typically displayed in a dialog box, or available via hyperlink). This approach is typically used in two significantly different contexts: (a) the "click acceptance" is required before a copy of the software can be downloaded over the Internet, and (b) the "click acceptance" is required before the software can be installed. Often, where the click acceptance is required for installation, the terms of the agreement are not available to the end user until after the software has already been acquired (paid for).

The efficacy of shrink-wrap and click licenses is governed by the applicable law of contracts. In general, a valid contract requires an "offer," an "acceptance," and "consideration." It is difficult to argue that there has been any manner of acceptance under circumstances where the consumer's first notice of the license agreement is only after the software is purchased. In determining the efficacy of shrink-wrap licenses it is necessary to, at the very least, distinguish situations where conspicuous prepurchase notice of a license agreement is provided from situations where its existence is apparent only after opening the box or attempting to install the software.

It can also be argued that sufficient steps have not been taken to preserve the trade secret, thereby forfeiting trade secret status. In this regard, an issue often arises as to how widely a software product can be licensed before the trade secret is lost. That is, how many people can be told a "secret" before it is no longer a secret? Can a product be considered a trade secret when almost everyone who would be interested knows or has access to it? These are questions of fact, and must be determined on a case-by-case basis.

Further, an issue has arisen in the courts as to whether it is now even possible to protect software as a trade secret if it is also protectable by copyright. Under the constitutional "Preemption Doctrine," when a federal statute is applicable in a given area, the states are precluded from also having statutes with respect to that area—the state law is "preempted" by the federal law. It has been argued that, since software may be protected under the federal copyright statute, state trade secret law is preempted. The courts have dealt with the "preemption" issue in a variety of ways.[9] The trend, however, appears to be against finding a state trade secret law preempted as it applies to software, so long as some element is required in addition to the requisite elements for a copyright infringement.[10]

Utility Patent Protection

Patent protection can, potentially, give you the right to prevent (exclude) others from making, using, or selling any product that incorporates the central idea or concept of an invention. Obtaining one or more patents on the inventive portions of a product can provide the broadest scope of legal protection. Conversely, as a basic proposition, absent some contractual obligation or likelihood of confusion as to source, anyone can make, use, or sell unpatented products.

In most countries, other than the United States, a patent grant originated as a gift or favor from the sovereign. In fact, many of the early "patents" granted in Europe had nothing to do with invention; they related to exclusive trading rights within a geographic region or to ownership of land. So, in part because of differing origins, the philosophy of the United States and the various foreign systems are subtly different. This tends to be reflected in subtle (and not-so-subtle) differences between the patent laws of the United States and other countries.

The U.S. patent system is designed to provide an incentive for inventors to bring their inventions to market for the benefit of the public, and to make their discoveries known (as opposed to keeping them secret). Consider this: Why would a business spend time and money on research and development if its efforts could be appropriated as soon as a product embodying the R&D was put on the market? How could a start-up possibly compete against the resources and market power of the "Big Boys"? The bottom line is that new businesses would be few and far between—for the most part they would be at the mercy of the established Big Boys. Other than perhaps the Big Boys (who could rely on market power for protection against competion), businesses would tend not to bring products to market unless they could maintain secrecy about some critical aspect of (or process of making) the product. This scenario is right out of history—my notion of the "dark ages." Most technology in medieval times was controlled by the guilds (or the church) and kept strictly secret. For someone outside of a guild to obtain guild knowledge could be worth that person's life. ("I'd tell you, but then I'd have to kill you.") During these "dark ages," technology and science were held at a standstill—if technology was developed, it was kept secret and was not available for others to build and improve upon, and competition against the Big Boys of those times was next to impossible.

This sorry state of affairs was something the founding fathers of the United States wanted to avoid. To do that, they built the basis for a patent system into the federal Constitution. Article I, Section 8 of the U.S. Constitution provides: "The Congress shall have the power . . . to promote the progress of science and useful arts, by securing for a limited time to authors and inventors the exclusive right to their respective writings and discoveries." Congress was then left the task of developing the particulars of a system for inducing an "inventor" to make the necessary investment of time and money in research, while at the same time ensuring that the work of the inventor would ultimately become available to the public. The result is the patent system that, today, is reflected in Title 35 of the United States Code and Chapter 37 of the Code of Federal Regulations.

> **The U.S. patent system originated in the Constitution**

In a nutshell, a patent in the United States is a quid pro quo ("give-and-take") agreement between you and the government. The inventor teaches the public, in enough detail to enable a person "of ordinary skill" in the field of the invention (the average engineer, technician, scientist, or worker in the particular area of technology of the invention), how to make and use the invention without undue experimentation. In return, the inventor is given the right to exclude the public from making, using, importing, offering for sale, or selling the invention for a period of up to twenty years from the date that the application for patent is filed.

The award of "exclusive rights" to the invention protects the inventor's investment. In return, the public is provided with the knowledge of how to use the invention. While the public cannot make, use, offer for sale, or sell the invention during the term of the patent (unless licensed by the patent owner), further research can begin at the point where the invention left off. In addition, after the patent lapses, the public is free to use the invention. In this way, the patent system provides both protection to the inventor and a very real benefit to the public.

Because of this quid pro quo between the inventor and the government, a patent grant is divided into two major parts: the written description, which includes a detailed description of the invention; and the claims, which define the rights of the inventor. This will be discussed in more detail later in the book.

Of course, there are certain safeguards included to make sure that the public receives a true benefit from the bargain. Threshold criteria must be met before an inventor is awarded exclusivity to an invention. The inventor must actually add something new and useful to the public knowledge (and observe the spirit of the patent law). As will be discussed, in order to be patentable an invention must be: (a) within certain broad categories of subject matter,[1] (b) "novel,"[2] and (c) "nonobvious."[3]

> **Patentable?**
> - Within statutory categories of patentable subject matter
> - Novel and not obvious

The categories of patentable subject matter encompass essentially "anything under the sun made by man," and exclude only those things that logically could not be subject to exclusivity, or with respect to which exclusivity could not realistically be enforced, such as laws of nature, natural phenomena, or abstract ideas.

Novelty, and nonobviousness, are measured against what is often referred to as the "prior art." Novelty is defined in the patent law[4] by exception; an invention is considered novel unless specific circumstances (referred to as "statutory bars") have occurred. In effect, when a statutory bar occurs, the subject matter of the statutory bar becomes "prior art" against which the patentability of an invention is measured. In essence, prior art with respect to invention claimed in a patent includes: (a) things that were (i) commercialized by the applicant for the applicant's business, or (ii) ascertainable from publicly available information more than one year before the application for patent was filed; and (b) things that either (i) the inventor knew, or (ii) were ascertainable from publicly available information, or (iii) were invented by someone else (and not maintained as a trade secret), before the invention was made. Under the novelty and nonobviousness sections of the law, a claimed invention is not patentable if the prior art fully anticipates (includes each and every element of), or renders obvious, the claim.[5]

The requirements for patentability will be discussed in more detail later in the book.

Exclusive Right

In order to promote improvements on inventions by providing patent protection for the improvements without degrading the protection provided for basic inventions, a patent provides an "exclusive" (exclusionary) right to the inventor. That is, if you hold a patent (if you are a patentee), you have the right to exclude (prevent) others from practicing the invention. *However, just because you have a patent does not necessarily mean that you have the right to* practice *your invention.*[6]

An unauthorized item infringes a patent if it includes elements corresponding to each and every element in any claim in the patent. It is irrelevant that the item includes additional elements, even if the additional elements (or combination) are patentable in their own right.

To illustrate the "exclusive" nature of patent protection, let's take a trip back in time to when the "stool" and "chair" were patentable inventions (and take the liberty of assuming that there was a patent system in place). Assume that I have just invented and obtained patent protection on the "stool," claiming: "Apparatus comprising a seat and a support structure for maintaining the seat at a predetermined level from the ground." You thereafter purchase a stool and find that you have difficulties remaining seated—every time you lean back, you fall off! Ultimately, you develop a back for my stool and invent the "chair." You then obtain patent protection on the "chair," claiming: "Apparatus comprising a seat, a support structure for maintaining the seat at a predetermined level from the ground, and a back extending above the seat."

You and I both have patents. However, notwithstanding the addition of the "back," your "chair" still includes elements corresponding to each and every element of my basic patent on the "stool." Similarly, while I am free to make, use and sell my "stool" (assuming that no other patents cover the stool structure), I cannot put a back on my "stool" without infringing your patent on the "chair."

How does this promote the advancement of technology? As a practical matter, the result is that you and I each obtain a license from the other under the respective patents, and, where before there was only one "stool" manufacturer, there are suddenly two "chair" manufacturers.

This example is overly simplistic, and obviously quite some time has passed since the stool or chair per se have been patentable inventions. However, the example does illustrate the "exclusive" nature of patent protection and improvement patents.

The "exclusive" nature of the patent grant is of consequence with respect to the procedures that should be followed by a business before introducing a new product. The issue of whether any aspect of the product is patentable is entirely different and distinct from the issue of whether the product infringes any patent held by another. Before introducing a new product you should study both of these issues thoroughly.

Patentable Subject Matter: Applicability to Software Inventions and Business Methods

Patent protection is available for "any new and useful process, machine, manufacture or composition of matter, or new and useful improvement thereof"—categories of subject matter that have been characterized by the

> ### Patentable Subject Matter
>
> • Anything under the sun that is made by man

Supreme Court as "anything under the sun that is made by man."[7] An invention in any one of those categories is generally patentable if it is neither "anticipated" by (identical to)[8] or "obvious"[9] in view of technology already known or dedicated to the public (referred to as the "prior art"). As a general proposition, there is no question that electronic or mechanical apparatus, electronic systems and components, and methods of performing industrial processes are patentable subject matter.

But what about software and methods of doing business?[10] Historically, there has been a great deal of controversy in the courts as to whether software and firmware developments, not to mention methods of doing business, come within any of the categories specified by the statute. It is now clear, however, that the majority of software and firmware inventions and methods of doing business are, in fact, patentable subject matter. Of course, in order to be patentable the inventions must still meet the novelty and nonobviousness criteria.

The courts have determined that certain things are definitely outside the categories of patentable subject matter—"laws of nature, natural phenomena, and abstract ideas."[11]

> ### Outside Statutory Classes
>
> • Abstract Ideas Divorced from Structure—
> • Mathematical Algorithm
> • Natural Phenomena
> • Laws of Nature

ABSTRACT IDEAS OR INFORMATION

Abstract ideas or a set of words cannot be patented. I could not patent the fact that my name is Mike Lechter or the set of words that make up this book. (However, patent protection might be available for embodiments of the *idea* or *concept* described by the words or the way paper is folded or perforated relative to printed matter.)[12]

NATURAL PHENOMENA; THINGS UNALTERED FROM A NATURAL STATE

For example, a rock taken unaltered from the earth is not, per se, patentable. (However, a given *method of using* the rock might be patentable.)

LAWS OF NATURE

Abstract principles, divorced from any physical structure (e.g., laws of nature) are not, per se, patentable. For example, Newton could not have patented "gravity." (Everybody has to use it.)

How do software and business methods inventions fit into a permissible category? Let's look at software inventions first. Since mere printed matter (a set of words) is generally not patentable, neither software code per se, nor documentation describing a program is, in itself, typically patentable. *The issue, however, is typically whether the underlying idea of the program is patentable as a "new and useful process."* If so, the execution of a patented program in a machine or computer, or the sale of a disk or ROM containing the program, would be an infringement of the patent.

The controversy over the availability of patent protection for computer programs arose because, at one time, some courts equated computer programs with mathematical algorithms. Mathematical algorithms, in the abstract, are considered to be mere manifestations of scientific principles. Consider, for example, the equation $e = mc^2$. The equation is, in effect, an abstract scientific principle.

The issue with respect to whether methods of doing business are patentable subject matter was more straightforward—business methods were considered abstract information (my name is Mike Lechter) and therefore not susceptible to patent protection.

However, it is now settled that both computer programs and methods of doing business are patentable subject matter. The law in this regard developed in stages. The first step was recognition by the courts that a computer program is not necessarily equivalent to a mathematical algorithm or law of nature. The Supreme Court decided two cases related to the patentability of software[13] and firmware[14] in 1981. In essence, the Court held that the fact that the inventive concept of an otherwise patentable invention resides in a programmed computer or in firmware does not make the invention un-patentable. The Supreme Court did not, however, specifically reach the issue of whether software or firmware, outside the context of a hardware system or process, is patentable subject matter, and the two cases did not in them-selves end the controversy. Methods of doing business, unless embodied in a hardware system, were still not considered patentable subject matter.

In October 1982, the Court of Appeals for the Federal Circuit (Federal Circuit) was created, with jurisdiction over all appeals from the U.S. district courts relating to patent matters (and, in most cases, appeals from the Patent and Trademark Office decisions). The Federal Circuit was formed by com-bining the Court of Customs and Patent Appeals (CCPA) and the U.S. Court of Claims, and has expressly adopted the body of law developed earlier by the CCPA and Court of Claims.[15] This is particularly significant because the Supreme Court has tended to defer to the Federal Circuit's expertise in patent and other technological matters, and, therefore, as a practical matter, the ultimate "law" on the patentability of software is determined by the Fed-eral Circuit. The CCPA (and thus the Federal Circuit) has for a number of years recognized that "computer program" and "mathematical algorithm" are not synonymous, and considers only mathematical algorithms to be un-patentable subject matter. In this regard, the CCPA has adopted a two-part test to determine whether a given patent claim covers patentable subject matter. The CCPA has construed the early Supreme Court cases to support this two-part test.

Under the CCPA test, the claim is first analyzed to see if a mathematical algorithm (defined as a "procedure for solving a given type of mathematical problem") is directly or indirectly recited. If not, the claim is directed to patentable subject matter. If a mathematical algorithm is found, the claim as a whole is then analyzed to determine whether the algorithm is "applied in any manner to physical elements or process steps." If the physical elements or process steps are present, the claim "passes muster" under the patent statute.[16]

In applying the first part of the two-part test to a compiler program, the CCPA has stated:

> It is [a mathematical] algorithm that constitutes nonstatutory subject
> matter, and this court has consistently rejected attempts to enlarge the

"mathematical algorithm" exception to .the definition of patentable subject matter in section 101 to include nonmathematical algorithms.[17]

The court held that patent protection was available for the compiler program:

> Appellants' method claims are directed to executing programs in a computer. The method operates on any program and any formula that may be input, regardless of mathematical content. That a computer controlled according to the invention is capable of handling mathematics is irrelevant to the question of whether a mathematical algorithm is recited by the claims.[18]

The court found that the steps of examining, compiling, storing, and executing used to describe the program do not involve any mathematical algorithm, and thus define patentable subject matter. Thus, patent protection is available for computer programs per se, except perhaps in the case of pure "number-cruncher" type programs where the inventive concept is a particular mathematical formula implemented by the program (as opposed to the particular manner in which the mathematical formula is implemented by the program).

Moreover, under the CCPA test, even where a mathematical algorithm is involved, patent protection may still be possible so long as the algorithm is "applied in any manner" to physical elements or process steps.[19] Thus, patent protection may be available for even a number-cruncher program, when used in a physical system or apparatus. Of course, in practice, the majority of number-cruncher programs are either used in conjunction with physical systems or processes, and are therefore protectable, or are valuable because of some economy in memory or execution time provided by the implementation of a formula rather than the formula itself. It is the feature that saves memory or time that is to be protected—not the formula—and the feature, defined in terms of the steps of examining, storing, executing, and so forth, is patentable subject matter.

In light of the Supreme Court and Federal Circuit decisions, the PTO for a time adopted the CCPA two-part test for patentable subject matter.[20]

More recent cases in the Federal Circuit have established a more expansive definition of patentable subject matter.[21] These cases establish that processes, such as business methods, that do not necessarily even involve a computer (although most do, one way or another) may be patentable subject matter. The process or business method need only produce "a useful, concrete and tangible result." So what is a "useful, concrete, and tangible result"? Frankly, there is no clear definition. However, the Federal Circuit has confirmed the patentability of processes or methods (e.g., methods of doing business) that are performed by a computer in accordance with a program, or that use newly available modes of information exchange (e.g., the Internet), or that use databases (assuming of course the novelty and nonobviousness requirements are met). For example, transforming data into a more meaningful form has been found to be a "useful, concrete and tangible result." Some examples might be: the transformation of data, representing discrete dollar amounts, by a machine through a series of mathematical calculations into a final share price momentarily fixed for recording and reporting purposes and even accepted and relied upon by regulatory authorities and in subsequent trades;[22] data, transformed by a machine through a series of mathematical calculations to produce a smooth waveform display on a rasterizer monitor;[23] electrocardiograph signals from a patient's heartbeat transformed by a machine through a series of mathematical calculations to indicate the condition of a patient's heart.[24]

Business Method Is Patentable If:

- It produces a useful, concrete, and tangible result
—and—
- It is novel and not obvious

The PTO Board of Patent Appeals and Interferences (the body that hears appeals from actions taken by patent examiners) has clearly adopted the logic of the Federal Circuit, which noted that a "practical application" was "a useful, concrete, and tangible result."[25] The court further stated:[26]

> Today, we hold that the transformation of data, representing discrete dollar amounts, by a machine through a series of mathematical calculations into a final share price, constitutes a practical application of a mathematical algorithm, formula, or calculation, because it produces "a useful, concrete and tangible result"—a final share price momentarily fixed for recording and reporting purposes and even

accepted and relied upon by regulatory authorities and in subsequent trades.

Although this statement is made with respect to mathematical calculations, it is manifestly intended to apply to the analysis of other "abstract ideas." Thus, a "process" no longer requires a physical transformation of something to a different state or thing: transformation of data is sufficient if it produces "a useful, concrete and tangible result." This reasoning appears intended to be broadly construed.

The examining corps of the PTO appears to be somewhat reluctant to embrace the Federal Circuit standard. A version of the broadened standard has now been adopted by the PTO.[27] The PTO has stated that in order to cover patentable subject matter, "[t]he claimed invention as a whole must accomplish a practical application. That is, it must produce a 'useful, concrete and tangible result.'"[28] However, the embellishments to, and application of, the "useful, concrete and tangible result" standard by the PTO are anything but clear.[29]

One thing is for sure. Even when an invention is clearly patentable subject matter, unless the claim defining the invention is properly drafted it will run into trouble in the PTO and/or courts. Claims intended to cover an invention can be drafted in many different ways, and in some cases form is exalted over substance. The specific manner in which the claim is drafted can be determinative as to whether or not the claim is found to define a "useful, concrete and tangible result."[30]

The migration of business onto the Internet has given rise to a multitude of patentable methods of doing business (many of which are the subjects of patents, or pending patent applications). Patent protection for software and/or business methods has successfully been obtained and exploited. Patents on software and business method inventions are now common.[31] According to the PTO,[32] of the applications filed in 1999, 2,658 were classified as claiming Automated Business Data Processing Technologies (Class 705); 3,898 as claiming Display Data Processing (e.g., graphical user interfaces, Web browsers) (Class 345); 3,190 as claiming Networked Computer Data Processing (Class 709); 3,068 as claiming Databases and Word Processors (Class 707); and 2,905 as claiming Dynamic Information Storage (e.g., disk drives) (Classes 360 and 369). Software patents have been obtained by numerous companies, notably

Adobe, Amazon.com, Apple, AT&T, AutoDesk, Bay Networks, Borland International, Bull, CASHFLOW Technologies, Cisco Systems, Citrix, Columbia University, Compuware, Computer Associates, Corel, Cybercash, Dragon Systems, Electronic Data Systems, Executive Software, Hewlett-Packard, IBM, Inso, Intel, Lotus, Micrografx, Microsoft, Mijenix Corporation, Netscape, Network Associates, Novell, Oracle, priceline.com, Raptor Systems, Sun Microsystems, Symantec, Trend Micro, Veritas Software, and WebTV Networks. Patents relating to financial systems (typically involving software) have also been obtained by numerous companies, notably Advanced Investment Technology, Affinity Technology Group, Albert Einstein Healthcare Network, Cedel Bank, Checkfree Corporation, Citibank, Citicorp Development Center, Columbia University, Financial Engineering Associates, General Electric, HSX, Merrill Lynch, Morgan Stanley Group, Proprietary Financial Products, Signature Financial Group, and the Evergreen Group. The courts have upheld patents on purely software/business method inventions.[33] Over the years, I have been involved in obtaining and successfully exploiting patents on various aspects of both compiler-type and applications-type programs, as well as on microprocessor-based systems that have an inventive concept embodied primarily in the software or firmware (as opposed to the hardware) of the system. More recently, my colleagues and I have been regularly called upon to develop protection strategies (often involving patent protection) of Internet-based business methods.

Requisites for Patentability

As noted above, the patent system incorporates safeguards to make sure that the public receives a true benefit in return for awarding exclusivity. Threshold criteria must be met before an inventor is awarded exclusivity to an invention. In addition to covering patentable subject matter,[34] to be patentable an invention must also be: (a) "novel,"[35] and (b) "nonobvious."[36] Under the novelty and nonobviousness sections of the law, a claimed invention is not patentable if the "prior art" (defined by "statutory bars") fully anticipates (includes each and every element of) or renders obvious, the claim.[37]

Statutory Bars

The patent statute expressly precludes obtaining a patent under certain circumstances. In theory, under specific circumstances set forth in the patent statute, the invention is considered either to have already passed into the public domain, that is, become public property, or to have already become the property of another and hence not be patentable. These circumstances are referred to as statutory bars. The patent statute regarding "novelty" sets forth the statutory bars.[38] In effect, when a statutory bar occurs, its subject matter becomes prior art against which the patentability of an invention is measured.

Statutory Bars

• Circumstances that would prevent obtaining a patent on an otherwise patentable invention

Under the novelty section of the law, a claimed invention is not patentable if the prior art fully anticipates (includes each and every element of) the claim.[39] However, the novelty section of the statute is also incorporated by reference into the nonobviousness section;[40] a claimed invention is not patentable if the prior art defined by the novelty section renders the claim obvious.[41] Because of the conjunctive use of the novelty (§102) and nonobviousness (§103) sections, the statutory bars are sometimes referred to as the section 102/103 bars.

Statutory Bars—Purpose

• Establish Threshold—prevent obtaining a patent on something already owned by another or in the public domain
• Hold Patentee to Bargain—prevent extension of patent rights beyond the term of the patent

The statutory bars are the pitfalls that so often trip up the unwary. Each of them will be discussed individually below.

PRIOR PUBLIC KNOWLEDGE

An inventor is not entitled to a patent on an invention if the invention is publicly known before the inventor conceives it. The statute states:

§102 A person shall be entitled to a patent unless—

(a) the invention was known or used by others in this country, or patented or described in a printed publication in this or a foreign country, before the invention thereof by the applicant for patent. . . .

This bar has been construed to mean the invention must not have been *publicly* known or used by others in the United States, or patented or de-

> **Statutory Bars—Not New**
>
> - Invention publicly known by others BEFORE CONCEPTION by applicant:
> - Publicly known/used by others in U.S.
> - Patented or described by others in U.S.
> - Patented or described in printed publication around world
> - Described in U.S. or PCT patent filed before conception

scribed in a *printed* publication anywhere in the world, before the "inventor" *conceived* the invention. In other words, if the public knew about an "invention" before the applicant for a patent conceived the idea, the invention is public property (or already the property of another) and the applicant cannot obtain a patent on it. As will be discussed, secret (non-public) use of the invention *by another* will not necessarily operate as a bar.[42]

Patents that are already issued are proof of that which the public knows at the time of an invention. In this regard, the statute also states:

§102 A person shall be entitled to a patent unless—

. . . .

(e) the invention was described in a patent granted on an application for patent by another *filed* in the United States before the invention thereof by the applicant for patent, or on an international application by another who has fulfilled the requirements of paragraphs (1), (2), and (4) of section 371(c) of this title *before the invention thereof* by the applicant for patent. . . .

This paragraph of the statute establishes the *filing* date of a patent (the date when the application for the patent was filed) as the date that the patent becomes "prior art." In other words, the patent is considered proof that the invention was known "by others" at least as early as the filing date of the patent (i.e., is either public property or the property of another). Therefore, if a patent describing the invention was filed before the person applying for a patent conceived the invention, it is clear that the invention was "previously known by others," and the later applicant is not entitled to a patent.

PREMATURE DISCLOSURE OR SALE

The inventor can also lose rights by prematurely disclosing, selling, or using the invention in public. The statute states:

§102 A person shall be entitled to a patent unless—

. . . .

(b) the invention was patented or described in a printed publication in this or a foreign country or in public use or on sale in this country, more than one year prior to the date of the *application* for patent in the United States. . . .

The so-called publication, public use, and on-sale bars of section 102(b) are traps that have caught many an unwary company. For example, recall Horror Story 2 (p. 2). Z-Corp is out of luck because of the "public use" and "on-sale" bars. Once the microcomputer had been on the market (on sale and/or in public use) for a year, Z-Corp was precluded from obtaining a patent to protect its R&D investment.

> **Statutory Bars—One-Year Grace Period**
>
> - Disclosure more than 1 year before U.S. application filed
> - Patented or described in printed publication
> - Publicly used or offered for sale in U.S.

There are two reasons for this section of the statute. The first is to prevent a patentee from, in effect, extending the term of a patent beyond the statutory limit (twenty years from filing) by filing a patent application only after first exploiting the invention until competitive products begin to appear. The second reason is to provide a degree of certainty as to whether or not technology is within the public domain. If technology is available or known to the public for a certain period of time and is not the subject of a patent or patent application, the public should be entitled to assume that the technology is in the public domain. Accordingly, under the statute, if an application is not filed, the technology is deemed to be in the public domain after being available to the public for more than one year. By not seeking a patent until more than one year after introducing the product, Z-Corp in effect dedicated its R&D investment to the public.

PATENTED

The term "patented" in this portion of the statute has been construed to mean that the invention is already "claimed" or "protected" under the laws of the particular country that issued the patent. The effective date of the "patent" is also a function of the particular country. A patent, of course, can also be a printed publication bar, as will be discussed below. It should be noted that it does not matter who the patentee is; depending on timing, the inventor's own prior patents can become prior art under this section.

DESCRIBED IN A PRINTED PUBLICATION

To constitute a possible "publication" bar, an item must (1) describe the invention, (2) be "printed," and (3) be "published." In this context "printed" means any visually reproducible form, such as print, xerographic reproductions, microfilm, and so forth. The requirement for "publication" under the patent statute is very different from publication in the copyright sense. *"Publication" under the patent statute has come to mean only that the document be accessible to that class of persons concerned with the field of technology to which the document relates and thus most likely to avail themselves of its contents.*[43] Factors bearing on whether a document is published under the patent statute include the number of copies made, availability, accessibility, dissemination, and, sometimes, the intent of the author.[44] Depositing copies of an "unpublished work" (in the copyright sense) with the Library of Congress constitutes publication under the patent statute. Making a document available on an Internet Web site that is accessible to search engines is likewise a publication under the patent statute.[45]

A document is published when it actually becomes accessible. For example, a magazine becomes "published," in the patent law sense, not as of the date it is placed in the mail, but rather on the date that it reaches its subscribers. The author of the publication is irrelevant. A document placed on an Internet Web site is "published" when the site comes online. Depending on timing, published writings *by the inventor* describing an invention can constitute a bar to a patent on the invention.

PUBLIC USE

In the context of the statute, "public use" means used in public, either by a third party or by *the inventor*. Any use of the invention by the inventor or the inventor's business in the ordinary course of business for trade or profit puts the invention in "public use," even if the use itself is secret and the public would have no way of ascertaining the use.[46] For example, if the invention is a new manufacturing technique, the sale of products made by that manufacturing technique by the inventor or his company constitutes a public use and may be a bar.

Similarly, any *nonsecret* use of the invention by a third party in the ordinary course of business is a potential bar to obtaining a patent. Even if a third party uses the invention in secret, a potential public use bar arises if inspection or analysis of a resulting product sold or publicly displayed by the third party can determine the invention.[47] However, if it could not be determined from the product that the invention was used by the third party, the use is not considered "public."[48] For example, if the invention is a manufacturing technique maintained as "trade secret" by a third party, and one could not analyze the products and "reverse-engineer" the manufacturing techniques, the use is not considered public. Similarly, if the invention is a program or programming technique maintained as a trade secret (even if licensed as such) by a third party, it is not considered a public use. In contrast, however, as noted above, where it is the *inventor* who sells or displays a product made using the manufacturing technique, the sale or display is a potential bar whether or not the manufacturing technique can be reverse-engineered.[49]

Most important, when an invention is shown or demonstrated to one or more prospective purchasers or licensees, the demonstration is frequently considered to be a "public use." A "public use" can be avoided in such situations if the persons viewing the demonstration sign confidentiality agreements. However, even with confidentiality agreements, the demonstration may constitute a potential "on-sale" bar, as will be discussed later.[50]

There is an exception to the public use bar for experimental uses under the strict direction and control of the inventor (and/or the inventor's business). In general, to qualify as an experimental use, the subjective intent of the inventor (or the inventor's business) must be to *test* the invention, rather than a profit motive.[51] There must be direct and continual feedback of the results of the "testing" to the inventor.[52] There should also be as little "publicity" as possible.[53] You must also distinguish an experimental use to test the invention—that is, prove that it works—from market testing designed to determine market acceptance of a product, a regulatory testing procedure, or to test features not part of the invention claimed.[54]

Whether or not a use is experimental is a very technical (in the legal sense) question, and it is prudent to not have to rely on the experimental use exception. The issue, however, is easily avoided by taking timely actions to protect inventions.

ON SALE

In the context of the statute, the term "on sale" is interpreted to mean "offered for sale, or sold."[55] The on-sale bar applies when two conditions are satisfied before the critical date: (a) a product is the subject of a commercial offer for sale; and (b) the invention is "ready for patenting" (for example, reduced to practice before the critical date; or there exist drawings or other descriptions of the invention that are sufficiently specific to enable a person skilled in the art to practice the invention). In effect, what was offered for sale before the critical date becomes a prior art reference against which the patentability of the claimed invention is measured.[56] The on-sale bar applies if "there was a definite sale or offer to sell more than one year before the application for the subject patent, and . . . the subject matter of the sale or offer to sell fully anticipated the claimed invention or would have rendered the claimed invention obvious by its addition to the prior art."[57]

A mere offer to sell or license a product embodying the invention is a possible bar, even if a prospective purchaser never receives the offer. The important factor is the date that the offer is made, not the date that a sale is consummated or product delivered.[58] Also, a sale or offer to sell need not be "public." Even a "secret sale" (offer to sell or license, under a confidentiality agreement) is a potential bar to obtaining a patent.[59] An advertisement in a trade journal or a direct mailing of brochures typically constitutes an offer for sale (as well as a printed publication) that can bar patent protection.

A distinction is drawn between an offer to sell a product embodying the invention, and seeking financing or co-venturers/partners for a business to exploit the invention.[60]

Can an offer for sale that is made before development of the product is complete be an on-sale bar? Absolutely! The invention need only be developed to the point where it is "ready for patenting" sometime before the critical date. As noted above, the on sale-bar applies if two conditions are satisfied before the critical date: (a) an offer for sale and (b) the invention becomes "ready for patenting." The order in which the conditions are satisfied is not important. It does not matter that the invention was not "ready for patenting" at the time the offer for sale was made as long as it becomes "ready for patenting" before the critical date.[61]

It is important to realize that you must focus on the invention *defined by the patent claim* as opposed to the ultimate commercial product.[62] Continued development of aspects or features of product that are not called for in the claim will not prevent application of the bar, if all of the elements of the claim were "ready for patenting" before the critical date. Likewise, continued market acceptance testing will not prevent application of the bar.

Let's put it in perspective by falling back on our old friends the stool and chair, but changing the scenario somewhat. Assume that you have just come up with the idea of a three-legged stool and that I am a merchant with a strong customer network. You come to me and propose, in essence, an exclusive distributorship. You offer to sell the stools exclusively to me and to provide enough stools to meet whatever my requirements might be. You show me a hand drawing and a sketch of your stool and explain to me how it works. The sketch illustrates a seat and support structure, where the support structure comprises three legs and three interconnecting members. The legs, connected at one end to the seat, form a tripod, with each leg connected to the other two legs by the interconnecting members. (Isn't it amazing how complicated something simple sounds when you try to describe it with words?)

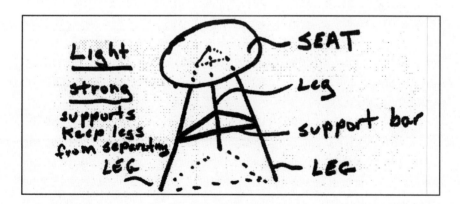

I respectfully decline your offer. I don't think that the stool will sell to my customers. Disappointed but undaunted, you go back to your shop determined to come up with additional features that would make the product marketable. The result is the development of the chair—the addition of a back to the stool—and, one month after our initial meeting, you make the same "exclusive distributorship" proposal to me with respect to the chair. This time, I accept. A year and one day after our initial meeting you decide to file a patent application on your product. You intend that the application describe and claim both the stool and the chair.

Do you have an "on-sale" problem? The on-sale bar applies if, more than one year before the application is filed: (a) a product is the subject of a commercial offer for sale; and (b) the invention is "ready for patenting."

Was there a commercial offer for sale more than one year prior to filing the application? Yes. Your initial proposal to supply me with product was a commercial offer for sale. It doesn't matter that I did not accept the offer or that no stools were actually delivered. The result might have been different if you were offering to sell me rights in your invention, seeking financing, or perhaps even seeking a partner in a new venture that would exploit the stool. However, in our hypothetical, you are clearly offering to sell stools.

But was the stool ready for patenting? In our scenario, I (the potential reseller) rejected the stool as a viable product. It was not until you added the back to the stool to create the chair that I found the product viable, and you are still within the one-year grace period with respect to the chair. The subject matter of an offer for sale is "ready for patenting" if, for example, it has been reduced to practice or there are drawings or other descriptions that are sufficiently specific to enable a person skilled in the art to make and use it. In this case, while the drawings are only a rough sketch, they do show all of the elements of the stool. This is probably enough to establish the stool as ready for patenting.[63] There is no requirement that the drawing or description be formal or in any particular form. The only requirement is that they be sufficiently specific.

Since there was a commercial offer to supply product (stools), and the stools were ready for patenting, both more than one year prior to filing the application, your initial proposal with respect to the stool constitutes an on-sale bar. This makes the stool prior art with respect to both the claims on the stool and on the chair. The claims on the stool would be anticipated and therefore unpatentable. The issue then becomes whether the claims on the chair (adding a back to the stool) are rendered obvious by the stool. If they are not, even though anyone would be free to make stools, you would still be able to obtain exclusivity with respect to chairs.

You may ask yourself how the Patent and Trademark Office could ever find out that you had offered to supply me with stools. The answer is really very simple. You would tell them. There is a very strict requirement of absolute candor with the PTO. You are required to advise the PTO of any information that might be relevant to the prosecution of the application. We will discuss this again later in the book.

STRICT NOVELTY IN MOST FOREIGN COUNTRIES

The law in the United States is very strict with regard to the publication, on-sale, and public use bars. *A single publication, sale, or public use more than one year before the patent application is filed in the United States is deadly.* Yet the United States is considered charitable when compared to many foreign countries. The United States, in effect, provides you a one-year grace period from the sale, use, or publication in which to legitimately claim his rights.

**Foreign Rights—
No Grace Period**

• Any description of the invention published before the application precludes most foreign patent protection

Most foreign countries, however, do not provide any grace period. Any description of the invention published prior to the filing of a patent application bars the inventor from obtaining patent protection. Recall Horror Story 3 (p. 2). Y-Corp has run afoul of the strict novelty requirements of Germany and Japan—Dr A's publication prior to an effective filing in those counties barred patent protection.

If proper procedures are followed (and timing requirements met), filing a patent application in the United States can preserve one's ability to obtain patent protection in most "strict novelty" countries. The United States has entered into treaties with most of the technologically developed countries, which give the inventor the benefit in the foreign country of the date that the inventor's U.S. application was filed, as long as a corresponding patent application is filed in the foreign country within a predetermined period (typically one year). Thus, publications made after filing the U.S. application generally do not prejudice the inventor's rights in those foreign countries. If Dr. A had waited until after a U.S. patent application had been filed before publishing the paper on his devices, Y-Corp would not have been barred from obtaining protection for the device in Japan and Germany, as long as corresponding patent applications were filed on time in Germany and Japan.

It is not always wise, however, to publish a paper on an invention before a patent is actually granted. Patent application files in the United States are maintained in secrecy for at least eighteen months from the effective filing date of the application.[64] If a patent application is filed on a process or programming technique and the program is later determined to be unpatentable in the United States, it may still be possible to maintain the program as a trade secret if there has been no publication in the interim.

ABANDONMENT

Another way to lose patent rights is through abandonment. The statute states:

§102 A person shall be entitled to a patent unless—

. . . .

(c) he has abandoned the invention. . . .

Someone who abandons an invention may not thereafter be entitled to a patent on the invention. For example, recall Horror Story 12 (p. 8). "Abandonment" is a matter of the subjective intent of the inventor, as well as the facts surrounding the inventor's activities.[65] However, as a rule of thumb, anytime someone "sits on" an invention, doing nothing for more than two years, the person is presumed to have abandoned the invention.

CORRESPONDING FOREIGN PATENT APPLICATIONS

An inventor in the United States can lose patent rights in the United States by filing a foreign patent application prematurely. Anytime a U.S. company files an application for a patent on an invention in a foreign country prior to, or within six months after, filing an application on the invention in the

United States, the company must first obtain a "Foreign Filing License" from the PTO, or a U.S. patent will be barred.[66]

An inventor can also lose patent rights in the United States through delay after filing a patent application on the invention in a foreign country. The statute provides:

§102. . . . A person shall be entitled to a patent unless—

(d) the invention was first patented or caused to be patented, or was the subject of an inventor's certificate, by the applicant or his legal representatives or assigns in a foreign country prior to the date of the application for patent in this country on an application for patent or inventor's certificate filed more than twelve months before the filing of the application in the United States. . . .

Under this paragraph of the statute, a bar arises if: (1) the inventor or the inventor's business or legal representatives; (2) files an application for a patent on the invention in a foreign country; (3) more than one year before filing an application in the United States; *and* (4) the foreign application issues as a patent prior to the filing of the application in the United States.

Statutory Bars—Foreign Patent Applications

Premature filing of foreign application—foreign filing license

—Delayed filing of U.S. application—
* Foreign application filed more than one year before U.S. application

—and—

* Foreign application issues as patent before U.S. application filed

ACTUAL INVENTOR

A U.S. patent on an invention can be obtained only by the actual inventor. This is in contradistinction to most other countries in the world; most other countries permit a patent to be filed in the name of its owner, such as an employer, rather than in the names of the actual individual inventor(s). This distinction in the United States patent law relates back to the constitutional origins of the U.S. patent system. The Constitution provides that "The Congress shall have power . . . to promote the progress of science and useful arts by securing for limited times to *authors and inventors* the exclusive right to their respective writings and discoveries." Accordingly, the statute provides:

§102 A person shall be entitled to a patent unless—

. . . .

(f) he did not himself invent the subject matter sought to be patented. . . .

In order to obtain a patent, the entity (one or more persons) named on the patent as the inventor must have, in fact, invented the invention claimed in the patent and not derived it from another.[67] Recall, for example, the situation in Horror Story 4 (p. 2). Ms. E is barred from filing a patent in her own name, even though there had been no public use, printed publication, or offer for sale more than one year prior to the date of the application. Ms. E was not an actual inventor and therefore, is not entitled to a patent. The application for a patent must be in the name of the actual inventor (even though Ms. E may be the owner of the patent application). Care must be taken to apply for the patent in the name of the correct inventors. There are presently provisions for correcting certain errors in the named inventorship of a patent.[68] However, it must be shown that any errors in naming the inventors arose "without deceptive intent." Thus, since Ms. E, who all knew had nothing to do with the invention, is named as an inventor, the patent is likely invalid for failure to name the correct inventorship.

**Statutory Bars—
Improper Inventorship**

- Application must be in name of actual inventor

Patent Application

~~True Inventor~~

*D.E. River
President*

In patent law, joint inventors are considered to be a single entity, separate and distinct from the individual inventors.[69] For example, if you invent a new semiconductor device, and thereafter you and I invent an improvement on the original semiconductor device, your initial invention is generally considered to be by a different entity than our joint subsequent improvement. This can have serious consequences. Under certain circumstances your original invention could be considered "known by others" prior to the joint invention of the improvement and thus prior art (against which patentability is measured) under, for example, 35 U.S.C., section

102(a) and/or (e). However, if an invention is adequately disclosed in an earlier application, a subsequent application on the invention filed while the earlier application is still pending by any one or more of the named inventors of the first application can claim the benefit of the earlier filing and will be treated as if filed on the date of the earlier application[70] (see description of divisional, continuation, and continuation-in-part applications in the section titled "The Patent Application"). Further, the work of a coworker (technology owned by the same entity that owns the invention at issue) that has not otherwise passed into the public domain (§102[a][b][d][e]), cannot render the invention unpatentable for being obvious.[71] (See the section entitled "Obviousness.")

FIRST TO MAKE THE INVENTION

To obtain a patent, the applicant must also have been the first to have "made" the invention in the United States. The statute states:

§102. . . . A person shall be entitled to a patent unless—

(g) (1) during the course of an interference conducted under section 135 or section 291, another inventor involved therein establishes, to the extent permitted in section 104, that before such person's invention thereof the invention was made by such other inventor and not abandoned, suppressed, or concealed, or

(2) before such person's invention thereof, the invention was made in this country by another inventor who had not abandoned, suppressed, or concealed it. In determining priority of invention under this subsection, there shall be considered not only the respective dates of conception and reduction to practice of the invention, but also the reasonable diligence of one who was first to conceive and last to reduce to practice, from a time prior to conception by the other.

> **Statutory Bars—First Made by Another**
>
> - Applicant must be first to have "made" and not abandoned, suppressed, or concealed the invention in U.S.
> - "Making" an invention:
>
>   —Conception
>   —Reduction to practice
>   —Diligence

The situation sometimes arises where two different inventors develop the same invention independently. In such a case, the U.S. patent law provides that the first to have "made" the invention in the United States, who did not abandon, suppress, or conceal the invention, is the person entitled to the patent. Conversely, if someone else makes an invention first, assuming that the invention was not abandoned, suppressed, or concealed (for instance, maintained as trade secret),[72] you can be precluded from obtaining a patent.[73] Where two inventors both file applications relating to the same invention, the relative priority of the inventors is determined by what is called an "interference" proceeding conducted by the PTO. It is possible that the first to file a patent application will not be the one who ultimately obtains the patent. (There are, however, certain procedural advantages that accrue to the first to file a patent application.)

> ### Interference Proceeding
>
> * Applicant must be first to have "made" and not abandoned, suppressed, or concealed the invention in U.S.
> * Two entities both apply for patents on the same invention
> * Litigation-like proceeding to determine who was first

The concept of the first to have "made" the invention is significant. "Making" an invention is considered to be a two-step process. The first step is conceiving the invention. This is basically the mental portion of the inventive act. Conception requires possession of every feature of the invention as claimed.[74] However, as will be discussed, the date of conception must be proven by more than just the inventor's word.[75] The second step is referred to as "reducing the invention to practice." In basic terms, "reducing to practice" is building the invention

> ### Making an Invention
>
> * Conception
> * Reduction to practice
> * Diligence

and proving that it works for its intended purpose.[76] The filing of a patent application is considered to be a "constructive" reduction to practice.[77] The diligence of the inventor between conception and reduction to practice of the invention is also a factor as to who will win the interference. Let's assume that both you and I have filed patent applications claiming the same invention. As a general proposition, if you were both the first to conceive and the first to reduce the invention to practice, you will win the interference. Further, if you conceived the invention before I did, but I reduced the invention to practice before you, you will still win the interference if you can prove that you were "diligent" in pursuing the reduction to practice from a time period prior to my conception of the invention. However, if you cannot prove that you were reasonably diligent in pursuing the reduction to practice before I conceived the invention, I will win the interference and will be awarded the patent.

The law of interferences is exceedingly complex, and far beyond the scope of this book. However, you should be aware of the concept of the two-step process of making an invention, and also of one all-important fact—each aspect of the two-step process must be proven by more than just the word of the inventor. As a basic proposition, the word of the inventor (or even co-inventors) as to when an invention was conceived or reduced to practice is worthless without "corroboration."[78] Corroboration can be in the form of dated documents, drawings, time records, and oral testimony by "noninventors."

> **Reduction to Practice**
> - The invention must be demonstrated to actually work for its intended purpose
> - The important date is when the inventor appreciated the success of the demonstration. Test results should be analyzed immediately by the inventor and witnesses
> - Tests should be performed under conditions approximating actual use. However, mere construction is enough for your simple inventions

> **Diligence**
> - Even a few days of "unexcused" inactivity may show lack of diligence
> - Vacation and illness are acceptable excuses for gaps in activity. Waiting for an exceptionally qualified assistant to become available is not

Recall Horror Story 5 (p. 3). Ms. B lost the interference because she did not maintain adequate records of the process of developing the invention. Had she obtained a witness to sign and date her sketch of the system architecture, she might have won the interference and obtained her patent. As it was, however, the disclosure to her employers was the earliest date of conception that she could possibly prove.

Many independent inventors, upon conceiving an invention, will write out a written description of the invention, put the description in a sealed envelope, and mail the envelope to themselves. The sealed envelope is argued to be proof of the date of conception, the postmark (showing the date of mailing) supposedly corroborating the inventor's word. This practice, without more evidence, is not generally recommended. If the seal on the envelope is broken, the proof becomes suspect. Also, envelopes can often be opened and resealed without great difficulty. Thus, absent some additional proof, this method of proving a conception date is subject to attack.

The best way to ensure positive proof of a conception date is for the inventor, when an invention is conceived, to prepare a document that fully describes the invention, sign and date the description, and also explain the invention to another person (who cannot be considered a co-inventor) and have the person read, sign, and date the description. It may also be helpful to have the document notarized.

Many companies utilize formal "invention disclosure" forms that elicit a description of the invention from the inventor, and specifically provide for dated signatures by noninventor witnesses who have "read and understood" the disclosure. As a practical matter, however, formal disclosure documents are generally not contemporaneous with the actual conception of an invention. Conceptions are typically first reflected in the notes and working papers of the inventor. For this reason, the importance of well-kept laboratory notebooks cannot be stressed enough. All engineers and programmers should maintain a bound engineering notebook. All computations, flowcharts, circuit diagrams, test results, and so forth should be contemporaneously entered into the notebook. Every entry should be signed and dated and, if possible, signed and dated by a "witness." Where software development is involved, a hard-copy listing of each iteration (at least each significant iteration) should be maintained. It is especially important that all loose papers, such as blueprints, flowcharts, etc., be signed and dated. The value of an entry in a laboratory notebook as proof of conception and/or reduction to practice of an invention is directly proportional to the care that was taken to date and sign each entry and have each entry read, signed, and dated by a witness.

The context of the entry in an engineering notebook can also sometimes be used to prove a date. For example, if an entry showing conception is found in a bound engineering notebook, between entries dated January 3

and January 5, it is relevant proof that the invention was conce
time between the third and fifth of January. It would not be so rel
ever, if a loose-leaf engineering notebook had been used.

Records should be maintained in contemplation of proving nc
dates of conception and reduction to practice, but also diligence in between.
To this end, it is desirable that careful time records be kept. In addition, the
documentary evidence and, in particular, dated notebook entries should describe all testing performed, the particular types of equipment used, and the
results of the testing (both good and bad). Physical results of tests, such as
samples, models, strip charts, oscillographs, or the like, should be carefully
dated and retained, preferably mounted (taped or stapled) in the body of
the appropriate notebook entry. All persons involved in the work should be
identified in the corresponding notebook entries. In all, a documentary
record should be maintained capable of establishing each of the elements of
"making" an invention, as well as identifying noninventor witnesses who can
provide testimonial proof. The process of keeping records of development
will be further discussed later in this book.

Other areas where the two-step concept of invention is of particular consequence are those of research contracts, particularly those with the federal
government, and licensing agreements relating to "all improvements made
during the term of the agreement."

Obviousness

In addition, the statute[79] requires that the invention *as a whole* be "unobvious" to a person of "ordinary skill
in the art." To assess the nonobviousness of an invention, a number
of factors must be reviewed: (1)
the scope and content of prior
patents and publications; (2) the
"level of ordinary skill in the art"
(typical education level in the pertinent area of technology); (3) the
differences between the invention
as claimed and the prior art; and
(4) whether the invention provides

It's Prior Art Against Which Patentability Is Measured If It Is:

- Prematurely commercialized by applicant
- Known to applicant before invention
- Readily ascertainable from public information
- TRADE SECRET INFORMATION IS NOT TYPICALLY ART AGAINST THIRD-PARTY APPLICATIONS

unexpected results, fulfills a long-felt need, and/or is commercially significant. In making this review, technology that is owned by the same entity
that owns the invention at issue,
and has not passed into the public
domain (by virtue of §102[a][b]
[d][e]), should not be considered.
The nonobviousness of the differences is then measured, not
against what was subjectively obvious to the inventor, but rather
against the general knowledge of

> **Nonobvious Factors**
>
> - Scope and content of prior art
> - Level of ordinary skill
> - Difference from art
> - Unexpected results
> - Commercial success

practitioners in the pertinent area of technology at the time of the invention.[80] The invention must be considered in total context and without hindsight.[81] For example, the solution
to a problem may be patentable
even though the solution, with the
benefit of hindsight, is very simple;
the identification of the problem
can constitute a patentable invention.[82] As a practical matter, if one
or more elements of an invention
as claimed are not disclosed in

> **Nonobvious If:**
>
> - Element of invention not in prior art
>   —or—
> - Prior art doesn't suggest combining elements of invention

prior patents or publications, or if the invention as claimed combines
known elements, but no prior patent or publication expressly or by implication suggests combining those specific elements, the invention is probably nonobvious.[83]

Personal Prior Inventor Defense with Respect to Business Method Patents

As briefly noted above, the statute provides a limited personal "prior inventor"
defense to charges of patent infringement by virtue of the use of a business
method, or the sale or disposition of
a "useful end product" made by the
method.[84] To establish the defense,
the accused infringer must prove, by
clear and convincing evidence, that:

> **Prior Inventor Defense Relates Only to Business Methods**

(a) the defense is being asserted for a method of doing or conducting business;[85] and

(b) the accused infringer:

- independently developed the method (i.e., did not derive the method from the patentee)[86]
- actually reduced the method to practice at least one year prior to effective filing date of patent;[87] and
- had commercially used (whether or not accessible or known to the public) the method before the effective filing date of the patent[88]
- had not abandoned the method.[89]

The defense applies only to methods of doing or conducting business[90] and does not apply if the accused infringer derived the method from the patentee.[91] In addition, while the defense extends to a customer's use of the end product of the accused method (as opposed to using the method itself),[92] the defense does not provide the accused infringer with a general license under the patent; the defense is limited to the specific claims met by the defense.[93] As a general proposition, the defense is also nontransferable. It can only be transferred as "an ancillary and subordinated part" of a good faith sale or transfer of an entire line of business,[94] and even then, the defense is good only with respect to those sites where the method was in use prior to the later of the effective filing date of the patent, or the date of the transfer of the business.[95] There is also a risk to raising the prior inventor defense; if the defendant is found to infringe, and not to have a reasonable basis for raising the defense, the court will award attorneys' fees to the patentee.[96]

The Patent Application

A patent application is, in effect, a proposed patent, submitted to the PTO for its approval. As previously noted, a patent is divided into two major sections (three if you count the drawing separately): the written description, which teaches the public how to use the invention; and the claims, which define the particular intellectual property to which the inventor obtains rights. The written description, drawing, and claims submitted in the application (either in the original or in an amended form) are ultimately printed as the patent grant.

In practice, there are a number of different types of applications: regular (in general, when the term "application" is used in this book, it means regular application); continuation; divisional; continuation-in-part applications; and provisional.

CONTINUATION APPLICATIONS

A continuation application is an application, filed while a "parent" application is still pending, that is substantively identical (except perhaps as to the claims) to an earlier-filed "parent" application by one or more of the applicants for the continuation, and which contains a specific reference to (claims the benefit of) the parent application.[97] The continuation is treated as if it was filed on (is accorded the benefit of) the date that the parent application was filed. This is particularly significant with respect to defining the prior art against which patentability is measured. However, the term of the patent issuing from the continuation application is measured against the filing date of the parent application, that is, twenty years from the effective filing date of the application.[98]

Continuation applications are often filed when some but not all claims in an application are allowed (indicated patentable), and for one reason or another the early grant of a patent is desirable. In that case, a continuation (or, in some instances, a continuation-in-part) application is filed. The continuation application is typically identical to the originally filed application, except that an amendment is filed adding the specific reference to the original application, and changing the claims to reflect only those still being prosecuted (and perhaps adding new claims). Theoretically, a continuation application can be filed to permit you to present new arguments regarding patentability that, for procedural reasons, could not be considered in the parent application. However, this practice is being supplanted in large part by a "Request for Continued Examination" procedure,[99] which in effect permits you to request continued examination (effectively to restart prosecution) upon payment of a fee (in an amount generally corresponding to the fee for filing a new application).

DIVISIONAL APPLICATIONS

A divisional application is, in effect, a continuation application filed in response to a restriction requirement by the PTO.[100] How does this come about? A patent application will often include separate claims covering different aspects of an invention. Occasionally, the PTO will take the position that the aspects of the invention are so different that they in fact constitute separate inventions. It will then issue a "restriction requirement," requiring the applicant to restrict the application to an "elected" one of the inventions. With respect to the "nonelected" aspects, the applicant has the option to file a "divisional" application at any time while the original (parent) application is still pending. The divisional application typically includes a written description identical to that of the "parent" application, but includes claims covering the nonelected aspect of the invention.

CONTINUATION-IN-PART APPLICATIONS

Once a formal application has been filed with the PTO, no new matter can be added to the application. In this context, "new matter" refers to new embodiments or details not described or shown in the originally filed application. In the event that further details or embodiments of the invention that, in and of themselves, warrant protection are developed after an application has been filed, a "continuation-in-part" (CIP) application may be filed. The CIP application includes an additional description of the further details or embodiments of the invention and claims relating to those new features. The claims relating to the material described in the original or "parent" application are given the benefit of the original filing date. The claims covering the additional details are given the filing date of the CIP application. However, the term of the patent issuing from the CIP application is measured against the filing date of the parent application, even with respect to the claims relating to the new matter.[101] A CIP application can be filed at any time before the original application issues as a patent or is abandoned.

PROVISIONAL APPLICATIONS

In general, the patent statute[102] requires that an application for a patent include a written description of the invention, a drawing (where necessary for understanding of the invention), at least one claim, and an oath or declaration by the applicant (although the oath can be filed and fees paid after the fact).[103] The statute also provides for what is referred to as a "provisional application,"[104] which does not require a claim or declaration.[105]

A provisional application, however, is not intended to itself provide any enforceable rights. It is not examined[106] and is automatically abandoned twelve months after filing. It does not itself ever mature into a patent. For a patent to issue on the subject matter described in the provisional, a regular continuation application claiming priority on the provisional application must be filed within a year of the provisional.[107] Once a provisional application has been filed, however, you are permitted to mark products including the invention described in the application with "patent pending."[108]

The ability to file a provisional application was provided primarily to place U.S. inventors in parity with inventors from outside the U.S. With the change in the U.S. law tying the term of the patent to the filing date of the application (as opposed to the date the patent was granted), U.S. inventors were perceived as being put at a disadvantage relative to foreign inventors. As discussed earlier, most foreign countries (outside of NAFTA) observe a strict novelty standard and have no grace period. Most of those countries, however, have entered into treaties with the U.S., by which the filing date of a application filed in one country becomes the effective filing date of a subsequent corresponding application in another country, as long as the subsequent application is filed within one year of the first application. This in effect gives foreign inventors the ability to delay filing in the U.S. for up to a year after they filed in their home country.[109] The provisional application is intended to give U.S. inventors an analogous ability. Claiming the benefit of an earlier-filed provisional application (like claiming the benefit of an earlier-filed foreign application) can establish the effective filing date of the continuing application for the purpose of defining prior art.[110] However (like the corresponding foreign application), the pendency of the provisional application is not included in the calculation of the term of the continuing application.[111] This in effect shifts the effective term of patent protection in time by up to one year.

For a provisional application to establish an early effective filing date for a patent claim for purposes of defining the prior art: (a) a corresponding complete continuation application claiming priority on the provisional must be filed within a year of filing the provisional, and (b) the provisional application must include the *required level of detail* for the elements of the claim.

This last point is particularly significant; in order to be effective, the provisional application requires the *same* level of detail with respect to an invention as in a regular nonprovisional application.[112] According to the PTO,[113] a provisional application "should preferably" conform to the arrangement guidelines for regular applications (discussed below). In practice, since provisional applications are not examined, considerably more latitude is taken with respect to the format of provisional applications as compared to nonprovisional regular applications. Under exigent circumstances (for instance, a statutory bar sneaks up on you and your attorney), an "information dump" can be filed as a provisional application. There is, however, significant risk that some necessary detail may not be included or described with sufficient clarity. The more different the provisional application is from the ultimate regular continuation application, the more likely that the sufficiency of disclosure of the provisional application and support for the claims of the continuation application will become issues.

It must also be kept in mind that filing a provisional application starts various clocks. As noted above, the provisional application is automatically abandoned twelve months after it is filed (if not earlier abandoned). Accordingly, if a corresponding U.S. continuation application claiming benefit of the provisional is to be filed, it must be filed within that one-year period. *Any corresponding foreign applications must also be filed within that one-year period.* The filing of a provisional application starts the one-year clock under the treaties. lightening cream too

Contents of an Application

As discussed above, the patent statute[114] requires that an application for a patent include a written description of the invention, a drawing (where necessary for understanding the invention), and with respect to a regular application, at least one claim, as well as an oath or declaration by the applicant (although the oath can be filed and fees paid after the fact).[115]

While it is not mandatory, a particular format is recommended for a U.S. patent application. Each section of the suggested format will be discussed in order.[116]

1. TITLE OF THE INVENTION
The title should describe the invention in as short and specific terms as possible.

2. CROSS-REFERENCES TO RELATED APPLICATIONS
This section is merely a listing of prior U.S. applications, if any, that are related to the present application. In order for a regular, divisional, continua-

tion, or continuation-in-part application to claim benefit of an earlier-filed (parent) application (regular or provisional), it must include a statement specifically referring to the parent application. The parent application would be noted as such in the "cross-references" section.

3. BACKGROUND OF THE INVENTION

This section includes a brief description of the field of art to which the invention pertains, followed by a description of the problem(s) solved by the invention, and any known prior art. Where no prior art is known at the time of preparing the application, a statement of the problem(s) solved by the invention or advantages of the invention is sufficient.

4. SUMMARY OF THE INVENTION

This section provides a brief description of the essential elements of the invention as claimed.

5. BRIEF DESCRIPTION OF THE DRAWING

Most patent applications include a drawing showing each element of the invention claimed. The particular format, standards, and conventions to be used in the drawing are specified in the statute and regulations.[117] This section of the application provides a brief description of each of the figures in the drawing.

6. DETAILED DESCRIPTION OF THE PREFERRED EMBODIMENT

This section is the primary vehicle for teaching the public how to use the invention. Each element of a "preferred exemplary embodiment" of the invention is described, with specific reference to the drawing. Each element shown in the drawing is designated in the drawing by a numeral. The designation used in the drawing is used to specify the element when mentioned in the specification.

The patent law requires that the description be in sufficient detail to permit a person "skilled in the art" to make and use the invention. Expertise in determining just how much detail is necessary in the specification is something that is acquired only by experience. As a basic proposition, however, it is desirable to include as much detail as possible in the description and to be exceedingly careful to fully describe each and every feature that is to be protected. Where an element or procedure is commercially available (or well-known), it can be described by its commonly known name, and shown in the drawings schematically as a "functional box." For example, one element of an invention could be referred to in the specification as "a filter circuit." However, the "give-and-take" nature of the patent must be recalled: any detail that is not disclosed in the application normally cannot be explicitly protected. For example, if an element is described in the application only as a "microprocessor," and it later becomes apparent that the only feature that actually distinguishes the invention from the prior art is the use of a particular type of microprocessor, for example, a microprocessor capable of calculating an arithmetic result and sensing the sign of the result in a single 100-nanosecond operational

> **Disclosure Requirement**
> - Need not have actually built device
> - Description must:
>   —enable average person working in relevant technology to make operative device
>   —describe "best mode" of the invention
> - So long as presently contemplated best mode is described, device need not be efficent, cost effective, or commercially viable

state (cycle), the applicant would not be able to claim that distinction, and would be forced to file a continuation-in-part (CIP) application in order to add the detailed description of the microprocessor. In the meantime, rights could be lost. This is not to say, however, if broader protection can be obtained, that the *claims* should all be limited to protecting the details of the apparatus, as will be discussed later.

Another requirement of the patent law is that the example of the invention described be of the "best mode contemplated by the inventor of carrying out his invention." Again, this reflects the give-and-take nature of the patent. The inventor must teach the public how to use the best mode of the invention contemplated by him at the time the application is prepared and filed. In other words, the inventor cannot "hold back" what he or she considers to be the best mode of the invention, teaching the public only how to use an inferior mode. For example, if at the time that you file an application, you have developed a production model of a product embodying your invention, you should not describe an inferior prototype as the exemplary embodiment in the specification. You are not, however, normally required to "update" the application once it is filed.

If desired, a number of alternative embodiments of the invention can be described in the patent. However, the inventor does not have to disclose all of the different variations of the invention in the specification. The application is only required to disclose what the inventor contemplated as the "best mode" at the time of filing. An alternative embodiment is generally disclosed when there is some particular feature of the alternative embodiment that in and of itself warrants protection, or to help establish the range of equivalents to be accorded the claims.

7. THE CLAIMS

The claims define the rights that the inventor obtains in return for teaching the public how to use his invention. A claim is analogous to a deed to a piece of real property—it defines the boundaries of the invention, a piece of "intellectual property." However, unlike a piece of real estate, the boundaries of an invention cannot be measured with a transit and tape measure. The scope of an invention is not something that can be calculated and set down in precise figures. The art of drafting patent claims is one that is developed only by years of experience.

The claims of the patent define the scope of protection provided by the patent. The broader and less specific the terms of the claim, the broader the protection afforded by the patent. For another's device or process to infringe (violate) the patent, the device must include elements corresponding to each and every element of the patent claim. Therefore, it is desirable that the claim be written in the most general terms possible while still defining the invention. However, if the claim is written in terms that are too general (i.e., the claim is too broad), and also reads on (describes and is not distinguishable from) the prior art, it is invalid. The language of the patent claim must, therefore, be drafted with the utmost precision to obtain the broadest definition of the invention without attempting to claim rights to something already in the public domain.

It is permissible to have a number of different claims in the patent application. As a matter of practice, claims of varying scope, ranging from the most general to the most specific, are submitted. In this way, if it appears after the fact that some relevant piece of prior art exists that invalidates the broad claims, the other, more specific claims are not necessarily invalidated. In this manner, the inventor not only can obtain protection on the broad aspects of his invention, but also on the specifics of the particular product that is put on the market.

8. ABSTRACT OF THE DISCLOSURE

The application also includes an abstract of the disclosure, which merely provides a summary of the description of specific preferred exemplary embodiment (as opposed to a summary of the claims).

9. THE DECLARATION AND POWER OF ATTORNEY

A declaration and power of attorney form is attached at the end of the application. If feasible, this declaration and power of attorney should be signed and dated by the inventor(s) before the application is filed with the PTO. Briefly, the declaration sets forth the address and citizenship of each applicant, and whether the applicant is the sole inventor or a joint inventor of the invention as claimed. The declaration also states that the applicant(s) has reviewed and understands the contents of the application, and believes the named inventor or inventors to be the original and first inventor or inventors of the invention claimed (i.e., the actual inventors). The declaration also acknowledges a duty of the applicant(s) to disclose to the PTO all information that is material to the examination of the application (e.g., all known prior art and potential statutory bars). In addition, the declaration may list the various circumstances that bar the issuance of the patent, and states that none of these circumstances have occurred.[118]

The declaration should be attached to the original copy of the application when it is signed by the inventor, and, in general, that particular original application—with the declaration attached—should be filed with the PTO. However, as will be discussed, procedures have been instituted for filing the application without a declaration and then supplementing the application at a later date with the declaration (and a surcharge).[119]

The law is very strict with respect to the declaration. Care must be taken that no changes to the application are made after the inventor has signed the declaration.

Information Disclosure Statement

As previously mentioned, a patent applicant (and those associated with the applicant, such as the applicant's business or attorney) has a strict duty of candor in dealing with the PTO. Any information known to be material to patentability must be disclosed to the PTO. This duty is typically

Strict Duty of Candor

observed through an "information disclosure statement," filed either with, or filed within three months of, the application.[120]

It is very important that the examiner be apprised of all relevant facts and prior art. If the most pertinent art is before the examiner, the patent is accorded a strong presumption of validity when it is enforced. It is, therefore, desirable that the examiner consider as much of the art as possible. On the other hand, if information is "withheld" from the examiner, the applicant may have committed a "fraud" on the PTO. Not only would any patent obtained be invalid, but if an attempt was made to enforce the patent, the patentee could be assessed for attorneys' fees, and be subject to a counterclaim of violating antitrust laws. When in doubt as to the materiality of the information, the safest course of action is to cite the information to the PTO.

Filing the Application with the Patent Office

After the application is prepared, it is filed with the Patent and Trademark Office. Application papers are deemed "filed" with the patent office when they are actually received by the Patent and Trademark Office, or when they are deposited as Express Mail with the U.S. Postal Service, together with an appropriate certificate of mailing by Express Mail.[121] There are also provisions for filing a patent application electronically.

The filing date accorded the application by the patent office is critical with respect to determining the relevant dates of potential statutory bars and prior art. The filing date may also be the effective date of invention (i.e., a constructive reduction to practice) if the invention was not actually reduced to practice prior to filing the application.[122]

Normally, if the situation permits, a complete application, including written description, claims, drawings, declaration, and filing fee, is filed to ensure obtaining the filing date. However, as previously mentioned, the application will be accorded a filing date, even in the absence of a signed declaration and the filing fee, upon the filing of a written description, at least one claim, and any required drawing in the name of the actual inventor or inventors,[123] so long as the filing is later supplemented with an executed declaration, the filing fee, and payment of a surcharge.[124] When the incomplete application is received by the PTO, a Notice to File Missing Parts form is mailed to the applicant and specifies a time period in which the missing parts of the application must be filed as well as a requirement that the surcharge be paid.[125]

Prosecution before the Patent Office

After the application is received by the PTO and accorded a filing date, the application is assigned to a patent examiner having expertise in the particular technological area of the invention. The patent examiner then conducts an investigation, searching the PTO files to determine if there is any relevant prior art in addition to that supplied by the applicant. The patent examiner then issues what is known as an "office action." In brief, the office action lists all of the references considered by the examiner and indicates whether he considers the claims to be of proper form, and whether he considers the claims to be anticipated by the prior art or rendered obvious by the prior art. The PTO mails the office action to the attorney, and the attorney immediately forwards it, with copies of the references cited, to the inventor.

A response to the office action (assuming one is necessary) should be filed within three months of the mailing date of the office action. The inventor typically provides the attorney with an analysis of the references, and the attorney then drafts the response. The response must answer each and every issue raised by the examiner by traversing (arguing against) the examiner's positions, amending the claims, or canceling the claims (that is, accepting the examiner's rejection). In effect, the attorney negotiates with the patent examiner to determine the exact scope of the claims to which the inventor is entitled.

Generally, when the inventor receives the office action, the inventor should analyze the office action and references and report back to the patent attorney to facilitate preparation of the response. Any errors in the positions taken by the examiner in the office action—for instance, mischaracterization of the references—should be identified. For each claim, and each rejection, the differences between the subject matter described in each individual reference and (1) the "claim language" and (2) the preferred embodiment described in the specification should be identified. If the examiner has rejected the claims as obvious over a combination of references, the inventor should also identify any reasons why the references cannot be combined as suggested by the examiner, and should establish or confirm that the references do not suggest that it would be desirable to make the modification or combination of features suggested by the examiner. In addition, the inventor should then assume for the purposes of argument that it is permissible to combine or modify the references as suggested by the examiner and identify the differences between modified or combination references as suggested by the examiner and (1) the claim language and (2) the preferred embodiment described in the specification.

If a response cannot be filed within the initial three-month period, it is possible to file a response to an office action at any time up to six months from the date of the office action. However, a cumulative fee must be paid to the patent office for each month after the initial three-month period.[126]

It must be stressed that it is the language of the *claims* that is controlling in arguing against a rejection; differences between the references cited and the preferred exemplary embodiment described in the specification are not controlling. The response must explain to the examiner how the specific language of the claims is distinguished from the references. The *claims*, however, can be amended to include any detail described in the specification.

After the examiner agrees with respect to the exact scope of the claims, the application issues as a patent.

"Patent Pending"

Filing a patent application does not in itself provide any enforceable rights. That is, *no enforceable rights are provided until the patent is actually granted*. However, during the period the patent application is pending before the PTO, a "patent pending" notice can be placed on products including the invention described in the application.[127] A patent pending notice can sometimes "scare off" certain types of potential infringers.

Care must be taken, however, not to mismark; marking a product with a patent pending notice when it is not actually described in a pending application can put you in violation of the false marking statute.[128]

Enforcing a Patent

The patent statute provides that anyone who infringes a patent is liable for damages to compensate for the infringement (no less than a reasonable royalty), plus interest and costs.[129] A patent is infringed when someone engages in any of the following activities: "makes, uses, offers to sell or sells" the patented invention in the U.S.; imports a patented invention into the U.S.; actively induces infringement of a patent; knowingly contributes to an infringement; supplies all or a substantial portion of the components of a patented invention in or from the U.S., and actively induces activities outside the U.S. that would be an infringement if the activities occurred inside the U.S.; or imports a product into the U.S. made outside the U.S. by a process patented in the U.S.

Contributory infringement occurs when someone sells a component of a patented machine or process knowing that the component is specially made or is specially adapted for use in the infringement of the patent, and the article in question is not a staple of commerce suitable for substantial noninfringing use.[130] Inducement of infringement occurs where one intentionally aids or suggests (such as by giving instructions for the use of a device) the direct infringement of a patent by another.[131] Activities in the United States that would otherwise be inducing or contributory infringement constitute infringement even if the ultimate "infringement" occurs outside of the United States.[132]

A patent is enforced by bringing suit in an appropriate U.S. district court.[133] As a general proposition, suit can be brought in the district court for any jurisdiction where the accused infringer resides, or has committed acts of infringement and has a regular and established place of business. For a corporate defendant, the corporation is deemed to "reside" in any judicial district in which it is subject to personal jurisdiction.[134]

In the past, an appeal from the decision of a district court was taken to one of the eleven U.S. circuit courts of appeals. A difficulty that often arose in litigation was that the judges involved typically had no technical background and often had no contact with the patent system. In addition, each of the different appeals circuits had its own body of law interpreting the patent statutes. The interpretation of the law in some of the circuits was more favorable to the patentee than in others. Accordingly, great care was taken to choose the best possible court in which to bring the suit. Since October 1982, however, appeals in patent cases no longer go to the individual circuit courts of appeals, but rather are now heard by the U.S. Court of Appeals for the Federal Circuit (Federal Circuit). As a result of this change in the law, the enforcement of patents has become more uniform across the nation, and the particular forum in which the case is heard has taken on less significance. In addition, the judges in the Federal Circuit are, in general, familiar with the patent laws, and either have technical backgrounds themselves, or have technical advisers available to them.

Remedies for Patent Infringement

The patentee is entitled to damages for the infringement[135] and possibly an injunction against the infringer[136] and, in exceptional cases, reasonable attorneys' fees.[137]

Damages for patent infringement are intended to compensate the patentee for the infringement, and must be, at a minimum, at least equal to a reasonable royalty.[138] To the extent it can be proven, compensatory damages include any income that the patentee would have made "but for" the infringement. Compensatory damages can include lost profits, "convoyed sales," and the results of price erosion.[139]

"Convoyed sales" are sales of products or services not actually covered by the patent, but that were lost because of the defendant's infringement. A typical example is aftermarket parts sales, and service or maintenance contracts.

To obtain lost profits the patentee must prove: (1) that there is a demand for the patented product; (2) that there are no acceptable noninfringing alternatives; (3) that it has the capacity to satisfy the additional demand created if the defendant is forced to leave the market; and (4) the amount of profit it would have made from the sales lost to the infringer.[140]

As a general proposition, damages can be obtained only with respect to infringement of the patent, occurring during the term of the patent. Damages are typically not awarded for sales prior to the grant of a patent or after its expiration. However, with respect to patents issuing on applications filed after November 29, 2000, that were published eighteen months after filing,[141] you can obtain "provisional rights damages" (a reasonable royalty) for infringement during the time period between publication of the application and ultimate grant of the patent, if: (a) the infringer had actual notice of the published application; and (b) the claims in the issued patent asserted against the infringer are substantially unchanged from in the published application.[142]

As noted above, the minimum damages are a reasonable royalty—the royalty a willing licensor and a willing licensee would have agreed to at the time infringement began. Factors to be considered include the profitability of the product, established royalties in the industry, and the length of time the patent has to run.[143]

In addition, the court can, at its discretion, increase damages by up to a factor of three.[144] Increased damages, however, are typically awarded only when there has been willful infringement or some form of misconduct,[145] and are not available for "provisional rights" damages for infringement.[146]

> **If infringement is charged, unless a formal opinion from a patent attorney is obtained, you can be found a "willful infringer"**

However, damages for any infringement committed more than six years prior to the institution of the suit cannot be recovered.[147] Nor can damages be recovered from an infringer who did not have either actual or constructive notice of the patent. Constructive notice is provided by placing the word "patent" and then the patent number on each article covered by the patent that is sold by the patentee. If such a patent marking is not on the device, an infringer is not liable for damages unless he has actual notice of the patent, that is, unless it can be proven that he actually knew that the patent existed.[148] The patent marking requirement relates back to the basic proposition that any hardware that is not patented can be freely used and copied by others (absent some contractual obligation, or a likelihood of confusion as to the source or origin of the goods). An innocent party might copy a product if he found the product on the market apparently not covered by a patent. For this reason, a patent marking is effective only if it is put on essentially every apparatus sold.

Provisions are also made for a patent holder to bring an action before the International Trade Commission[149] to prevent the importation of articles infringing the patent. The ITC has the power to bar the importation into the United States of goods that "unfairly compete" with "an efficiently and economically operated" domestic industry, where injury or a tendency for injury occurs. One form of "unfairly competing" is the infringement of a valid U.S. patent, or the importation of articles made by a process covered by a U.S. patent.[150]

Post-Issuance Actions

Under the present law, maintenance fees must be paid at various intervals throughout the term of the utility patent to keep it in force. The basic term of the utility patent is twenty years from the date that the application for patent is filed. At three and a half, seven and a half, and eleven and a half years after the patent issues, maintenance fees must be paid to the PTO. The fees must be paid either before the date due, or, upon payment of a late charge, within six months thereafter. If the maintenance fee is not paid, the patent expires. There are, however, provisions in the statute that permit, under certain circumstances, revival of a patent that has lapsed due to nonpayment of the maintenance fees.[151] No maintenance fee is required for a design patent.

Reexamination

Unlike in many countries, the U.S. patent laws do not provide for any proceeding directly analogous to trademark opposition or cancellation proceedings (through which a party can actively participate in opposing the grant of a patent). However, anyone can submit to the PTO patents or printed publications that have a bearing on the patentability of a particular patent claim (together with a written explanation of their relevance).[152] The submission is made part of the patent file[153] and available to any third party reviewing the file. Any party (including the patent owner) can initiate either of two types of limited "reexamination" proceeding in the PTO with respect to an issued U.S. patent:[154] a standard reexamination procedure,[155] and an "inter partes" procedure.

In both cases, the reexamination process is initiated by filing a request for reexamination, together with a fee set by regulation (a portion of which is refunded if the request for reexamination is denied, as will be explained). The request for reexamination must include a statement showing that a "substantial new question of patentability" exists with respect to at least one claim. A "substantial" new question of patentability exists where prior art patents or publications are shown to be material to at least one claim and the same questions of patentability have not been decided by the PTO during a previous examination of the claim. The "new questions of patentability" must be based upon prior patents or printed publications. Issues of prior use or prior sale cannot be raised.

The PTO then considers the reexamination request and, within three months, determines whether or not a substantial new question of patentability has been raised by the request. This initial determination is based solely upon the reexamination requested, and no submission by the patent owner is permitted. If the PTO determines that a new question of patentability is raised by the request, an order for reexamination of the patent is issued. If no substantially new question of patentability is found, the reexamination proceeding is terminated and the requester is refunded a portion of the initial fee.

After a reexamination order issues, the patent owner is permitted to file a statement in response to the reexamination request and to propose amendments to the claims. The patent owner is not permitted to enlarge the scope of the claims of the patent over the original claims or introduce any new matter during the reexamination proceedings. If the patent owner files a statement, the requester is then permitted to file a reply.

In a standard reexamination proceeding, the PTO then proceeds with an expedited ex parte examination of the patent claims with respect to prior art patents and publications.[156] These proceedings are strictly between the PTO and the patent owner. While the requester is entitled to receive copies of all papers filed during the further proceedings, no submissions by the requester are permitted. The third-party requester is not permitted to participate in appeals to the Board of Patent Appeals and Interferences.[157]

In an inter partes reexamination proceeding, the PTO likewise proceeds with an expedited examination of the patent claims with respect to prior art patents and publications.[158] However, the third-party requester not only receives copies of all papers filed during the examination process, but is also permitted (within thirty days of service) to file a response to documents submitted by the patentee.[159] The third-party requester may also participate in appeals to the Board of Patent Appeals and Interferences.[160] There is, however, a catch: if someone participates in an inter partes reexamination proceeding, and they become involved in litigation, they will be estopped (precluded) from contesting the validity of any claims found valid during the reexamination process.[161]

Upon conclusion of the ex parte examination, the PTO issues a reexamination certificate, which, among other things, cancels any claims determined to be unpatentable, confirms any claims determined to be patentable, and incorporates into the patent any amended or new claims found to be patentable. The reexamination certificate is mailed to both the patent owner and the requesting party.

Advantages of Obtaining a Patent

A patent grant provides a number of substantial benefits. As a general proposition, any product that is not covered by the claim of a patent is fair game for the competition, so long as there are no contractual obligations or likelihood of confusion as to the source or origin of the respective products. The only mechanism for protecting against an independent development of an invention is by obtaining a patent. In this sense, a patent is necessary to adequately protect an investment in research and development. Also, a patent on an improvement to a basic invention can sometimes be used, through cross-licensing, to offset patents held by others on the basic invention (as with the chair versus the stool).

A patent is demonstrative evidence of expertise in the technological area of the invention. This can often be a great aid in obtaining contracts with, for example, the federal government. Moreover, a patent can also be the source of a substantial royalty income, through the institution of a licensing program.

A patent is also a demonstrative asset that aids in obtaining capital from investors and loans from commercial institutions.

Ownership of a Patent

The rules with respect to ownership of patents are far from intuitive. You would think that if you paid for the development of an invention, you would own the rights to it. However, that is not necessarily so! As a basic proposition, in the United States, unless there is an express or implied contractual agreement to the contrary, the actual inventor (not the inventor's employer or entity financing the development) owns the invention and any patent on the invention. Where there are joint inventors, each owns an equal undivided interest in the whole of the invention (and any patent on the invention). Absent an agreement to the contrary, all joint inventors are entitled to make, use, and

> **The Default Rule:
> Inventor Owns**

sell (and license others to make, use, and sell) the invention, without accounting to the other co-inventors.[162] Of course, these are default rules, and may be (and, in the world of sophisticated businesses, typically are) varied by (written) agreement.

Under certain circumstances, for example, where an employee is "hired to invent," there is an implied agreement that the employer will own all rights to that invention.[163] Similarly, where an invention is made on company time and/or using the businesses's facilities, the business may acquire "shop rights" (in essence a royalty-free license) to the invention.[164] However, in order to avoid any disputes it is best to require each of your employees to execute an "employee's invention agreement" as a condition of employment—obligating the employee to assign all rights in inventions to the business. The ownership of rights in inventions is discussed in more detail in the section of this book called "Making Sure You Own What You Pay For."

Design Patent Protection

The patent statute also provides for obtaining a design patent for protecting the *ornamental* appearance of a product. Design patent protection has also been held applicable to information icons for the display screen of a programmed computer system, so long as the icon is an integral part of the operation of a programmed computer (rather than merely a displayed picture).[1]

In general, the same considerations as noted above with respect to utility patents apply to design patents. To be patentable, a design must be new, original, and ornamental.[2] In the context of the statute, "original" means that the design must originate with the patentee (as opposed to being derived from another). "Ornamental" requires that the particular features of the design to be protected not be functional.[3] In addition, a design is not patentable if the differences between the subject matter of the design and prior designs are such that the design *as a whole* would be obvious to a "designer of ordinary skill" at the time the design was made.

> **Design Patent**
> - Protects ornamental appearance of product
> - New, original, and ornamental—not functional
> - Design as a whole not obvious
> - Terms 14 years

The term of the design patent is fourteen years. A design patent typically

includes a drawing showing views of each side of the product having an ornamental feature, followed by a single, formalized claim.

In testing whether the single, formal claim of a valid design patent is infringed, the issue is typically whether the ordinary prospective purchaser or
user of the product, "giving it the amount of attention that such a purchaser
or user would be expected to give," would be likely to mistakenly assume
that the article in question was of the patented design.[4] The test assumes
that the ordinary person is aware of the patented design; it does *not* call for
a side-by-side comparison. Basically, the test is on the overall appearance of
the accused design.

In addition to the usual remedies for infringement of a patent, the
statute provides that the design patentee can recover the total profit made
by the infringer on the infringing product, in lieu of actual damages.[5]

Copyright Protection

Like the patent law, the basis for copyright protection in United States is in the Constitution.[1] Article I, Section 8 of the U.S. Constitution provides: *"The Congress shall have the power . . . to promote the progress of science and useful arts, by securing for a limited time to authors . . . the exclusive right to their . . . writings. . . ."* Congress's answer was copyright system.

The owner of a copyright on a "work of authorship" (often referred to by the shorthand "work") has the exclusive right (subject to certain limitations) to reproduce the copyrighted work; to prepare derivative works based upon the copyrighted work; to distribute copies of the copyrighted work to the public by sale, rental, lease, or lending; and to publicly display or perform the copyrighted work (in the case of musical, dramatic, and other such works).[2] In addition, an artist/photographer who creates single-copy or limited-edition (fewer than two hundred copies, signed, and consecutively numbered) paintings, drawings, sculptures, or still photographs has an additional "right of attribution and integrity."[3] (This right does not apply,

---

Works of Authorship

- Literary
- Musical
- Dramatic
- Pantomimic/Choreographic
- Pictorial, graphic, and sculptural
- Motion pictures and other audio-visual
- Sound recordings

however, if the piece was a "work for hire," or certain types of commercial art such as posters, advertising, and merchandising items.)

Over the years, the copyright law of the United States has undergone a number of changes. Major revisions were enacted in the Copyright Act of 1976 (Title 17, U.S. Code), which became effective on January 1, 1978. Under the 1976 Copyright Act, a copyright arises automatically as soon as an "original work of authorship" becomes "fixed" in a tangible form of expression. In other words, copyright protection is secured automatically as soon as the "work" is "fixed" in a form that can be read or visually perceived either directly or with the aid of a machine or device. Copyrightable "works of authorship" include booklets, advertising brochures, artistic designs, maps and architectural blueprints, "phonorecords," including audiotapes and records, and, at least to some extent, computer programs. However, copyright protection is expressly not available for ideas, methods, systems, mathematical principles, formulas, and equations.

Securing a Copyright

- Arises automatically as soon as work is fixed in tangible form
- Publication Issues
  —Copyright notice
  —Deposit
- Registration not a prerequisite for protection but is for enforcement

Neither publication nor registration is necessary to secure copyright protection under the 1976 act. In addition, as of March 1, 1989, the United States became a signatory to the Berne Convention for the Protection of Literary and Artistic Work. In compliance with the Berne Convention, most of the formalities involved in securing and maintaining a copyright, including that of the copyright notice, as will be discussed below, have been relaxed.

The Digital Millennium Copyright Act (DMCA)[4] created, as of October 28, 2000, a new set of civil and criminal penalties for persons who directly or indirectly circumvent "a technological measure that effectively controls access to a [copyrighted] work."[5] The DMCA prohibits the manufacture, importation and trafficking in technology for circumventing technological protection mechanisms,[6] as well as the removal or alteration of copyright management information.[7] It also provides certain limitations on copyright infringement liability on the part of online service providers (OSPs).[8]

Copyrightable Subject Matter

Copyrights are intended to provide protection for "original works of author-ship." Exemplary categories of works of authorship are listed in the statute.[9] These include: literary works; musical works; dramatic works; pantomimes and choreographed works; picto-rial, graphic, and sculptural works; motion pictures and other audiovi-sual works; and architectural works. Certain aspects of computer pro-grams are also considered literary

> **Copyright**
>
> Protects only expression of an idea—not the idea itself

works.[10] As will be discussed, copyright protection is also available for original "compilations" (creative selection or arrangement of preexisting materials or data).[11]

Copyright protection, however, is expressly limited by the statute[12] to nonutilitarian expression:

> In no case does copyright protection for an original work of author-ship extend to any idea, procedure, process, system, method of oper-ation, concept, principle, or discovery, regardless of the form in which it is described, explained, illustrated, or embodied in such work.

In addition, copyright protection is available only for "*original* works of authorship." To be "original" a work must be independently created by the author, and it must possess a minimal degree of creativity.[13] Those aspects of a work that are not created by the author are not copyrightable subject mat-ter. For example, facts are in essence "discoveries,"[14] and are not created by an act of authorship. The same is true with respect to those elements of a work that are in the public domain, and, arguably, those elements of a work that are dictated by function.[15] Accordingly, none of those elements are protected by copyright. In addition, some types of works are simply considered to be in-sufficiently creative to warrant copyright protection. These include, for ex-ample: a numbering scheme for replacement parts;[16] command codes;[17] and "fragmentary words and phrases."[18] Page numbering schemes have received different treatment depending upon the specific court involved.[19]

So what does all this mean? Assume you hold a copyright on a work (say, a book or computer program) that expresses, describes, or embodies ideas, facts, and utilitarian elements.[20] The copyright gives you exclusive rights with respect to the way in which the ideas, facts, and utilitarian elements are expressed or described. It does not give you any sort of exclusivity with respect to the use of the ideas, facts, and utilitarian elements that are expressed or described.

A classic example is found in the case of *Baker v. Selden*.[21] Mr. Baker, an accountant, wrote a book describing a double entry accounting system that he had developed. Mr. Selden, also an accountant, bought the book and began using the system developed by Mr. Baker. Mr. Baker contended that the use of his accounting system by Mr. Selden constituted copyright infringement. The Supreme Court, however, disagreed. The use of the ideas described in a copyrighted work does not constitute infringement of the copyright.[22]

Expression that is inseparable from an idea, either because (a) protecting the expression would, in effect, give exclusive rights to the underlying idea, or (b) because the expression serves a functional purpose or is dictated by external factors, is likewise not protectable under the copyright law.[23] In this regard, two "tests" have been developed: the "merger" and *"scènes à faire"* doctrines. The merger doctrine is intended to make sure that no one obtains exclusive rights to an idea by obtaining exclusive rights to the only, or one of only a few, means of expressing that idea. The *scènes à faire* doctrine is intended to prevent someone from obtaining exclusive rights to those expressions that are standard, or common for a particular topic, or that necessarily follow from a common theme or setting, and thus are dictated by subject, function, or other external factors.

However, just because some aspects or elements of a work are an "idea," utilitarian, or unoriginal does not mean that other aspects or elements of the work are not copyrightable subject matter. In essence, all of the different aspects of the work are considered individually, as well as in combination (as a compilation). While ideas, utilitarian elements, public domain materials, and facts themselves are not protectable, if you create an original compilation, comprising an arrangement or selection of those unprotectable elements that is itself nonutilitarian and sufficiently original, the compilation is protected by copyright.[24] However, "the copyright is limited to the particular selection or arrangement. In no event may copyright extend to the facts themselves."[25] If the selection or arrangement of a compilation of uncopyrightable material is not sufficiently original, then the work is not protected by copyright. This is true even if assembling the compilation took considerable effort. For example, the Supreme Court[26] held that a telephone directory comprised merely of names, addresses, and phone numbers organized in alphabetical order was not copyrightable. The Court rejected the notion that copyright law was meant to reward authors for the "sweat of the brow," instead concluding that protection only extends to the original components of an author's work.

A copyright infringement analysis involves what is typically referred to as "abstraction-filtration-comparison" process. The work is dissected into varying levels of generality (aspects). Each level of abstraction (aspect) is then examined to filter out unprotectable elements, such as ideas, facts, public domain information, merger material, *scènes à faire* material, and other unprotectable elements. The remaining protectable elements are then compared with the allegedly infringing program to determine whether the defendants have misappropriated substantial elements of the plaintiff's program.

Actually applying this test to nontextual aspects of a work is easier said than done. For example, assuming that the precise text of an earlier work is not copied (and ignoring the issue of trademark infringement/unfair competition),[27] how much of the plot/sequence of events/characters of an earlier story must be appropriated before there is copyright infringement? Is the unauthorized use of a "well-delineated" character or the copying of a sequence of incidents from an earlier work a copyright infringement?[28] It depends on whether the copied elements are characterized as a general theme, or as including sufficient similarities of treatment, details, scenes, events, and characterization to be considered a particular expression of the theme.[29] There is an issue as to whether merely using a "well-delineated" character is a copyright infringement.[30] In any event, for there to be an infringement the characters have to be substantially similar, not merely reminiscent of each other. (Frankly, when a character is copied, *trademark* rights should be considered.) Similar issues arise with respect to architectural drawings; infringement tends to be a function of the level of detail copied.[31]

Which aspects of an audiovisual work, such as a television commercial, are copyrightable expression, and which are uncopyrightable ideas? Nontextual aspects of audiovisual works that have been found to be copyrightable artistic expression include a combination of such things as: background; a particular montage style of rapid close-ups of a particular model; a model's attire and hairstyle; camera angles; and framing. As will be discussed, a similar conundrum occurs with respect to determining which aspects of a computer program other than literal code constitute protectable expression as opposed to noncopyrightable idea. Similarly, if an aspect of any "work" is dictated by function, or is otherwise primarily utilitarian, it is not copyrightable subject matter.[32]

Copying Required

In addition, a copyright only protects against *copying* of a work; it gives no protection whatsoever against another person independently developing the work. To establish a copyright infringement, a plaintiff must prove ownership of a valid copyright and "copying" of protectable expression by the defendant.[33] Copying is typically inferred from proof of access to the copyrighted work and substantial similarity as to protectable expression between the accused and copyrighted works.[34] Thus, even if computer programs are identical in every respect, there is no copyright infringement if there was no copying, that is, if the subsequent program was independently developed.

For this reason, it is very important that appropriate records of developmental efforts be generated and maintained. For evidentiary purposes, it is recommended that a hard copy of each version of a program throughout its development be generated, signed, and dated by a witness (preferably someone not directly involved in the development). The records should be retained for at least three years after the product is placed on the market, and preferably kept for the lifetime of the product plus three years.[35]

The copyright is also subject to a number of limitations set out in the statute,[36] including the doctrine

---

Limitations on Copyright

- Limited to nonfunctional expression
- Fair use doctrine
- Archival/Machine Use Rights §117

---

of fair use, compulsory licensing in certain instances, and a number of limitations pertaining to computer programs, including so-called archival rights.[37]

The Fair Use Limitation

The limitation of most general applicability is the "fair use" limitation, which permits copying "for purposes such as criticism, comment, news reporting, teaching (including multiple copies for classroom use), scholarship, or research."[38]

There is no litmus test to determine whether a particular use of a copyrighted work is a permitted fair use or a copyright infringement. However, the statute specifies a number of factors to be considered. These include: the purpose and character of the use (such as whether the use is of a commercial nature or for non-profit educational purposes); the nature of the copyrighted work; the amount and substance of the portion used in relation to the

> **Fair Use Factors**
> - Commercial or nonprofit use
> - Nature of copyrights work
> - Portion of work copied
> - Effect of use on market for/value of work

copyrighted work as a whole; and the effect of the use upon the potential market for or value of the copyrighted work.[39] As a rule of thumb, if neither the value of the work nor the market for the work are affected by a use of the work, it is a fair use.

No single factor is dominant in a fair use analysis, and the fact that a use is commercial in nature is not necessarily dispositive.[40] In some instances, the nature of the work tends to justify substantial copying as fair use. For example, a parody, at least in part, comments on the original work. In order to do that, at least some elements of the parodied work must be used. While there is no presumption of fair use when a parody is at issue, and each case must be analyzed on its own merits, parodies are typically "transformative" (provide something new) rather than a substitute for (supplanting) the parodied work, and therefore have little effect on the value or market for the work.[41] This tends to make parody a fair use.

In other instances, copying is considered fair use because it is necessary to make transitory/intermediate copies in order to get access to the underlying information/idea. For example, making necessary intermediate copies in connection with the reverse-engineering of software has been held to be fair use.[42]

Playing Background Music and Nondramatic Performances

Technically, in the absence of a provision to the contrary, any public "performance" (playing) of music or a play constitutes a copyright infringement (subject, of course, to the doctrine of fair use). However, as of August 1999, the copyright statute[43] incorporated specific (qualified) exceptions relating to: classroom performances and displays of works;[44] the transmission of a performance of a nondramatic literary or musical work or the display of a work (e.g., a movie) to a classroom;[45] the transmission, performance, or display of works to accommodate disabled persons;[46] the performance and display of works in the course of religious services;[47] free or charitable fund-raising performances of nondramatic literary and musical works;[48] the playing/display of works received through public transmissions (e.g., playing a radio in public); and the display of/playing of works in bars and restaurants and in other types of establishments.[49]

Some of these exceptions demand that very specific requirements be met in order to qualify. For example, qualified small commercial establishments[50] of the type that merely augment a home-type receiver to display/play radio or TV transmissions, and that are not of sufficient size to justify, as a practical matter, a subscription to a commercial background music service, and that do not charge a fee to see or hear the transmission, would be exempt.[51] However, specific requirements must be met. Different rules[52] apply depending on whether an establishment is a "food service or drinking establishment"[53] or another type.

An establishment will qualify for the exception if it has less than a specified maximum square footage (3,750 gross square feet of space[54] for restaurants and bars, and 2,000 gross square feet of space for other types of establishments, in each case excluding space used for customer parking and for no other purpose), or, if it has more space than the specified maximum, the equipment used falls below certain thresholds. For audio performances (e.g., radio) the establishment can employ no more than a total of six loudspeakers, of which not more than four are located in any one room or adjoining outdoor space. For audiovisual performances (e.g., playing a TV), the limitations on audio systems must be met, and in addition, there can be no more than four audiovisual devices (TV screens), with none having a diagonal screen size greater than 55 inches, and with no more than one located in any one room.

If a commercial establishment does not qualify for one of the exemptions, it must obtain a license, typically from an appropriate copyright collecting agency, such as for example, ASCAP (http://www.ascap.com) or BMI (http://www.bmi.com).

Practical Considerations with Respect to Software Works

As previously noted, copyright protection is available for "works of authorship," including booklets, advertising brochures, artistic designs, maps and architectural blueprints, phonorecords,[55] and, at least to a limited extent, computer programs. Certain aspects of computer programs are also considered literary works.[56] However, you must keep in mind that ideas, facts, and utilitarian elements embodied in the software are not protected by copyright.

Historically, there was much debate as to whether software was a "work of authorship" and thus qualified for copyright protection. It is well settled that copyright protection is applicable to human-readable software, such as flowcharts, documents, machine-readable source code representations of a program, and audiovisual displays in game programs. In a number of cases in the federal courts, it has been argued that a video game as a whole is an audiovisual work, and is protectable as an "expression" of the game.[57] Similarly, copyright infringement has been found based upon copying of the audiovisual screens (e.g., menus) of a program.[58] Other courts have, however, expressly rejected the proposition that the screens, per se, are covered by a copyright on the underlying program code; copyright infringement by copying the screens would require the screens to be the subject of a separate copyright registration.[59]

Historically, the courts have drawn a distinction between object code and source code representations of a computer program. Questions have been raised as to whether object code representations of a program (not intended for communication to humans, but rather for direct communication to machines) are even within the scope of the copyright statutes; at least one federal court has taken the position that object code programs are not copyrightable.[60] Others, however, have adopted the contrary position.[61]

The courts have also been divided as to whether a copyright on a source code program is sufficient to protect an object code version of the program,[62] and as to the copyrightability of firmware and microcode.[63] "Firmware" is defined for the purposes of this discussion as software in hardware form; that is, program information stored in a physical medium such as read-only memory (ROM). "Microcode" is defined as encoded instructions controlling the details of execution of one or more primitive functions of the computer.

In more recent cases, however, the courts have found (or assumed) object code and microcode programs to be copyrightable, irrespective of storage in a physical device such as a ROM,[64] and that the loading of an unauthorized copy of software into memory in the course of using the unauthorized copy is a copyright infringement.[65]

In addition, it is now generally accepted that the audio/visual aspects of program screens (user interfaces) are copyrightable as audio/visual works[66] or as compilations.[67] However, it is not universally accepted that a copyright registration of the underlying program code that generates the displays extends to the screen displays generated by the program; arguably, the screens must be subject to a separate copyright. It is prudent to consider copyright protection of the various screens separately from the copyright protection of the underlying program code; it may be advantageous to register copyrights on the respective screens as audio/visual works separate and apart from the program code.[68]

The most important limitation on the scope of copyright protection, as it applies to software, however, is the nature of the copyright itself. As previously discussed, copyright protection is limited to original nonutilitarian works of authorship.[69] A copyright protects only the author's particular form of expression and does not extend to the underlying idea or concept of the program. The copyright, in essence, protects the owner against actual copying of substantial portions of the program code by others.

Recall Horror Story 1 (p. 1). In the hypothetical, Ackman was unsuccessful in enforcing his copyright against conceptually similar competing games because a copyright protects only the author's particular form of expression and does not extend to the underlying idea or concept of the program.

It is often extremely difficult to categorize aspects of a computer program other than literal code as constituting a protectable expression as opposed to an idea or a utilitarian aspect. The extent to which a copyright protects against the copying of nonliteral aspects of a program (such as the modularity, organization structure, or sequence of instructions) tends to vary as a function of the particular court addressing the issue. At one extreme, it is clear that (absent patent protection or contractual obligation) the functionality of a copyrighted program can be freely copied.[70] On the other hand, some courts have found that a direct translation from a higher-order to a lower-order language (or vice versa), or from one high-order language to another, is a derivative work.[71] There have been a number of cases that have tended to accord relatively broad protection to nonliteral aspects of software.[72] Other, more recent, cases,[73] while recognizing that some nonliteral elements of a program may be copyrightable, have taken a much more restricted view of those nonliteral elements of software that are subject to copyright protection. These cases have for the most part employed the "abstraction-filtration-comparison" process. The program is dissected into varying levels of generality (aspects). For example, a computer program can often be parsed into at least six levels of generally declining abstraction: (i) the main purpose, (ii) the program structure or architecture, (iii) modules, (iv) algorithms and data structures, (v) source code, and (vi) object code.[74] Each level of abstraction (aspect) is then examined to filter out unprotectable elements—ideas, facts, public domain information, merger material, *scènes à faire* material, and other unprotectable elements. For example, under the *scènes à faire* doctrine, elements of a computer program that are necessary to comply with hardware standards and mechanical specifications,[75] software standards and compatibility requirements,[76] computer manufacturer design standards, industry practices and demands,[77] and computer industry programming practices[78] are not copyrightable subject matter. The remaining protectable elements are then compared with the allegedly infringing program to determine whether those protectable portions of the original work that have been copied constitute a substantial part of the original work—that is, matter that is significant in the plaintiff's program.[79] Depending upon the nature of the elements at issue, the courts require either "substantial identity," or "substantial similarity" between the elements in order for there to be an infringement.[80] In general, a substantial similarity test is applied to literal elements of the software, and a virtual identity test is applied to nonliteral elements and compilations.

In any event, a copyright does not in any way protect the owner from the independent creation of a similar program by another person, even if the other is generally aware of the copyrighted program. A competitor can, in general, study a copyrighted program, determine the central concept and basic methodology of the program, then write his own program to accomplish the same results. In practice this is often done using so-called clean rooms.

Right to Make Archival and Transitory Copies

Specific provisions in the statute additionally limit the scope of copyright protection accorded to computer programs.[81]

§117. Limitations on exclusive rights: Computer programs.

(a) . . . Notwithstanding the provisions of section 106, it is not an infringement for the owner of a copy of a computer program to make or authorize the making of another copy or adaptation of that computer program provided:

> (1) that such a new copy or adaptation is created as an essential step in the utilization of the computer program in conjunction with a machine and that it is used in no other manner, or
>
> (2) that such new copy or adaptation is for archival purposes only and that all archival copies are destroyed in the event that continued possession of the computer program should cease to be rightful.

(b) . . . Any exact copies prepared in accordance with the provisions of this section may be leased, sold, or otherwise transferred, along with the copy from which such copies were prepared, only as part of the lease, sale, or other transfer of all rights in the program. Adaptations so prepared may be transferred only with the authorization of the copyright owner.

At least one court, however, has read section 117 to pertain only to inputting a copy into a machine and to "destructible" copies.[82] (It appears that the court interpreted the statute to fit what it perceived as the equities of the case: the defendant provided disks containing programs printed in the plaintiff's magazine to the plaintiff's subscribers in competition with the plaintiff.)

Other courts have interpreted section 117 to preclude prohibitions against disassembly by rightful holders of copies.[83] In at least one subsequent case, however, the protection of section 117 was limited to owners of copies of the software, as distinguished from mere licensees.[84]

It can also be argued on the basis of section 117 that once a copyrighted program is sold, the copyright owner cannot prevent the purchaser from adapting the program to other machines (CPUs) owned by the purchaser. A corollary argument, however, also arises that the copyright owner can stop someone who does not rightfully "own" a copy of the program (i.e., a licensee) from making such "adaptations."

Fair Use As Applied to Computer Programs

The application of the doctrine of fair use, particularly when applied in conjunction with a recognition of the utilitarian nature of software, has also tended to limit the scope of copyright protection for software. The fair use doctrine has been held to permit disassembly of a program for the purposes of reverse-engineering, that is, study or examination, so long as the copy disassembled was rightfully obtained.[85]

Publication

While publication is no longer necessary to secure statutory copyright protection, it is still an important concept. Several significant consequences follow from publication of a work: works published before March 1, 1989, must include "proper copyright notice"; a deposit of copies with the Library of Congress becomes mandatory; and various time periods begin to run.

Under the Copyright Act, a work is published upon distribution of, or an offer to distribute, copies of the work to the public by sale or other transfer of ownership, or by rental, lease, or lending. In this context, the "public" means any person who is under no explicit or implicit restrictions with respect to disclosure of the contents of the work. If a document is distributed under a proprietary notice to licensees or the like, it is not "published" under the Copyright Act.

Notice

Until adoption of the Berne Convention, a proper copyright notice was required on all published works. Indeed, omitting or misplacing the copyright notice was fatal to obtaining copyright protection for works prior to the effective date of the 1976 act. As to works subject to the 1976 law, however, omission of or error in the copyright notice on a publication does not necessarily invalidate the copyright, as long as an application for registration of the copyright on the work was made before the publication, or is made within five years after the publication, and a reasonable effort is made to add proper notice to all of the copies that are distributed to the public after discovery of the omission or error. Under the Berne Convention, a copyright notice is no longer necessary on works published after March 1, 1989.

The Berne Convention notwithstanding, it remains advantageous that all published copies of a work bear a notice of copyright. Access to a copy of the work bearing a proper copyright notice precludes interposition of an "innocent infringement defense."[86] Basically, the notice of copyright includes three elements: the copyright symbol ©, the word "copyright," or the abbreviation "Copr."; the named owner of the copyright; and the year of first publication of the work. An example of a copyright notice can be found on the copyright page at the beginning of this book. Care

> **Copyright Notice**
> - © 2001 Michael A. Lechter
> - Copyright 2001 Michael A. Lechter
> - COPR 2001 Michael A. Lechter

should be taken, however, not to include a date of publication in a notice on an unpublished work, such as software distributed under a trade secret license.

There are various requirements as to where the copyright notice must be placed on the work.[87] However, in general, the placement of the notice should be sufficient if it is placed in a prominent position on the work, in a manner and location as to "give reasonable notice of the claim of copyright."

Term

The term of the copyright for all works created after January 1, 1978, is the author's life plus an additional 70 years after the (last surviving) author's death.[88] The term for a work for hire is 95 years from publication or 120 years from creation, whichever is shorter.[89]

Deposit with Library of Congress

Two copies of a work are required to be deposited in the Copyright (
the use of the Library of Congress within three months of publication of any
work bearing notice of copyright. Where a program is not copy protected,
only one complete copy of the "best edition" must be filed.[90] However, while
failure to make the deposit can give rise to fines and other penalties, it does
not affect the copyright protection itself, and special relief from the deposit
requirement can be applied for through the Copyright Office.[91]

Registration

Except in the case of publication with omission of a proper copyright notice
on works first published before March 1, 1989, copyright registration is not
a prerequisite for copyright protection. However, registration is significant
in three respects. A registration is normally necessary before the copyright
on works originating in the United States can be enforced, that is, before an
infringement suit may be filed in court.[92] If the registration is made before
publication, or within five years after publication, the mere fact of registration establishes the validity of the copyright and of the facts stated in the
copyright certificate in court.[93] Also, the copyright statute provides for
"statutory damages and attorneys' fees" that may range, according to the
circumstances, from $750 (in the case of an innocent infringer) to up to
$150,000 (in the case of a willful infringer).[94] If a registration is made within
three months after publication of the work or prior to the infringement of
the work, the copyright owner has the option to elect to take statutory
damages instead of the actual damages and profits that he can prove, as well
as attorneys' fees.[95] Unless made within three months after the publication
of the work, a registration not made until after the infringement only entitles the copyright owner to be awarded the damages and profits that can actually be proven.[96]

Procedure for Obtaining a Registration

A registration is obtained by filing (in the same envelope or package) the appropriate completed application form, a specified fee for each application,
and two complete copies of the work.

There are different application forms for different types of works. For example, Form TX must be used for published and unpublished nondramatic literary works, while Form VA must be used for published and unpublished works of the visual arts (pictorials, graphics, etc.). Form TX should be used with respect to applications pertaining to program code, while Form VA should be used with respect to the screen output (user interfaces) of programs as visual arts. The Copyright Office is very exacting with respect to the forms. However, the forms are available online from the Copyright Office Web site (http://lcweb.loc.gov/copyright/). The Copyright Office also insists that the application fee and complete deposit copies be sent together in the same envelope or package.

With respect to works first published after January 1, 1978, two complete copies of the "best" edition must be filed. If the work was first published in the United States before January 1, 1978, two complete copies of the work as first published must accompany the application. Under the Copyright Office regulations, special provisions are made for deposit of "identifying portions" of machine-readable works, in lieu of two complete copies.[97] More specifically, for unpublished works that are fixed, and published works that are published only in machine-readable form, other than a CD-ROM format, the deposit may take any of the following forms:

Deposit Requirements

- Identifying portions
- First and last 25 pages
- Source code required
- Dynamic works—new version

- The first and last twenty-five pages or equivalent units of the source code, together with the page or equivalent unit containing the copyright notice. However, with respect to revised versions of computer programs, if the revisions do not occur in the first and last twenty-five pages, the deposit must consist of the page containing the copyright notice and any fifty pages of source code representative of the revised material. Trade secret material within the first and last twenty-five pages of source code can be blocked out or redacted, provided that the blocked-out portions are proportionately less than the material remaining, and the deposit reveals an appreciable amount of original computer code;

- The first and last ten pages or equivalent units of source code without blocked-out portions;
- The first and last twenty-five pages of object code, together with any ten or more consecutive pages of source code with no blocked-out portions;
- With respect to copyright claims in a revision that is not contained in the first and last twenty-five pages of source code, the deposit shall consist of either twenty pages of source code representative of the revised material with no blocked-out portions, or any fifty pages of source code representative of the revised material with portions of the source code containing trade secrets blocked out, again provided that the blocked-out portions are proportionately less than the remaining material, and an appreciable amount of original computer code remains.
- Where work is fixed in a CD-ROM format, the deposit must consist of one complete copy of the CD-ROM, together with any accompanying operating software, an instruction manual, and a printed version of the work embodied in the CD-ROM, if the work is fixed in print.

The deposit of only "identifying portions" of lengthy programs, which can often be the equivalent of over a thousand pages, has given rise to another area of controversy. Programs tend to be dynamic products; improvements are constantly being made. Thus, the question arises as to which particular version of a program the identifying portion was taken from. It is, therefore, prudent for the software developer to maintain proper documentation to protect against possible controversy. If the "identifying portions" are not sufficient to "identify," arguments may be raised that the registration is invalid or inapplicable.[98]

Enforcing a Copyright

The copyright statute[99] provides that anyone who violates any of the exclusive rights of a copyright holder (or, in the case of "visual art," copyright holder or the author), or imports unauthorized copies of the work into the U.S., is an infringer. As we discussed earlier, subject to certain limitations, the owner of the copyright on a work has exclusive right to: reproduce the work;

prepare derivative works based upon the work; distribute copies of the work to the public by sale, rental, lease, or lending; and publicly display or perform the work (in the case of musical, dramatic, and similar types of works).[100] In addition, where single-copy/limited-edition visual art[101] is concerned, the artist/photographer who created the visual art has an additional "right of attribution and integrity."[102]

Contributing to (knowingly encouraging) unauthorized copying of a copyrighted work can also create liability for (contributory) infringement.[103] However, there are certain limitations on copyright infringement liability on the part of online service providers (OSPs)[104] arising from certain separate and distinct categories of conduct (transitory communications; system caching; storing information at the direction of users; and information location tools).

To qualify for the limitation of liability, an entity must qualify as a "service provider." A "service provider" is defined,[105] for the purposes of limitation of liability for transitory communications, as "an entity offering the transmission, routing, or providing of connections for digital online communications between or among points specified by a user, or material of the user's choosing, without modification as to the content of the material as sent or received." For the purposes of the other three categories of activities, a "service provider" is more broadly defined as "a provider of online services or network access, or the operator of facilities therefor."

The definition of "service provider" is extremely broad. The House Judiciary Committee Report explains that the definition includes "services such as providing Internet access, e-mail, chat room and Web page hosting." Hence, companies that are not in the business of providing online services can still benefit from the DMCA's protection—provided that certain conditions and requirements are met. Consequently, a company that maintains an Intranet for its employees may be a service provider under the statute. Similarly, a company may qualify as a service provider if it maintains a bulletin board where customers can post comments concerning the company's products.

However, the rules pertaining to the limitation of infringement liability are complicated and rigid. Unless an OSP fully complies with the rules specified in the statute, it faces loss of the exemption and may be exposed to potentially large copyright monetary claims. These rules are summarized in the table below.

Prerequisites for OSP Limitation of Liability		
Activity	**Requirements**	
Transitory communications §512(a) Transmitting, routing, or providing connections for material through a system or network control or operated by or for the service provider, or by reason of the intermediate and transient storage of that material in the course of such transmitting, routing, or providing connections	Transmission of material initiated by, or at the direction of, other than the OSP	§512(a)(1)
	Services provided through automatic process, without selection of material by the OSP	§512(a)(2)
	Service provider does not designate recipients	§512(a)(3)
	Only anticipated recipients have access to copies of material	§512(a)(4)
	Copies are maintained no longer than is reasonably necessary to effect transmission	§512(a)(4)
System caching §512(b) Intermediate and temporary storage of material on a system or network control or operated by or for the service provider	The material is made available online by Party A (a person other than the OSP); The material is transmitted from Party A through the system to Party B at the direction of Party B; The material is stored for the purpose of making the material available to users of the system that subsequently request access from Party A	§512(b)(1)
	The material is transmitted without modification	§512(b)(2)(A)
	The OSP complies with reasonable refreshing/reloading/updating specifications of Party A	§512(b)(2)(B)
	The OSP does not unduly interfere with information gathering by Party A	§512(b)(2)(C)
	The OSP restricts access in accordance with restrictions (e.g., password, payment) imposed by Party A	§512(b)(2)(D)
	The OSP expeditiously takes down allegedly infringing material removed from the originating site	§512(b)(2)(E)
Storage at user direction §512(c) Storage of material at the direction of a user of the material on a system or network controlled by the OSP	The OSP does not have actual knowledge of infringement	§512(c)(1)(A)(i)
	The OSP is not aware of facts or circumstances from which the infringement is apparent	§512(c)(1)(A)(ii)
	The OSP expeditiously takes down the infringing material upon becoming aware of infringement	§512(c)(1)(A)(iii)
	No direct financial benefit from the infringing activity	§512(c)(1)(B)
	The OSP expeditiously takes down material after receiving Notice pursuant to §512(c)(3)	§512(c)(1)(C)
	The OSP designates an Agent to receive Notice (Web site link and filing contact information with Copyright Office)	§512(c)(2)

Activity	Requirements	
Information location tools §512(d)	The OSP does not have actual knowledge of infringement	§512(d)(1)(A)(i)
Referring or linking users to an online location containing infringement, or using information location tools such as directory, index, reference, pointer, or hypertext link	The OSP is not aware of facts or circumstances from which the infringement is apparent	§512(d)(1)(A)(ii)
	The OSP expeditiously takes down the infringing material upon becoming aware of infringement	§512(d)(1)(A)(iii)
	No direct financial benefit from the infringing activity	§512(d)(2)
	The OSP expeditiously takes down material after receiving Notice pursuant to §512(c)(3)	§512(d)(3)

To establish a copyright infringement, a plaintiff must prove ownership of a valid copyright and "copying" of *protectable expression* by the defendant.[106] Copying is typically inferred from proof of access to the copyrighted work and substantial similarity (or virtual identity, depending upon the aspects at issue) as to protectable expression between the accused and copyrighted works.[107] Of course, even if programs are identical in every respect, there is no copyright infringement if there was no copying, that is, it can be shown that the subsequent program was independently developed.

A copyright is enforced by bringing suit in an appropriate U.S. district court.[108] However, as previously noted, a copyright registration is a prerequisite to bringing the action.[109] As a general proposition, as with respect to patent infringement, suit can be brought in the district court for any jurisdiction where the accused infringer resides, or has committed acts of infringement and has a regular and established place of business. For a corporate defendant, the corporation is deemed to "reside" in any judicial district in which it is subject to personal jurisdiction.[110] An appeal from the decision of a district court in a copyright infringement matter is taken to one of the eleven U.S. circuit courts of appeals.

Remedies for Copyright Infringement

The copyright owner is entitled to actual damages and profits or statutory damages for the infringement[111] and may also obtain an injunction against the infringer,[112] and seizure and impoundment of infringing articles.[113] In addition, a court, at its discretion, may award costs and attorneys' fees to the prevailing party.[114]

As previously noted, if a registration is made within three months after publication of the work or prior to the infringement of the work, the copyright owner has the option to elect to take statutory damages instead of the actual damages and profits that he can prove, as well as attorneys' fees.[115] Statutory damages may range, according to the circumstances, from $750 (in the case of an innocent infringer) to up to $150,000 (in the case of a willful infringer).[116] Unless made within three months after the publication of the work, a registration not made until after the infringement only entitles the copyright owner to be awarded the damages and profits that can actually be proven.[117]

Ownership of a Copyright

Copyright ownership is one of the areas of IP law that tends to turn the unwary into casualties. It is counterintuitive. You would think that if you paid for something to be created then you would own it. Not necessarily so under the copyright law. Unless there is a written assignment, or the work qualifies as a "work for hire," the creator/originator of a work owns the copyright.[118] If the work quali-

> **The Default Rule:
> Owned by Author**

fies as a "work for hire," then the employer of the creator, or the entity that commissioned the work, is considered to be the author and holder of the copyright.[119] To be a work for hire the work must either: (1) have been prepared by an employee within the scope of the employee's duties; or (2) fall within one of certain specified categories of works, be especially ordered or commissioned, and be the subject of an express written agreement specifying that it will be a work for hire.[120] The specified categories include: collective works (a work including a number of contributions, each constituting a separate and independent work that is assembled into a collective whole); audiovisual works, such as motion pictures and phonorecords; compilation works (a work formed by the collection and assembly of preexisting materials or of data that are selected, coordinated, or arranged in such a way that the resulting work as a whole constitutes an original work); supplementary works (works prepared as a secondary adjunct to another work, such as illustrations, forewords or afterwords); instructional texts, tests, and test answers; translations and atlases.

The requirements to qualify as a work for hire are very strictly construed. Unless the creator qualifies as an employee, and the work is created within the scope of employment, the existence of an express written agreement specifying that the work is a work for hire is imperative.[121] Employee status is determined under the law of agency and is based upon such factors as: the skill required to do the work; where the work is done (for instance, at the facility of the entity that commissioned the work?); who supplies the facilities and tools; the right to assign additional work; discretion over when and how long to work; who hires and pays the creator's assistants; whether the creator is a separate business entity; the provision of employee benefits; and tax treatment (are Social Security and income tax withheld?).[122] While no single factor is determinative, as a practical matter, unless the creator is treated as an employee for tax and Social Security purposes, the person is likely to be deemed an independent contractor and the owner of the copyright in the absence of a written agreement.

As discussed below, even if a work does not qualify as a work for hire, a party commissioning a work can still obtain ownership of the copyright by assignment. There is, however, a practical difference between obtaining the copyright by assignment and being the author by virtue of work for hire; as will be discussed below, assignments by individual authors are subject to a right of termination.[123]

It should also be noted that, with respect to a periodical or other "collective work," the copyright to the compilation of works is separate and distinct from the copyright in each separate contribution. The copyright in the separate contribution is thus initially with the originator of the contribution (unless it is a work for hire, in which case the person commissioning the work is considered the author).

Absent agreement to the contrary, authors of a joint work (a work prepared by two or more authors with the intention that the respective contributions be merged into inseparable or interdependent parts of a unitary work) are co-owners of the copyright. Each co-author owns a proportionate share of the copyright, and, in the absence of an agreement, is entitled to contribution, that is, a share of any royalties received from licensing. A joint owner may generally use or license the use of the work without the consent of co-owners, but must account to them for their shares of profits derived from any license to a third party. Potentially, contribution to other co-owners may be required for use of the copyrighted work by a particular co-owner.[124]

The author of a work can assign the copyright to another. The assignment requires a written agreement[125] that must be recorded in the Copyright Office in order to be effective against a subsequent recorded transfer to a party that did not have notice of the earlier transfer and that paid a valuable consideration for the copyright.[126]

However, under the statute,[127] any license or transfer of right in a copyright in other than a work made for hire may be subject to a right of termination that cannot be assigned; during a five-year period beginning thirty-five years after the transfer, the author, or the author's heir, may terminate the rights granted.[128] Termination, however, does not require the grantee to cease the use of derivative works that were prepared under the authority of the grant before it was terminated,[129] but the preparation of further derivative works is not permitted.

Trademark Protection

A trademark (or service mark) is used to identify the source or origin of a product (or service)—that is, a trademark distinguishes the goods or services of one company from those of another. It is through a trademark that a customer connects the goodwill and reputation of the company to its products. Under the law, a competitor is prevented from capitalizing on your reputation and goodwill by passing off possibly inferior goods as those made by, or for, you. Thus, in a manner of speaking, proper use of a trademark can protect the sales value of your reputation and that of the product,

> **Trademark:**
> **Anything nonfunctional that is capable of distinguishing the goods or services of one entity from those of others**

as well as your investments in advertising and other promotional activities used to develop goodwill. However, trademark protection does not prevent the competition from copying or reverse-engineering your product unless the competition misrepresents or creates confusion as to the source, origin, or sponsorship of the product (or

> **Trademarks**
>
> - Identifies source of goods—protects reputation
> - Protects as long as used with goods
> - No protection against copying or reverse engineering, unless confusion as to source of goods

copies a feature of the product having "secondary meaning," as will be discussed later).

Acquiring Rights

In the United States, trademark rights are acquired through use of the mark in legal commercial transactions. That is, you simply adopt a proper mark, begin to use it commercially, and through that use you acquire proprietary rights in the mark. In general, the first to use a given mark in connection with particular goods in a given geographical area obtains the exclusive right to the mark for use with those goods in that area.

Acquiring Trademark Rights

• By use of mark with goods
• By filing application based on intent to use
• First to use mark or file intent-to-use application obtains rights

---

Once the mark is used in interstate commerce (or a good faith bona fide intent to use the mark in interstate commerce is formed), a federal registration may be obtained.

Under common law, as a general proposition, if you are the first to use a given mark in connection with particular goods or services in a given geographical area you obtain the exclusive rights in the mark for use with those particular goods or services in that particular geographical area. However, if someone else adopts the mark somewhere outside of that geographical area (such as in a distant state), without knowledge of your prior use of the mark, that person (not you) will acquire valid common-law rights to the mark in the remote area. That is where federal registration comes in; as will be discussed, through federal registration you can prevent subsequent remote users from obtaining rights.

"Use" of a trademark requires physical association of the mark on or in connection with the product or service. With a trademark, it is sufficient to apply the mark to labels or tags affixed to the product or to the containers for the product, displays associated with the product, or the like. "Trademark" usage cannot be established just through the use of the mark in advertising or product brochures, although, if the nature of the goods is such that that placement of the mark on the product (or on labels or tags) is impracticable, then the mark may be placed on documents associated with the goods or their sale.[1] On the other hand, if services are involved, rather than a physical product, the use of a mark in advertising is a proper usage for a "service mark" (a mark used in sales, advertising, or services to identify the source of the services). In either case, in order for a use to qualify as "use in commerce" under the federal statute, the use of a mark must be bona fide and in the ordinary course of trade. A use made merely to reserve a right in a mark (sometimes referred to as a token use) is not sufficient.

APPLICATION BASED ON "INTENT TO USE"

In general, prior to the Trademark Law Revision Act of 1988 (enacted November 16, 1988; effective November 16, 1989), once a proper mark (not "confusingly similar" to a mark already being used by another) has been used (sold or transported) in *interstate* commerce ("commerce which may lawfully be regulated by Congress"), it is eligible for registration with the PTO. Under the prior law, obtaining a federal registration, while providing constructive notice and many procedural advantages, did not generate any substantive rights in the mark; all rights were based upon actual use of the mark. This, however, was changed by the Trademark Law Revision Act of 1988. After November 16, 1989, substantive rights can be created by filing an application for registration based upon a bona fide intent to use the mark.[2] Once a registration based upon intent to use is obtained, the registrant is accorded a "constructive use" priority, effectively equivalent to actual use of the mark on the date of the application for registration.

> **Intent-to-Use Application**
>
> - Bona fide intent to use
> - As if actual use began on date of filing
> - Verified statement of actual use within six months of notice of allowance, with specimens
>   —Time period can be extended for fee
>   —Can convert to application based on actual use at any time prior to notice

More specifically, an application for registration of a mark may be filed on the basis of a good faith, bona fide intention to use the mark in commerce.[3] To obtain a registration, however, actual use of the mark must commence within a predetermined period (six months, extendable to one year upon request, and up to twenty-four additional months for good cause) of a notice of allowance from the PTO indicating that subject to a proper showing of the use in commerce, the mark is entitled to registration.[4] An application based on an intent to use will establish constructive use of the mark as of the filing date of the application. This creates trademark rights that are superior to any other, unless the other (1) actually used the mark prior to the filing date, (2) filed an intent-to-use–based application prior to the filing date, or (3) can claim a treaty priority date based on a corresponding foreign trademark application.[5]

The intent-to-use provisions of the law make it important that you be particularly careful about disclosing ideas for new marks—it is important that security be maintained to prevent someone else from winning a race to the PTO. Careful records should also be kept to show good faith intent to use the mark.

The Strength of a Mark

A symbol or word that cannot effectively identify the source of the goods cannot be used as a trademark. For example, putting a label "Oscilloscope" on an oscilloscope does not identify the origin of the oscilloscope. The protection afforded by (the strength of) a particular trademark is a direct function of the "distinctiveness" of the mark; that is, how closely associated the mark is with the source of the product, as opposed to the product itself. Marks can be categorized with respect to the degree of protection accorded by the mark, as "generic," "descriptive," "suggestive," and "fanciful" ("coined" or arbitrary).

UNPROTECTABLE GENERIC MARKS
A "generic mark" uses a term that refers to (or has come to be understood as referring to) the genus of the particular product, such as the mark "Oscilloscope" used with an oscilloscope apparatus. A generic term does not serve to identify the source of the goods, and therefore cannot be utilized as a trademark.

DESCRIPTIVE MARKS
A "descriptive mark" is a term that conveys an immediate idea of the ingredients, qualities, or characteristics of the goods. It describes the intended func-

tion, purpose or use of the goods, size of the goods, class of user of the goods, effect upon the user, and the like. A descriptive term is just one step removed from a generic term. An example would be using the trademark "Electronic" for an oscilloscope apparatus. However, a descriptive term can possibly come to be associated with a particular manufacturer and, thus, serve as identification of the origin of the goods. In trademark parlance, the initially descriptive mark has acquired a "secondary meaning." Absent such secondary meaning, a descriptive term does not accord a great deal of protection. You cannot stop someone else from using a term in its normal descriptive sense. (That type of use of a mark is referred to as a permissible "fair use.")

SUGGESTIVE MARKS

A "suggestive mark" requires imagination, thought, and perception to conclude the nature of the goods from the term used as the mark. For example, "Waveshape" would be a suggestive term when used with an oscilloscope.

FANCIFUL AND ARBITRARY MARKS

The highest degree of trademark protection is provided through the use of a "fanciful" ("coined") term or arbitrary term. A fanciful term is a word created strictly and entirely for use as a trademark. For example, the mark "ZOAZ" would be a fanciful term if used as a trademark for an oscilloscope. An arbitrary term is a common word used in a "fanciful sense." For example, "Bigfoot" would be an "arbitrary" mark when used for an oscilloscope.

It should be noted, however, that a misspelled word or a term combining commonly used words is not a "fanciful" or "coined" word. Acronyms, initialisms, abbreviations, phonetic variations, and foreign words all afford the same protection as the corresponding correctly spelled English word.

It should be apparent that a given term may be generic in one market and arbitrary in another market; for example, the mark "Oscilloscope" for an oscilloscope apparatus is generic. However, the mark "Oscilloscope" for chewing gum is arbitrary. Terms can, however, change from one category to another. At one time "escalator," "cellophane," "aspirin," and "shredded wheat" were valid trademarks. However, through improper use, these marks became associated with the goods in general, that is, became generic terms for the goods. This is the reason why some companies are fighting a continual war against people who are improperly using their trademarks. In the past, some goods that have found themselves in a generic status have, in effect, made a comeback. For example, the marks "Goodyear" and "Singer" at one time were considered to be generic, but eventually reacquired the status of protectable trademarks.

Choosing a Mark

There are certain basic guidelines with respect to choosing a mark. The strongest word mark (as opposed to a symbol mark) is a relatively euphonious, easily pronounced, coined word that does not include components commonly used in marks. It is desirable that the mark be simple—a simple mark is more easily protected. Where a mark includes a large number of elements, there is the possibility that someone else could adopt some of, but not all of, the elements of the mark and (at least arguably) avoid infringing it. If both a word mark and a symbol mark are adopted, they should, if possible, be completely separate in at least some of the instances where they are used, to ensure that each can be protected separately. It should also be noted that a simple mark is more easily remembered by purchasers. Finally, it has been found that a mark that can be depicted and put into words is more easily remembered than a mark that can only be depicted or verbalized but not both.

> **Choosing a Mark**
> - Must identify source of goods
> - Simple design and/or coined word
> - Trademark search

It should be apparent that you do not want to choose a mark and expend large sums in advertising and so forth, only to learn that someone else has proprietary rights in the use of that mark. If you begin using a mark on a product that is so similar to a mark already in use by someone else on similar goods and/or services that there is a "likelihood of confusion" as to the source of the product, you have in all likelihood violated state unfair competition common laws, as well as the federal trademark law.[6] As will be discussed later, this can have rather dire consequences.

Accordingly, before you adopt a mark for a product or service, it is prudent to undertake an investigation to ensure that no one else is using the particular mark. That is, you should have a "trademark search" performed.

Basically, this involves examining trademark registration files maintained at the PTO to see whether any similar mark is already registered to another party, or whether an application has been made for registration of a similar mark for similar goods and/or services. You can do this yourself over the Internet using the Trademark Electronic Search System (TESS) database made available by the U.S. PTO at http://www.uspto.gov.

"Confusingly Similar"

Potential trademark problems arise when the proposed trademark is "confusingly similar" to another mark, that is, it so resembles the other mark that it is likely to cause deception or confusion as to: (a) the source of the particular goods involved; or (b) affiliation, connection, or association with or (c) sponsorship or approval by the owner of the other mark. Three rule-of-thumb criteria for determining whether or not a mark resembles another are:

1. Do the marks look alike?
2. Do the marks sound alike? and
3. Do the marks have the same meaning or suggest the same thing?

The similarities and dissimilarities of the goods themselves must also be considered. In this regard, the manner of marketing the goods is relevant. Do the respective goods move in the same channels of trade? Are they sold in the same type of store? Are they bought by the same people? What degree of care is likely to be exercised by the purchasers?

Trademarks, when used on products purchased by relatively sophisticated purchasers, are less likely to cause confusion as to the source of goods, sponsorship, or affiliation than when used on goods typically sold to unsophisticated purchasers. The ultimate answer as to whether marks are "confusingly similar" is the cumulative effect of the differences and similarities in the marks and in the goods or services.

Prior to 1988, the test for confusing similarity was essentially limited to whether or not there was confusion as to the source (origin) of goods. While that was the case, the similarities and dissimilarities in goods or services, channels of trade, and relevant markets had particular significance. However, in about 1988 the test was expanded to include confusion as to *affiliation or sponsorship*. In part because merchandising—the use of the trademark with numerous types of goods to take full advantage of goodwill associated with the trademark—has become commonplace, the expansion of the confusing similarity test to include affiliation and sponsorship has made issues of similarities and dissimilarities in goods, channels of trade, and relevant markets much less significant in most cases.

"Dilution"

Even in the absence of confusing similarity because of dissimilarities in goods or channels of trade, if a mark has achieved "famous" status (as with Coca-Cola, Harley-Davidson, McDonald's) it is possible to obtain an injunction against commercial use of the mark by another, under the principle of "dilution."

In 1996, the federal trademark law was amended to include a federal antidilution provision.[7] The federal statute defines dilution as "the lessening of the capacity of a famous mark to identify and distinguish goods or services, regardless of the presence or absence of (1) competition between the owner of the famous mark and other parties, or (2) likelihood of confusion, mistake, or deception."[8] Dilution is not applicable to: fair use of the mark in comparative advertising or to identify the authorized goods or services sold under the famous mark; noncommercial use of the mark; or news reporting and commentary.[9]

Dilution statutes, in contradistinction to the classical trademark infringement based upon likelihood of confusion, *relate to use on goods that are not the same or similar to goods in connection with which the trademark is used and are limited to trademarks that are so famous that they are recognized as a source indicator even in the absence of a reference to particular goods or services.*

In order to prove a violation of the Federal Trademark Dilution Act, you must show that: (1) the mark is famous; (2) the defendant is making a commercial use of the mark in commerce; (3) the defendant's use began after the mark became famous; and (4) the defendant's use of the mark dilutes the quality of the mark by diminishing the capacity of the mark to identify and distinguish goods and services. Dilution can be caused by, for example, "blurring" (where your mark is used to identify someone else's goods or services, creating the possibility that the mark will lose its ability to serve as a unique identifier of your product), or by "tarnishment" (where your mark is improperly associated with an inferior or offensive product or service).[10]

For example, assume you began selling chewing gum under the mark "Xerox," and that you can prove that, since the goods are so dissimilar, the use of the mark on the chewing gum would not be likely to "cause confusion, or to cause mistake or to deceive" the public as to the source of the goods or as to sponsorship or affiliation. If this were the case, the use would not be a classical trademark infringement. However, if the Xerox mark qualified as "famous" before you began using the mark on the chewing gum, there could still be dilution.

How can you tell whether a mark qualifies as "famous"? There is no hard-and-fast rule. However, the federal statute[11] does provide a (nonexhaustive) list of factors that may be considered:

(A) the degree of inherent or acquired distinctiveness of the mark;
(B) the duration and extent of use of the mark in connection with the goods or services with which the mark is used;
(C) the duration and extent of advertising and publicity of the mark;
(D) the geographical extent of the trading area in which the mark is used;
(E) the channels of trade for the goods or services with which the mark is used;
(F) the degree of recognition of the mark in the trading areas and channels of trade used by the mark's owner and the person against whom the injunction is sought;
(G) the nature and extent of use of the same or similar marks by third parties; and
(H) whether the mark was federally registered .

It is clear that in order to qualify as famous, a mark must be strong and well recognized.[12] National renown is an important factor.[13] A mark that is weak because it describes the goods, or is a common term, typically will not qualify as famous.[14] In any event, there is a high threshold for fame; in order to qualify as famous a mark has to be unique and out of the ordinary.[15]

There is a split among the courts as to the extent to which dilution must be shown. Certain courts require proof of actual dilution, that is, actual economic harm.[16] Other courts, however, have taken the position that a mere likelihood of dilution is sufficient for an injunction.[17]

Some states have their own antidilution statutes.[18] Typically, the state statutes effectively make any unauthorized use of another's trademark a misdemeanor, resulting in a fine or imprisonment, or create a private right of action to enjoin the unauthorized use. The existence and specific provisions of state antidilution statutes must be investigated on a state-to-state basis. In addition, other bodies of state law and statutes exist, such as the Uniform Deceptive Trade Practices Act, which may be applicable in various situations.

"Cybersquatting"

The federal trademark statute[19] also creates a specific civil cause of action for "cybersquatting." This practice will be dealt with in more detail in the section later in this book on the Internet and your intellectual property. Briefly, however, to establish a claim of cybersquatting, you must show:

(1) your mark was distinctive (or famous) at the time of the registration of the domain name;

(2) that the defendant "registers, traffics in, or uses a domain name" that is identical or confusingly similar to (and/or, if famous, dilutes) that mark; and

(3) that the defendant has "a bad faith intent to profit from that mark."

A parallel action on the part of a domain name registrant is provided for review of actions by domain name registrars who suspend, disable, or transfer a registered domain name based upon identity or similarity with someone else's mark.[20] The statute also deals with the problem of obtaining jurisdiction over foreign nationals who register domain names, by providing for in rem jurisdiction to permit civil actions to obtain forfeiture or cancellation of a domain name that violates a trademark right in instances where you otherwise would not be able to obtain jurisdiction over the registrant.[21]

Federal Registration

Common-law rights in a trademark inure to the user immediately upon use of the mark in a legal, commercial transaction. Even without registration of the trademark, the owner of a mark is entitled to prevent others from using a confusingly similar mark for related goods in the geographic area in which the rights are established. However, the owner of a common-law (unregistered) mark is typically not protected against a third party in a remote geographical area (such as a distant state) who, without knowledge of the prior use of the mark by the owner, subsequently adopts the mark and acquires valid common-law rights to the mark in the remote area. As noted above, that is where federal registration comes in; you can prevent subsequent remote users from obtaining rights through federal registration of the mark. Appropriate federal registration gives constructive notice of the use of the mark, and prevents subsequent remote users from obtaining rights. As will be apparent from the following discussion, there are a number of very substantial benefits that come with registering a mark with the PTO.

The PTO maintains two separate registers: the "Principal Register" and the "Supplemental Register." Registration on the Principal Register is most desirable, and provides a number of procedural and substantive advantages, as will be explained. However, registration on either register provides a number of very valuable rights.

Registration on either register provides the very practical benefit of tending to provide *actual* notice of the mark to would-be users. In the first place, marks on both the Principal and Supplemental Registers are available to the trademark examiners and can thus, as will be explained, prevent someone else from obtaining a registration on a confusingly similar mark. In addition, the mark may show up in any investigations made by a company prior to adopting a mark, causing the company to reconsider adopting the mark.

PRINCIPAL REGISTER

Registration on the Principal Register also affords various substantive and procedural advantages. In addition to providing actual notice of the mark, registration of a mark on the Principal Register also provides constructive notice of the registrant's claim of ownership of the mark.[22] This prevents someone else in a remote geographical area from subsequently adopting and obtaining rights in the mark. Some case law,

> **Principal Register**
> - Any mark capable of distinguishing source of goods, unless:
>   —Immoral
>   —Confusingly similar
>   —Merely descriptive or misdescriptive of goods

however, is to the effect that there is no "likelihood of confusion" as to the source of goods if the registrant is not doing business in the remote geographical area. Under those cases, the subsequent user will not be enjoined from using the mark until the registrant begins actually doing business in the same geographical area.

Registration of the mark on the Principal Register is prima facie evidence of the validity of the registration, the registrant's ownership of the mark, and the registrant's exclusive right to use the mark in commerce in connection with the goods or services specified in the certificate.[23] In addition, if an affidavit is filed with the PTO to the effect that the mark has been used continuously for five consecutive years subsequent to the date of registration and is still being used in interstate commerce,[24] the registered mark is incontestable and can be attacked only on certain limited bases.[25]

Once a mark is registered on the Principal Register, it can be filed with the U.S. Customs Service to prevent any article of imported merchandise that copies or simulates the trademark from entering the country.[26]

Any mark capable of distinguishing the goods of one company from those of another can be registered on the Principal Register *unless* the mark:

(a) includes immoral, deceptive, or scandalous matter or matter which may disparage or falsely suggest a connection with persons living or dead, institutions, beliefs, or national symbols, or bring them into contempt or disrepute;

(b) includes the flag or coat of arms or other insignia of the United States, or of any state or municipality, or of any foreign nation, or any simulation thereof;

(c) includes the name, portrait, or signature of a particular living individual or a deceased president during the life of his widow, unless by consent;

(d) is "confusingly similar" to the mark of another; that is, "consists of or comprises a mark which so resembles a mark registered in the U.S. Patent and Trademark Office, or a mark or trade name previously used in the United States by another and not abandoned, as to be likely, when applied to the goods of the applicant, to cause confusion, to cause mistake, or to deceive";

(e) consists of a mark which, when applied to the goods of the applicant, is merely descriptive or deceptively misdescriptive of such goods;

(f) consists of a mark which, when applied to the goods of the applicant, is primarily geographically descriptive or deceptively misdescriptive of the goods; or

(g) consists of a mark which is primarily merely a surname.[27]

SUPPLEMENTAL REGISTER

Any mark in actual use that is capable of distinguishing the applicant's goods or services, but is not registerable on the Principal Register because it is "merely descriptive" of the goods, a geographical origin of the goods, or a surname, can be registered on the Supplemental Register.[28] For the purposes of registration on the Supplemental Register, a mark can consist of any trademark, symbol, label, package, configuration of goods (such as the shape of a bottle), name, word, slogan, phrase, surname, geographical name, device, or combination thereof, so long as the mark is capable of distinguishing the applicant's goods or services from those of others and is not utilitarian or directed by the function of the goods (i.e., is ornamental). In other words, the trade dress— shape of packaging, color combinations, and so forth—can be registered on the Supplemental Register. The use, however, must be trademark use, to distinguish the goods, and not trade name use, that is, it must not merely be the name of the business. Registration on the Supplemental Register does not provide all of the rights accruing to registration on the Principal Register. A supplemental registration: is not constructive notice of the mark;[29] is not prima facie evidence of the validity of the registration; is not prima facie evidence of the registrant's ownership of the mark, or the registrant's exclusive right to use the mark;[30] and cannot be the basis for stopping importations through customs.[31] The primary difference in an infringement action concerning a mark on the Supplemental Register, as compared to a suit

> **Supplemental Register**
> - Any mark capable of distinguishing source of goods, but, for example, "merely descriptive"
> - After "secondary meaning" is acquired, the name can be registered on principal register

concerning a mark on the Principal Register, is that the registrant must actually prove that the mark is distinctive and identifies that the goods originate with a single source (e.g., the registrant).

On the other hand, registration on the Supplemental Register does not preclude subsequent registration on the Principal Register, and is expressly not an admission that the mark is not distinctive.[32]

Secondary Meaning

Things change. Just as a good trademark can, as noted above, become generic over time, a descriptive term can turn into a good trademark. If a descriptive mark becomes "distinctive" of the applicant's goods in interstate commerce and actually identifies the applicant as the originator of the goods to the public, that is, achieves what is referred to as secondary meaning, the mark can be registered on the Principal Register. In this regard, substantially exclusive and continuous use of the mark in commerce for five years is considered prima facie proof that the mark is "distinctive."[33] It is not necessary that such marks be first registered on the Supplemental Register, or that they necessarily must be in use for five years. If it can be demonstrated that an otherwise "descriptive" mark has acquired a secondary meaning that identifies you as the origin of the goods, the mark can be immediately registered on the Principal Register. "Distinctiveness" of the mark can be proven by testimony, surveys, and other evidence of recognition by the public.

Concurrent Registrations

There are also provisions for concurrently registering confusingly similar marks to different parties in different geographical locations. Concurrent registrations are generally issued only when the parties involved establish that they have become entitled to use the mark as the result of concurrent, lawful use in commerce prior to the earliest of the filing dates of the applications or when a court has determined that more than one person is entitled to use the same or similar marks in commerce.[34]

Registering a Trademark

Once a bona fide, good faith intention to use a mark in interstate commerce can be alleged, an application for registration of the mark may be filed. As noted above, if the mark is properly chosen, it can be registered on the Principal Register. To prepare a trademark application, an attorney will need the following information:

1. The name and citizenship of the applicant. If the applicant is a partnership, the citizenship of the general partners is required. If the applicant is a corporation or an association, the state or nation where it is organized must be specified.

2. The domicile and post office addresses of the applicant.

3. The name of the person who will ultimately sign the trademark application. If the applicant is a company, the person signing the application must actually be an officer of the corporation, with signatory authority. Both name and title should be provided.

4. A description (i.e., the identity) of the goods or services for which the mark is presently being used and the manner in which the mark is being (or is contemplated to be) used in connection with the goods or services (i.e., affixed as a tag, on the packaging, etc.). The description of the goods and services on which the mark is in use must be entirely accurate. Inclusion of any goods or services in the application on which the mark is not currently in use at the time of an application based on actual use can result in the registration being held invalid. Likewise, particular care must be taken in describing the goods or services in an intent-to-use application; understating the goods can cause loss of rights. Additionally, discrepancies between the goods stated in the intent-to-use application and those on which the work is actually ultimately used can cause severe complications in examination or result in denial of a registration.

5. A drawing of the mark. Care should be taken that the drawing depict the mark precisely as it ultimately will be used. Discrepancies between the mark as shown and the mark as actually used can preclude registration.

6. Whether the application is based on an intent to use or actual use, and if the application is based on actual use:

    a. The date of the first actual use of the mark with the goods or services in interstate commerce. Generally "use in interstate commerce" requires the movement across state lines of a product bearing the trademark. There are, however, provisions for obtaining a trademark registration based upon a prior foreign registration or application for registration, without requiring use in U.S. commerce.

b. The date of first actual use of the mark with the goods or services anywhere in the world (not necessarily in interstate commerce). Great care should be taken when specifying the date of first use. It is desirable that the specified date of first use be as early as possible; the first to use the mark generally wins in any contest of rights. However, error as to the date of first use may sometimes void the registration.

c. A prescribed number of specimens of the mark as actually used in interstate commerce. Where feasible (such as where the mark is used on labels or tags), actual specimens should be provided. If it is not feasible to provide actual specimens because, for example, the specimens are unreasonably large or painted directly on the goods, facsimiles must be provided. The facsimiles should be photographic or some other acceptable reproduction, which clearly show the mark and, preferably, how the mark is used on the goods.

7. The company should also be sure to inform its attorney of any possible concurrent users of which it is aware.

After the application is filed, a trademark examiner in the PTO reviews the application to determine whether the mark is, in fact, registerable, that is, capable of distinguishing the applicant's goods from the goods of others. The examiner also reviews both the Principal and Supplemental trademark registration files maintained at the PTO to determine if the mark is "confusingly similar" to any mark already being used by another. Thus, registering a mark and making it available to the trademark examiner tends to prevent registration of confusingly similar marks.

When an application for registration on the Principal Register survives examination, the mark is published in the "Official Gazette" of the PTO.[35] For thirty days after publication, any person who believes that he or she would be damaged by the registration of the mark may file what is known as an "opposition" to registration of the mark.[36] If no opposition is filed by the end of the thirty-day period, or if the applicant is successful in withstanding the opposition, a notice of allowance is issued. Oppositions are described in the following section.

If the application was based upon actual use of the mark, the registration is granted in due course. However, if the application was based upon an intent to use, additional procedures are followed. Specifically, the applicant must file a declaration of commencement of use, together with specimens of the use, within six months from the date of the notice of allowance. However, the six-month period can be extended for an additional six months by filing a request for extension together with a verified statement of continued bona fide intention to use the mark and payment of a specified fee. Up to four additional six-month extensions can be obtained upon showing good cause, and payment of additional fees.

After the declaration of commencement of use has been filed, the application is examined a second time. The examiner considers the specimens filed to ensure that the specimens reflect the same mark and goods described in the applications. Additionally, the examiner considers any new developments since the first examination, and the possibility of clear error in the first examination. Thus, the second examination will consider such issues as the mark having become generic since the first examination, or relevant prior registrations missed in the first examination.[37]

The use in commerce that must be alleged in the declaration of commencement of use must be the bona fide use of the mark in the ordinary course of trade, and not a token use made merely to reserve a right in the mark. Until the Trademark Law Revision Act of 1988, token sales of a product bearing the mark were sometimes made in an attempt to establish "use" of the mark. It was recognized that such a practice was questionable, but the theory was that a token sale was better than none at all. Therefore, if full-dressed commercial sales could not be commenced immediately, a token sale was made in an attempt to establish use, followed as soon as possible by the full-dress commercial sales. As of November 16, 1989, token sales are no longer effective to establish actual use. Of course, under the new law, rights can be obtained by filing an application based upon an intent to use.

Once the mark is actually used, and the registration granted, the registrant obtains a nationwide "constructive use" priority, effective as of the date of the application. The constructive use priority provides superior rights to the mark against all other persons except those who (a) used or applied to register the mark prior to the date of the application, or (b) obtained an earlier "effective filing date" by applying to register the mark under section 44 of the Lanham Act (obtained a priority based upon a filing in a foreign country).[38]

Contesting Registration: Opposition and Cancellation Proceedings

As previously noted, for a thirty-day period after a mark is published, any person who believes that he or she would be damaged by registration of the mark may initiate an "opposition" proceeding to prevent the grant of the registration.[39] An opposition is an inter partes procedure similar to litigation. The opposer is, in effect, in the position of a plaintiff, and the applicant for the registration is in the position of the defendant. The opposer initiates the proceeding by filing a verified (e.g., under oath) opposition paper stating facts that he contends show that the registration should be denied, and that the opposer would be damaged by the issuance of the registration. The grounds for the opposition can be that any of the requisites for the registration are not met, and that the opposer would be damaged by the registration. Typically, the opposer claims that he or she is presently using a mark or trade name that is confusingly similar to the applicant's mark and has been using that mark prior to use of the mark by the applicant. This situation establishes both the requisite damage and the grounds for opposition. The applicant typically counters with an argument that the applicant, in fact, is the prior user, or that there is no likelihood of confusion between the marks, or both. The parties then attempt to prove the facts. A "discovery" period occurs during which written questions (interrogatories) are answered by the parties, specified documents are requested and are produced for the other party to review, and oral depositions are taken. Evidence in the form of exhibits, affidavits, or oral depositions taken before a court reporter are then submitted, together with briefs explaining the parties' positions. An oral argument is then made before the Trademark Trial and Appeal Board, and that board ultimately renders a decision.

The trademark laws also provide for a "cancellation" proceeding.[40] The cancellation proceeding is similar to the opposition proceeding and can be brought by any party who believes that he is or will be damaged by the registration of a mark on the Principal Register. The cancellation proceeding is initiated by filing a verified petition stating facts showing the grounds for canceling the mark, and showing that continuing the registration will damage the petitioner. In general, if the cancellation petition is filed within five years after the registration issues, the cancellation proceeding can be based on any ground on which an opposition might have been brought. After five years, however, the cancellation proceeding can be filed only on the basis that: (a) the mark has become a common, descriptive name for the goods, that is, has become generic; (b) a registrant has abandoned the mark; (c) the registration of the mark was obtained fraudulently; or (d) the registrant is using the mark, or is permitting the mark to be used, to misrepresent the source of goods or services.[41]

Trademark Marking

Once a federal registration (on either the Principal or Supplemental Register) has been obtained with respect to a mark, the registrant is entitled to use a registration notice such as an asterisk, or an ® "bug" (typically as a superscript to the mark).

The use of a registration notice or "bug" is not mandatory under the statute. However, the notice or "bug" does provide constructive notice of the registration (obviates the need to prove actual notice of registration when seeking profits or damages against an infringer),[42] and "sets off" the mark. "Setting off" the mark signifies that the term or symbol is intended to be a mark that indicates the source or origin of the goods as opposed to a descriptive term for the goods.

Care must be taken with respect to the use of registration notices. A registration notice is appropriate only when used with the specific term or symbol shown in the registration, and only when the mark is used in connection with goods that are within, or are natural extensions of, the definition of the goods set forth in the registration. Accordingly, when a registered trademark is used in conjunction with a new product, a determination should be made as to whether or not the new product falls within the scope of the definition of goods of the registration. If not, a registration notice should not be used and consideration should be given to filing an application for a new registration.

It is not necessary that a registration notice accompany each instance or usage of a trademark in a publication or advertising copy. It is sufficient for constructive notice purposes that the registration notice be used prominently at least once in the publication. So long as the notice requirement is met, it is appropriate to use the registration notice only when the mark appears apart from a body of text. Within the body of text, using a distinctive typeface can generally best set off the trademark.

In circumstances where there is no applicable registration, a ™ symbol is often used to "set off" a mark. The use of the ™ symbol has no legal significance other than to indicate that the term or symbol is intended to be a source-identifying trademark.

Post-Registration Actions

Trademark law requires an affidavit of use (referred to as a "Section 8 Affidavit") to be filed with the PTO during the fifth year of registration.[43] The affidavit must state that the mark is still in use for at least one of the goods recited in the registration for each of the various classifications of goods. If an affidavit of use is not filed before the beginning of the sixth year, the registration is canceled.

As previously noted, if a mark is in continuous use for five consecutive years after the date of the registration, and is still in use, an affidavit to that effect can be filed (referred to as a "Section 15 Affidavit") to render the mark "incontestable." An "incontestable" status generally strengthens the mark.[44]

Term of the Registration

While trademark protection is of potentially infinite duration, the registration itself must be periodically renewed after each ten-year period. There is no limit on the number of times that the registration can be renewed. The registration is renewed for the next ten-year period by filing the appropriate papers and fees within six months before the expiration of the registration. There is no necessity to file a section 8 affidavit during the second or further terms of registration. However, when the registration is renewed, it is necessary to indicate that the mark is being used in interstate commerce. In addition, the renewal application must recite only the goods on which the mark is in actual use at that time.

Maintaining Trademark Rights

After rights in a mark are acquired, it is important to prevent the mark from losing its trademark significance. If the mark ceases to distinguish the company's goods or services from those of others, it becomes public property and can be used by anyone. In other words, if the primary significance of the mark to the consuming public becomes a descriptor for the nature or characteristics of the goods, rather than an indication of the source of the goods, the mark becomes a common descriptive term and any trademark rights in it are lost. Suggested procedures for maintaining trademark rights will be provided in a later section of this book.

Practical Considerations with Respect to Software Goods

Trademark protection is available for software products in the same manner as for other goods or services. The trademark should be included on packaging, in all documentation, and (where feasible) also in the body of the software in a manner that ensures the trademark is displayed whenever the program is used. Inclusion of the trademark in the body of the program provides a measure of protection against outright copying of the software. If an unauthorized person copies and sells or distributes the software in interstate commerce with the trademark still included in the software, irrespective of other remedies available (such as copyright, patent, or trade secret), the very powerful remedies for trademark infringement discussed above may be available.

The use of a trademark does not prevent competitors from copying or reverse-engineering a product unless some confusion as to the source or origin of the product is likely. However, the distribution of unauthorized copies of software incorporating the trademark can, in many instances, be a trademark infringement. Because of, for example, the lack of quality control of the magnetic media and copying process, and lack of access to support, maintenance, and updates, the unauthorized copy should not be considered to be the goods (or a service) of the trademark owner. Thus, in circumstances where an end user receiving an unauthorized copy including a trademark is likely to think that the source of the copy is the trademark owner, a trademark infringement occurs. Such a likelihood of confusion as to source commonly occurs where the unauthorized copies of the software

are obtained for a substantial fee from a commercial establishment in response to a request for the trademark owner's software, particularly if received in the packaging purporting to be that of the trademark owner.

A compelling argument that a likelihood of confusion exists can still be made where the parties to the original unauthorized copying or to distribution of the unauthorized copy were aware that the actual source was not the trademark owner. In many circumstances, potential purchasers of the software who were not party to the original transaction will have access to and use the software. In practice, once software is in the hands of the end user, "backup" copies (disks) of programs are typically used, or the program is installed on a fixed (hard) disk. Accordingly, those persons may well be confused as to the source after viewing the trademark in the displays. Under the laws of at least one state, likelihood of confusion is presumed when an unauthorized copy of software displays a registered mark.[45]

Further, market goodwill and recognition of the expertise of the originator (identified by the trademark) tends to give any follow-up or update services provided by the program originator more credence. The availability of follow-up or update services—that is, access to the expertise of the program originator—tends to enhance the value of authorized, relative to unauthorized, program copies.

Enforcing Trademark Rights

Trademark rights are one of the few areas of intellectual property law where an infringement suit can be brought in either state or federal court.[46] State courts, however, do not have the ability to alter registrations.[47] Your trademark rights are infringed if someone else uses a mark that is confusingly similar to yours (creates a likelihood that a consumer would be confused as to source, sponsorship, or affiliation) in interstate commerce,[48] dilutes your mark (if it is famous),[49] or commits "cybersquatting" with respect to your mark (in bad faith, adopts a domain name that is confusingly similar to your mark or that dilutes your famous mark).[50] In addition, false statements in someone else's advertisements or promotional materials (false advertising) regarding your products, or their products, is actionable under the federal trademark statute.[51]

As a general proposition, suit can be brought in the federal district court for any jurisdiction where the accused infringer resides, or has committed acts of infringement and has a regular and established place of business,[52] or in any state court that has jurisdiction under the applicable laws. For a corporate defendant under federal law, the corporation is deemed to "reside" in any judicial district in which it is subject to personal jurisdiction.[53] An appeal from the decision of a federal district court in a trademark infringement matter is taken to one of the eleven U.S. circuit courts of appeals; appeals in state actions are in accordance with state law.

Remedies for Infringement

A trademark owner can obtain not only an injunction against further use of the mark,[54] but also, subject to the principles of equity, recovery of all of the *profits* made by the infringer on the goods, any actual damages sustained due to the infringement (such as loss of sales), and the costs of the infringement action.[55] To recover the infringer's profits, the registrant is only required to prove the defendant's sales. The infringer then must prove all of the elements of cost. The court can, however, vary the award to an amount that it finds to be just according to the circumstances of the particular case.[56] In addition, all of the infringer's labels, packages, advertisements, and other material bearing the infringing mark must be destroyed.[57] In exceptional cases, the trademark owner can also recover reasonable attorneys' fees.[58]

In addition, if the infringement constitutes counterfeiting (unauthorized use of a mark that is identical with, or substantially indistinguishable from, a mark registered on the principal register),[59] the trademark owner can obtain: seizure of the goods bearing the counterfeiting marks, as well as the means of making the marks and manufacturing records;[60] and can elect at any time before a final judgment by a trial court to take, in lieu of actual damages and profits, statutory damages of between $500 and $100,000 (as determined by the court) per counterfeiting mark, per type of goods sold, or, if the counterfeiting was willful, up to $1,000,000 per counterfeiting mark per type of goods sold. Similarly, in instances of "cybersquatting" (bad faith adoption of a trademark as a domain name) the trademark owner can take, in lieu of actual damages and profits, statutory damages of between $1,000 and $100,000 (as determined by the court) per domain name.

Mask Work Protection

Historically, manufacturers and developers of semiconductor chips could not, as a practical matter, prevent competitors from appropriating the substantial investment inherent in developing circuit layout and production masks. None of the classical legal protection mechanisms were effective in protecting the developmental aspects of the chip. Notwithstanding the effort and cost of developing a mask, it is typically developed by the straightforward application of standard engineering principles and generally does not meet the novelty and unobviousness requisites for patentability.[1] Similarly, a mask typically does not constitute a work of authorship under the Copyright Act.[2] Further, as a general proposition, the technology presently available is not cost-effective in preventing competing companies from recon-

> **Mask Work Protection for Integrated Circuits**
>
> "A series of related images, however fixed or enclosed, that represent three-dimensional patterns in the layers of a semiconductor chip."

structing and copying the circuit layout and masks associated with the chip once it is placed on the market. (The author was privileged to have been one of the persons requested to submit testimony to Congress with respect to the protection of semiconductor products and proposed legislation in that regard.)

A new form of protection for mask works, that is, semiconductor chip products, is now available. The new form of protection is, in effect, a hybrid of the copyright and patent protection mechanisms.

Protectable Subject Matter; Requisites for Protection

Under the Semiconductor Chip Protection Act ("the act"), "mask works" are defined as a "series of related images, however fixed or enclosed" that represent three-dimensional patterns in the layers of a semiconductor chip.[3] Protection is available for any mask work unless:

1. The mask work is not original (that is, it was copied); or
2. The mask work consists of designs that are "staple, commonplace, or familiar in the semiconductor industry, or variations of such design, combined in such a way that, considered as a whole, is not original";[4] or
3. The mask work was first commercially exploited more than two (2) years before it was registered with the Copyright Office.[5]

In order to be eligible for protection, the mask work must also have a nexus to the United States. The owner of the mask work must either be a national or domiciliary of the United States or a foreign country that is party to a treaty with the United States that provides protection of mask works (at this time, there are no such treaties), or a stateless person. However, even if the owner does not fit in any of the above categories, mask work protection is available under the act if the mask work is first commercially exploited in the United States, or a special presidential proclamation with respect to the owner's country is applicable.[6] The United States nexus provisions were included to encourage other countries to enact similar legislation. A number of countries have now followed suit.[7]

Typically, the owner of a mask work (entitled to protection under the act) is the person(s) who created the mask work. Presumably, in analogy to the copyright statute, co-creators of the mask work would be co-owners of the mask work protection. However, where the mask work is made within the scope of the creator's employment, the employer is considered the owner of the mask work.[8]

The act includes various transitional provisions applying to chips that were first commercially exploited prior to the act, and to protection of mask works by foreign nationals. Under the transitional provisions, protection is available for any mask work that was first commercially exploited between July 1, 1983, and the passage of the act, so long as the mask work was registered with the Copyright Office before July1, 1985. However, the owner's rights are limited with respect to such chips. Infringing chips manufactured prior to the act may be imported and/or distributed in the United States until two years after the date of registration upon an offer to pay a reasonable royalty to the mask work owner on the units imported or distributed after the date of the act.[9] It is not clear exactly how the notice provisions of the Act (to be discussed) interact with the transitional provisions.

The transitional provisions also established interim protection for foreign nationals. A petition is made to the commissioner of patents and trademarks for an order extending protection under the act to nationals of a particular foreign country.[10] Guidelines for the submission of applications for interim protection of mask work have been published.[11] In essence, a showing must be made that the foreign country is attempting in good faith to comply with section 920(a)(1) of the act.

Scope of Protection

In essence, the Semiconductor Chip Protection Act protects against the use of reproductions of mask works in the manufacture of competing chips. However, the act makes it absolutely clear that competitors are not precluded from reverse-engineering the chip for purposes of analysis[12] or from using any (unpatented) idea, procedure, process, system, method of operation, concept, principle, ordiscovery embodied in the mask work.[13]

The owner of a protected mask work is provided the exclusive right to reproduce the mask work, and to import and distribute semiconductor chip products in which the mask work is embodied (i.e., chips using layouts according to the mask work).[14] However, the mask work owner's exclusive right is explicitly limited by the "reverse-engineering," "first sale (exhaustion of rights)," and "innocent infringer" provisions. The statute effectively limits infringement to instances of commercial exploitation of reproductions of the mask work, that is, to situations where competing chips are manufactured using outright copies of the protected mask work. It is permissible under the statute for competitors to reproduce the mask work solely for the purposes of reverse-engineering and to use the reverse-engineering analysis in the development of the competitor's chip.[15] Thus, competitors are permitted to study a semiconductor chip product, then develop their own corresponding masks (unless precluded by applicable patent rights).

Mask work owners' rights are of necessity limited with respect to the importation and sale of unauthorized chips by innocent purchasers of infringing chips. A person who purchases a chip without any reason to believe the chip to be subject to protection (purchases the chip "in good faith and without having notice of protection") is considered an innocent purchaser.[16] Where chips are purchased in good faith and without notice, the innocent purchaser does not incur any liability for importing or distributing the chips prior to being given notice that the chip is subject to protection, and is thereafter permitted to dispose of the remainder of the chips upon payment of a "reasonable royalty" on each unit of the infringing chip.[17] However, the innocent purchaser is somewhat at risk with respect to chips that are sold after his having been given notice of the protection. Unless the parties agree on a "reasonable royalty," the royalty will be determined by infringement litigation.[18]

The rights of the mask work owner are also limited to a certain extent with respect to the import and sale of authorized chips (chips embodying the mask work made by or with the permission of the mask work owner). The owner of the mask work exhausts his rights to control the importation and distribution of a particular protected semiconductor chip unit once it is sold. Once the owner of the mask work sells a chip to a third party, the third party is entitled to use the particular unit without the permission of the owner of the mask work. However, the third party does not have the right to reproduce the chip.[19]

Notice

The act provides for the constructive notice of mask work protection by use of a "mask work notice" similar to the copyright notice. The use of the mask work notice is not a prerequisite for protection. However, unless the notice is affixed to the semiconductor chips, in an action against an accused infringer it must be proven that the infringer was, or should have been, aware that the mask work was subject to protection. The mask work

Mask Work Notice

- Mask Work Michael A. Lechter
- *M* Michael A. Lechter
- Ⓜ Michael A. Lechter

notice consists of the words "mask work," the symbol *M*, or the symbol Ⓜ, followed by the name of the owner or owners of the mask work.[20]

Term; Registration

Under the act, mask work protection commences upon the first commercial exploitation of the chip (anywhere in the world) or upon registration of the mask work, whichever occurs first. The protection then runs for a term of ten years, expiring at the end of the tenth calendar year.[21] However, in order to maintain mask work protection, the mask work must be registered with the Copyright Office within two years of the first commercial exploitation.[22] Registering a mask work involves the filing of a Copyright Office form together with particular identifying material, and a fee.

Enforcement; Remedies

Registration of a mask work provides a number of very powerful remedies against infringers. Once a registration of the mask work has been obtained (or if registration is applied for and refused, in which case notice must be served on the Copyright Office), the mask work owner can bring an infringement suit in the federal courts[23] and, if successful, obtain not only injunctive relief and actual damages suffered as a result of the infringement, but also any profits made by the infringer that are not accounted for in the actual damages[24] and, at the court's discretion, all of the costs of the suit, including attorneys' fees.[25] Alternatively, in lieu of actual damages and profits, the owner can obtain an award of statutory damages up to $250,000 (the exact amount is determined by the court).[26] In addition, infringing chips and drawings, layouts, and so forth can be impounded or destroyed.[27]

The owner of a protected mask work can also prevent the importation of infringing chips into the United States. The Treasury Department and Postal Service have issued regulations with respect to the exclusion of infringing articles from the United States. It is probable that the regulations will require, as a condition for preventing imported articles from entering the United States, that the protected mask work owner either obtain a court order or an order from the International Trade Commission, prove that the mask work is protected and the imported articles are an infringement, and/or post a bond.

Practical Considerations

As a practical matter, the most difficult aspect of enforcing mask work protection is likely to be proving that the accused chip embodies the particular mask work; that is, that the protected mask work was reproduced. The dividing line between infringing reproduction and embodiment of a protected mask work, as opposed to permitted use of the result of reverse-engineering analysis, may be difficult to draw. Accordingly, mask work developers would be prudent to include "signatures" (arbitrary, nonfunctional elements) to facilitate proof of copying. Does an infringement occur when the masks used in manufacturing a chip are not actual reproductions of protected mask work, but rather are developed by reproducing the protected mask work and then calling out dimensions to a draftsman on the other side of the room? Arguably, such a practice is merely "incorporating" the results of the analysis or evaluation of the mask work. It remains to be seen how the courts will deal with such situations.

Comparison of the Protection Mechanisms

Each of the respective mechanisms for protecting intellectual property has advantages and disadvantages, as outlined and discussed below. A summary comparison of the term of effectiveness, scope of protection, and other compatible forms of protection that are available for concurrent use with each mechanism is provided in the Appendix.

- **A trade secret strategy** can provide protection of potentially infinite duration. However, the trade secret is no protection whatsoever

---

Trade Secret CONs

- No protection against:
  —independent development
  —Reverse engineering from publicly available information
- As a practical matter, trade secret protection is simply not applicable to technology in any product that is sold to the public

---

Trade Secret PROs

Trade Secret protection is available for anything that gives a competitive edge as long as it can be kept secret

---

against another party independently developing the technology, and/or possibly obtaining exclusive proprietary rights to it. For that matter, a trade secret provides no protection against someone copying the technology, as long as he obtains the technology legally and is not under any express or implied contractual obligation not to use it.

- **A trademark** provides protection of potentially infinite duration and protects against competition trading on a company's reputation. However, a trademark provides no protection whatsoever against the independent development of technology, or, for that matter, the copying of the technology, so long as there is no likelihood that the public will be confused as to the source or origin of the goods.

Trademark PROs	Trademark CONs
• Identifies source of goods and services • Protects against: —unauthorized attempts to capitalize on goodwill —false advertising • Protects for as long as the mark is used with goods and identifies source	• No protection against copying or reverse engineering, unless confusion as to source of goods or as to affiliation or sponsorship • Assignments in gross prohibited • Licenses must provide for quality control

- **Copyright protection,** while not potentially infinite, is still of relatively long duration. However, the copyright protects only the form of the expression of an idea, not its substance. Thus, copyrights provide very limited protection.

Copyright PROs	Copyright CONs
• Automatic • Inexpensive	• Limited to nonfunctional expression • Fair use doctrine • Archival/machine use rights §117

- **Mask work protection** is available with respect to semiconductor chip products, but may afford protection only against instances where a reproduction of a mask work is used in the manufacture of competing chips.

- **A design patent** has a term of only fourteen years, but provides substantial protection with respect to the ornamental features of a product, that is, the nonfunctional "trade dress" of the product. A design patent, however, does not protect the functional aspects of the product.

- **A utility patent** typically has a maximum term of only twenty years from filing, but provides the broadest scope of legally available protection. The utility patent can be used to protect the new and unobvious inventive concepts of a product. Of course, in return for this, the details of the product, or at least the details of the product relating to the inventive concepts, must be disclosed to the public. Those details become the property of the public at the end of the twenty years.

Patent PROs	Patent CONs
• If properly drafted, can protect the central concept of the invention—the FUNCTIONALITY of an invention • The only protection against independent development by others • Can be used to offset basic patterns held by others • Evidence of expertise/demonstrative asset • Can be a source of royalty income to the company	• Must meet criteria for patentability • Disclosure • Relatively expensive • Time factor

The various forms of protection are not necessarily mutually exclusive. In many cases, different forms of protection can be used concurrently with respect to a given product, as summarized in the Appendix.

As a basic proposition, trademark protection can be used in connection with any of the other modes of protection. For example, assume that a company is marketing a handheld instrument that has a particular ornamental (as opposed to functional) shape. A design patent may be obtained on the ornamental aspects of the casing. At the same time, those ornamental aspects can be used as a trademark. After actual use has commenced, the shape of the casing can be registered on the Supplemental Register. Moreover, after five continuous years of exclusive use, the secondary meaning is presumed; that is, it is presumed that the shape has become associated with goods originating from the company, and an application for registration on the Principal Register can be made.

In the meantime, the design patent has protected the design itself. Also, a utility patent could have been filed on the inventive aspects of the instrument, and if there were particular manufacturing techniques that provided the company a competitive advantage in producing the instrument, but were not related to the actual apparatus, these could be maintained as trade secrets without jeopardizing the validity of the patent. However, if a given technique is necessary to make the invention operable, or to make the best mode of the invention, it would necessarily be disclosed in the patent, and thus could not be maintained as a trade secret. Of course, a copyright could be claimed on any documentary material published with respect to the instrument, and mask work protection could be obtained with respect to any custom integrated circuits used.

Combined trade secret and copyright protection has also been attempted. The principal form of protection is a trade secret license, but a copyright notice is included on the distributed materials as secondary protection in the event that the trade secret is lost. However, the inclusion of an effective copyright notice on the product that is being maintained as a trade secret may in itself destroy the trade secret. A copyright notice, if it is to be effective, is required to include a date of *publication*. Thus, the copyright notice can be construed to be an admission that the work has been published, in the copyright sense; that is, distributed to the public on a nonconfidential basis. Moreover, use of a copyright notice may give rise to a requirement that a copy of the work (or identifying portions thereof in the case of a program) be deposited with the Library of Congress—the very antithesis of secrecy. For this reason, an alternative "provisional" copyright notice in the following form is suggested:

© Michael A. Lechter [Author's name], an unpublished work.

Since the "provisional" notice is not a form of notice expressly recognized by the Copyright Act, it is uncertain whether the "provisional" notice will prove adequate. However, as previously discussed, under the 1976 law, publication without a proper copyright notice will not destroy the copyright, so long as registration is made within five years of the publication, and proper remedial measures are taken. Further, works first published after March 1, 1989, require no notice under the Berne Convention.

. A sequential trade secret/patent protection strategy may also be employed, where the nature of the product permits. Initially (preferably after a patent application is filed on the product), the product may be marketed under trade secret licenses. A patent application is maintained in secrecy by the Patent and Trademark Office for at least eighteen months from filing and until the patent grant is actually issued if a request is filed, certifying that application will not be published in another country.[1] Accordingly, no conflict arises between the modes of protection during that time. In fact, the effectiveness of a license is often bolstered by the inhibiting effect of a "patent pending" notice on would-be copiers. If the application is abandoned prior to eighteen months from filing, the patent office files are never opened to the public (except in particular special circumstances), so that the trade secret can be maintained. If a patent issues, the license would still be effective, defining the rights licensed under the patents.

Concurrent use of the patent and trade secret mechanisms can also sometimes be used to protect different aspects of a product. Such interaction, however, must be carefully considered. An application for a patent must include a detailed description of the "best mode" of the invention known to the inventor at the time the application is filed. Certainly, any element or feature that is necessary to the operation of the invention or that makes the invention practical must be disclosed (and presumably should be claimed) in the patent application. Further, it has been argued that the application should include all major details relating to the invention

> **Patent Disclosure Requirements**
>
> - Need not have actually built device
> - DESCRIPTION MUST:
>   —enable average person working in relevant technology to make operative device
>   —describe "best mode" of the invention
> - So long as presently contemplated, best mode as described device need not be efficient, cost effective, or commercially viable

known to the inventor at the time the application is filed, to comply with the requirement that the application describe the "best mode" of the invention.

In the case of an inventive algorithm, such details could exclude the data manipulation techniques, and perhaps specific code, used in implementation.

On the other hand, the inventor is not required to (and in fact is prohibited from) adding new descriptive matter to a patent application after filing. Accordingly, details developed after filing the application legitimately may be either the subject of another patent application or may be maintained as a trade secret. For this reason, it is sometimes advisable to file a patent application at an early stage of the development of a product. However, it is imperative to thoroughly review the patent application as the commercial embodiment is developed, to ensure that all operationally necessary details are described in the application and that the claims provide proper coverage. If a review is not made in a timely fashion, it is possible that intervening publications or sales will ultimately bar the obtaining of patent protection.

> **Patent/Trade Secret Strategy**
>
> • Initially maintain all aspects as trade secret until placed on market
> • File application early in development cycle to minimize "best mode" disclosure requirement

In developing a protection strategy for a software product, consideration should be given to such issues as the difficulty of adapting the software to different hardware systems, as well as the medium of distribution (source code, object code, magnetic disk, cassette, ROM, PROM), the cost and volume of the products to be protected, the amount of administration that is acceptable, and the intended markets.

> **Strategic Timing of Patent Filings**
>
> • Aspects/details of product developed after filing (e.g., program code, specific circuits/components)
>   —Maintain as trade secrets
>   —or—
>   —File additional patent applications—continuous in part

Thus, with a little bit of forethought, an appropriate strategy using each of the various protection mechanisms to its best effect can be developed to protect a given product. The particular approach to protecting a product must be tailored to the specific characteristics and form of the product as marketed, as well as the specific marketing approach and distribution scheme contemplated.

The Internet and Your Intellectual Property

mlechter@richdad.com

The Internet has probably already affected the way you do business. If it hasn't yet, it probably should have, and sooner or later it certainly will. There is no question that the Internet has affected the way you must mind your intellectual property.

Just doing business over the Internet can have consequences. Expanding your business into other states and countries over the Internet may subject you to the jurisdiction of (make you subject to being sued in) those states and countries. Whether or not you subject yourself to the jurisdiction of a remote state by placing a site on the Web is, in large part, a function of the nature of your Web site—whether it is: (a) "passive" (does not accommodate an exchange of information with the host computer); (b) semi-interactive (allows exchange of information with the host computer, but does not actually effect business transactions); or (c) interactive (actually used to conduct business over the Web). Generally, at least in the United States, merely providing a passive site that is accessible from a state does not, by itself, subject you to personal jurisdiction in that state. However, if you actually transact business over the Net with someone in that state, you will probably be subject to that state's jurisdiction.[1]

Other issues arise from the straightforward (or not so straightforward) application of existing law and concerns to the new circumstances of the Internet. The existing regime of intellectual property laws, of course, applies to the Internet. For example, many (if not most) of the business method patents that have become so prevalent relate to Internet-based business, the contents of Web sites are subject to copyright protection, and trademarks are used to identify the source of goods and services related to, or provided over, the Internet, and are sometimes used as domain names. In addition, the availability of the Internet as a communication medium has made the creation of publication bars to patent protection much easier, as well as the disclosure (inadvertent or otherwise) of confidential information.

The global extent of the Internet has also made its mark. It is now much more important for you to consider international protection of trademarks (and technology) used, described, or advertised over the Internet relatively early in the game. In the "old days," foreign-based Pirates often were not aware of a trademark or a new product until the trademark or product found its way overseas. This often did not occur until you began to actually ship product or otherwise do business abroad. Today, these unscrupulous parties become immediately aware of a product or trademark as soon as the trademark is used (displayed) or the product is advertised or described on a Web site. Even more than that, in many cases trademarks are literally made available to the Pirates in ready-to-copy digital form.

Existing laws (such as defamation, trademark, copyright) also apply to common Internet practices (such as downloading or copying all or portions of files, the use of "metatags," "linking," and "framing"). It is important to know what you can and cannot do when referencing or using material from someone else's site to avoid inadvertently incurring liability. Of course, the flip side of that coin is also true; it is important to know what others can do when referencing or using material from your site.

Just because something (such as music or software) is copied through the Internet does not mean that it avoids the copyright law. Copying copyrightable material directly from someone else's Web site, or downloading files without permission, would be, unless it falls into one of the exceptions (such as fair use), a copyright infringement. On top of that, knowingly facilitating the unauthorized copying of copyrighted material say, music files, would be contributory copyright infringement.[2] Converting a file (e.g., music) into a compressed format (MP3), even if provided only to people who already have an uncompressed copy of the file, would probably be a copyright infringement rather than a fair use.[3]

As will be discussed, a "metatag" is an "invisible" piece of code in a Web page that provides information about the page without affecting how it is displayed, and is often used by search engines in locating and ranking pages relative to keywords. Using someone else's trademark keyword or description as a metatag can be a trademark infringement, or it can be "fair use," depending upon the circumstances. If someone else's trademark is used as a metatag in a site in an attempt to divert potential customers from the mark owner's Web site to the site, it can constitute trademark infringement and unfair competition.[4]

"Linking" refers to the use of hyperlinks that permit you to jump from one document to another simply by clicking on a "hot spot" (an associated area of a graphics object, or a section of text). If you are merely providing a link to someone else's home page there is likely no problem (unless created by the context of or graphics/trademarks used in the hyperlink itself). Since linking does not involve copying material, it is typically not a copyright infringement.[5] Depending upon the circumstances, the use of someone else's trademark as a hyperlink can be a trademark infringement, or it can be "fair use." If the link tends to cause confusion as to sponsorship or affiliation, it is a trademark infringement.[6] Also, depending upon the context, linking to someone else's Web site can be defamatory, an invasion of privacy, false advertising, or a contributory copyright infringement. A link may defame if its effect is to create an untrue statement that injures the reputation of a person or business (such as putting a link to someone's site under the heading "crook of the year"), or it can be false advertising if it creates an untrue or misleading impression of a product (such as putting a link to a competitor's site regarding a UL-listed product, under a heading "products not UL listed"). Contributory copyright infringement can arise from a link to a site that is known to provide unauthorized copies of copyrighted material, in a context that encourages unauthorized copying.[7]

Direct Linking—Potential Legal Issues	
Defamation	(From context of link)
Invasion of privacy	(Unauthorized publication of private site)
Unfair competition	(Suggestion of affiliation or sponsorship)
Trademark infringement and dilution	(Use of graphic trademark as link) *Playboy Enterprises Inc. v. Universal Tel-A-Talk Inc.,* 48 U.S.P.Q.2d 1779 (E.D. Pa. 1998)
Copyright infringement	(Contributory infringement) *Intellectual Reserve Inc. v. Utah Lighthouse Ministry Inc.,* 75 F. Supp. 2d 1290 (D. Utah 1999)
False advertising	(From context of link)

"Deep linking" refers to a hyperlink that bypasses information and advertising on a home page and goes directly to an internal page of the linked site. Revenues generated by a site are often tied to the number of viewers who pass through its home page. As a result, deep linking into a site can cause it to lose income. This of course tends to make the site owner unhappy. There is, however, no law against deep linking per se. Again, since no copying is involved, deep linking is not typically a direct copyright infringement. However, it may well be a trademark infringement by virtue of creating (a) an impression that the linked sites are associated or endorsed, or (b) creating a likelihood of confusion as to the source of products shown on the linked site. A form of trademark infringement occurs when one business creates the impression that it is the source of another business's products. (In trademark parlance, this is called "reverse passing off"). Deep linking tends to cause reverse passing off when, for example, it is not crystal clear that the products are actually being shown on a different, unrelated Web site. As with direct linking, deep linking to someone else's Web site can, depending upon the context, also be defamatory, an invasion of privacy, or a contributory copyright infringement.

Frames provide a means for dividing a Web page into scrollable portions, or windows, that are viewed in separate parts of the screen simultaneously,

Deep Linking—Potential Legal Issues	
Defamation	(From context of link)
Invasion of privacy	(Unauthorized publication of private site)
Unfair competition	(Suggestion of affiliation or sponsorship)
Trademark infringement and dilution	(Reverse passing off) *Ticketmaster Corp. v. Tickets.Com Inc.,* 54 U.S.P.Q.2d 1344, 1346 (C.D. Cal. 2000)
Copyright infringement	(Contributory infringement)
False advertising	(From context of link)

while functioning independently. "Framing" issues arise when one entity displays another entity's Web page (or part of the other entity's Web page) within a frame in its Web page. Framing does not actually involve making a new copy of the other entity's Web page—the other party's original Web page (or part thereof) is actually displayed within the frame. This is the basis for an argument that framing is not a copyright infringement. However, since the frame is viewed surrounded by the rest of the Web page, the framing may be considered to modify the appearance of the framed material, thus creating an infringing derivative work.[8] In addition, since framing one entity's site (or a part thereof) by definition makes it seem a part of another's, it can readily create (a) an impression that the sites are associated or endorsed, or (b) a likelihood of confusion as to the source of products shown on the framed site—and thus become a trademark infringement. Framing someone else's Web site can, depending upon the context, also be defamatory, or an invasion of privacy.

The Internet has also created what is in effect a new form of intellectual property—the domain name. Domain names can be extremely valuable. The exclusive right to use a particular term as a domain name on the Internet is acquired through registration; in general, the first to register a term as a domain name gets the exclusive right to that domain name. The choice of domain names is, however, subject to the trademark laws—use of someone else's trademark as a domain name can create liability under the long-standing trademark law.[9] In addition, the trademark law has been amended

Framing—Potential Legal Issues	
Defamation	(From context of link)
Invasion of privacy	(Unauthorized publication of private site)
Unfair competition	(Suggestion of affiliation or sponsorship)
Trademark infringement and dilution	(Reverse passing off)
Copyright infringement	(Infringement based on the creation of a derivative work)
False advertising	(From context of link)

to include provisions specifically relating to domain names. The amendments: establish limitations on the liability of domain name registrars for taking actions relating to domain names based on third-party trademarks;[10] create a civil action for "cybersquatting";[11] and create a parallel action on the part of a domain name registrant for review of actions by domain name registrars who suspend, disable, or transfer a registered domain name based upon identity or similarity with someone else's mark.[12] In addition, a new administrative procedure (similar to arbitration) has been created as an alternative to litigation to deal with the disputes over domain names.

Internet Basics

So what is the Internet anyway? Basically, it's hundreds of millions of computers tied together in a worldwide network—a network where every computer has agreed to a system for uniquely identifying each computer on the network, as well as certain common sets of rules (protocols). Those protocols ensure a common scheme for establishing connections and exchanging streams of data between the computers on the network, formatting and transmitting messages, and the particular meanings assigned to various commands.[13]

THE PHYSICAL SYSTEM

In terms of the physical system, the Internet includes a hierarchy of five different levels of "access providers":

Level 1—"network access points"(NAPs);
Level 2—"Internet backbone networks";

Level 3—"regional Internet service providers" and "private network access points" (pNAPs);

Level 4—"local Internet service providers" (ISPs); and

Level 5—consumer and business networks/connections (e.g., user PC "hosts").

The NAPs are specific designated public network exchange facilities[14] (each generally managed by a telephone company) that provide central points of interconnection between Internet backbone networks. An Internet backbone is a national (or worldwide) physical network interconnecting (all of) the NAPs. (How's that for a circular definition?)

There are a number of independent commercial Internet backbone networks.[15] Each services a number of geographical areas (which may or may not be serviced by other Internet backbone networks). While the individual Internet backbone networks may provide connections in a number of different cities and areas, each is, by definition, connected to each of the NAPs. In this way all of the Internet backbone networks are interconnected through the NAPs.

Regional ISPs provide their own physical networks similar to the Internet backbone networks, but they are regional (as opposed to national or international) and are not necessarily directly connected to even one (let alone all) of the NAPs. There are a few commercial regional ISPs (most have been consolidated into [acquired by] Internet backbone networks), and a number of government and educational institution run regional ISPs.

Local ISPs[16] are connected to (have a point of presence [POP] on) one of the Internet backbone networks (or in some cases to a regional ISP or directly to a pNAP or NAP). The local ISPs are the primary interface to the Internet for the typical host (user).

The hosts, each with a unique address, are connected (via some sort of modem) through some communication medium (such as the "plain old telephone system," DSL, leased lines, cable, satellite, power lines, wireless) to an ISP.

This network permits any host to communicate with any other host. Assume, for example, that you are host A, using ISP A, which in turn is connected to the Internet backbone network A, and you wish to access a particular Web site B. However, Web site B is not connected to your ISP or to Internet backbone A; it uses ISP B, which is connected to the Internet backbone B. Never fear: Internet backbones A and B are interconnected at the network access points (NAPs). So your data access request (and data packets) travels on backbone A to one of the NAPs, crosses over to backbone B, goes through backbone B to ISP B and Web site B.

But what if Web site B is on a host physically located directly across the street from you, and the nearest NAP is in another city? Absent other provisions, even though the Web site is on a host just across the street, the data access request (and data packets) would still have to travel all the way on backbone A to the NAP in the other city in order to cross over to backbone B, then all the way back on backbone network B to Web site B. This creates inefficiencies, and potential delays. To avoid this problem, private network access points (pNAPs) interconnecting particular Internet backbone networks, regional ISPs, and/or local ISPs have been created in a number of cities. These private NAPs permit "peering arrangements", that is, direct connections between ISPs on the participating backbone networks and/ or participating ISPs, and thus more efficient routing of data. The NAPs and pNAPs determine how traffic is routed. (They are also the points of most Internet congestion.) More information on pNAPs can be found at http://navigators.com/isp.html.

THE WORLD WIDE WEB

The Internet is the communication network for a number of different groups and services, notably e-mail systems, the Usenet, and the World Wide Web (WWW). The Usenet is a worldwide bulletin board system (electronic message center) with many different forums, called newsgroups, each corresponding to a particular interest or subject.

Many people tend to use the term Internet and World Wide Web interchangeably. However, this is not technically correct; not all computers on the Internet are part of the World Wide Web. The World Wide Web includes only those locations on the Internet that support specially formatted documents, which accommodate not only text, graphics, audio, and video files, but also "hyperlinks" to other documents. The hyperlinks permit you to jump from one document to another simply by clicking on a "hot spot" (an associated area of a graphics object, or a section of text).

Each location on the World Wide Web, typically referred to as a Web site, is owned and managed by an individual, company, or organization. Each Web site contains a home page, which is the first document users normally see when they enter the site. The site might also contain additional documents and files, which are typically accessed through hyperlinks on the home page. However, it is possible to address the additional documents and files directly, bypassing the home page. (This is referred to as "deep linking" into a site.)

INTERNET ADDRESSES, URLS, AND SEARCH ENGINES

Each location (host) on the Internet is identified by a unique numerical "IP address" (Internet protocol address). The format of an IP address is a 32-bit numeric address written as four numbers (from zero to 255) separated by periods. The network software generally requires this type of numerical Internet address in order to open a connection or send a datagram. However, humans tend to find it difficult to remember numbers. Names are easier. Accordingly, alphanumeric "domain names" are used to identify one or more IP addresses, correlated by a database. When the Internet was small, each system would have a file that listed all of the other systems, giving both their name and number. However, the growth of the Internet has made this impractical. As will be discussed, the individual database files have now been replaced by a set of name servers that keep track of host names (domain names) and the corresponding Internet addresses.

A standard format, referred to as a uniform resource locator (URL), has been adopted to specify the location and nature of resources (such as Web pages and files) on the Internet. In general, the URL identifies a scheme protocol (e.g., "http," "gopher," "ftp," or "news") associated with the resource (identifying the nature of the resource), followed by the IP address or the domain name where the resource is located (separated from the scheme by //), followed by the path to the particular file you want to access (separated from the domain name by /). If the path is omitted, you will go to the "home page" for the system. On the other hand, where http is concerned, you can reference a particular named anchor portion (e.g., frame) of an identified Web page (using a # separator from the path). For example, the URL for a section named "M_Lechter" in a (fictitious) document, "Worlds_Best_IP_Attorneys.html," in the "Advisors" folder at the rich dad.com Web site, would be "http://www.richdad.com/Advisors/Worlds_Best_ IP_ Attorneys.html#M_Lechter."

What is the ".html" in the document name? It indicates that the particular document was written/formatted in a language called HTML (hypertext markup language). Web documents are typically formatted in HTML (or a version thereof). HTML defines the structure and layout of a Web document by using a variety of commands (tags) inserted in the document that specify how the document, or a portion of the document, should be formatted and the attributes of the document or document portion. There are literally hundreds of different tags used to format and lay out the information in a Web page. For example, tags can be used, among other things to: specify the beginning and end of documents; set the size, color, font, and attributes of, and paragraph separations and headings in, text; set the page background; insert tables, images, objects, and applets; establish relative addressing within the document (assign addresses to the additional documents, files, and the like within the Web site). Tags are also used to assign names to particular portions of documents, create the hypertext links that permit you to jump from one document to another with a click, and to set up independent "frames" within the document. Frames allow you to divide Web pages into multiple scrollable regions. Each framed region can be assigned a separate addressable name (e.g., "M_Lechter" in the example) and separately targeted from other locations. Each framed region can reference a separate IP address, allowing you to display multiple Web pages at once on a single page. However, as will be discussed, displaying someone else's Web page in a frame on your site can create trademark and copyright problems.

A special HTML tag called a "metatag" provides information about a Web page without affecting how the page is displayed. Metatags provide information such as who created the page, how often it is updated, what the page is about, and which keywords represent the page's content. These keywords are important, because they are typically the basis for users to locate the Web site.

To access the World Wide Web you typically use a software application called a "Web browser" (such as Netscape Navigator or Microsoft's Internet Explorer) to locate and display Web pages. Generally, to go to a particular Web site, you just enter (type) the URL or IP address for that site into the browser. What if you do not know the URL for a site, or are just looking for information without any particular site on the Web in mind? When that is the case, you use a program called a "search engine" (like AltaVista or Excite), which searches documents on the World Wide Web and Usenet newsgroups for specified keywords and returns a list of (hyperlinks to) the documents where the keywords were found.

Typically, a search engine works by building a database correlating Web pages to keywords. The database is typically built using an automated "spider" or "Web crawler" and an indexer program. The spider or Web crawler mimics a browser to automatically download as many Web pages as possible and store them raw in a temporary database. Another program, called an indexer, then processes the temporarily stored documents and creates an index (database) based on the words contained in each document. Search engines look for keywords in places such as domain names, actual text on the Web page, and metatags. When a request for information (a query) is made, the search engine performs a search of its database and returns a list of (typically hyperlinks to) the documents where the keywords were found. The more often a term appears in the metatags and in the text of the Web page, the more likely it is that the Web page will be "hit" in a search for that keyword, and the higher on the list of "hits" the Web page will appear. Some web site developers have attempted to stack the deck—to ensure that their Web site shows up high in the list provided by the search engines—by including multiple instances of metatag keywords. This has given rise to an intellectual property issue when someone else's trademarks are used as metatags. If the third-party trademark is used as a metatag in a site in an attempt to divert potential customers from the mark owner's Web site to the site, it can constitute trademark infringement and unfair competition.[17]

THE DOMAIN NAME SYSTEM

As noted above, each location on the Internet is assigned a unique IP address, which is, to make it easier on us humans, associated with an alphanumeric "domain name." Keeping track of millions of domain names is no easy task. Making sure that each domain name is unique is even harder. A global distributed network of name servers, the Domain Naming Service, has been established to keep track of host names (domain names) and the corresponding Internet addresses.

Responsibility for the management of the Internet domain name system has been assigned to an organization known as the Internet Corporation for Assigned Names and Numbers (ICANN). According to ICANN, it "coordinates the assignment of the following identifiers that must be globally unique for the Internet to function": Internet domain names, IP address numbers, and protocol parameter and port numbers; and also "coordinates the stable operation of the Internet's root server system." Actual naming authority has delegated to individual institutions, "registrars" accredited by ICANN. A list of accredited registrars can be found at http://www.icann.org/.

The Internet domain name system (DNS) is basically a database correlating each domain name to a corresponding computer and the particular company or person to which it is registered. The Internet DNS, however, is organized in a hierarchical (tree) structure of "domains" and "subdomains" (see figure 2).

Internet Domain Name System Hierarchy

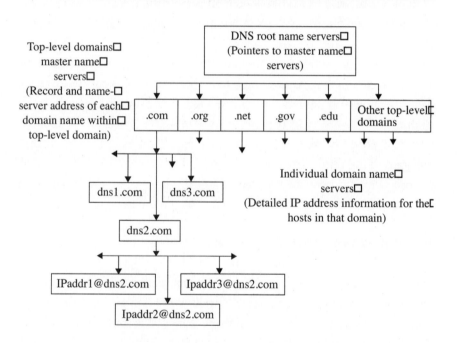

In general, the DNS database hierarchy runs, starting at the top, from: "root name servers"; to a set of "master name servers" corresponding to each of a set of top-level domains (e.g., .edu, .com, .net, .org, .gov, .mil, .int, and two-letter country codes); from each master name server to each of the individual domain servers within the corresponding top-level domain; and, perhaps, from individual domain servers to each of the individual subdomain servers within the individual domain. Each domain has a "registry" (database) of the names of all immediate subdomains, plus information about how to get to each one (its address) and a contact person for the domain. For example, the root name servers contain pointers to the master name servers for each of the top-level domains, the master name servers each contain a record and name-server address for each domain name under the particular top-level domain, and the individual name servers for each domain name (such as richdad.com) contain detailed address information for the hosts in that domain. The contact person is responsible for the domain, keeping the registry up to date, serving as a point of contact for outside queries, and setting policy requirements for subdomains. Each subdomain can decide who it will allow to have subdomains, and can establish requirements that all subdomains must meet to be included in the registry.

How can you tell what top-level domain a domain is in? This is where the ".com" designation comes in. The portion of a host name, immediately following the last "." (such as ".com" in www.richdad.com), is the top-level domain to which the host belongs. In addition to the .com domain, there are a number of other top-level domains, at least two of which are generally available: .org and .net. There is a set of what are called "top-level domain names" (TLDs). These are the generic TLDs (.edu, .com, .net, .org, .gov, .mil, and .int), and the two-letter country codes

Only registrars accredited by ICANN are authorized to register .com, .net, and .org names. (Some accredited registrars, however, offer their services through resellers. Nevertheless, the registration contract, will be with the accredited registrar, and that registrar will maintain the contact information.) Other top-level domains are reserved for specific types of institutions or industries, such as .gov (governmental entities) and .edu (educational institutions). Seven new top-level domains have been selected, and are expected to be available in the second quarter of 2001: .aero (air-transport industry); .biz (businesses); .coop (nonprofit cooperatives); .info (unrestricted use); .museum (museums); .name (for registration by individuals); and .pro (accountants, lawyers, and physicians).

The assignment and regulation of domain names for sites outside the United States is in the hands of a number of other organizations. Some ICANN-accredited registrars provide registration services in non-U.S. top-level domains in addition to registering names in .com, .net, and. org. However, ICANN does not specifically accredit registrars to provide those registration services. In most cases, top-level domains for non-U.S. hosts are two-letter domains, corresponding to a country, territory, or other geographic location, and sometimes called country code top-level domains (country code TLDs). The rules and policies for registering domain names in the country code TLDs vary significantly. Some are reserved for use by citizens of the particular country. Examples of country code TLDs include: .uk (United Kingdom); .de (Germany); .jp (Japan); .ac (Ascension Island); .sh (St. Helena); .io (British Indian Ocean Territory); .tm (Turkmenistan); .nu (Island of Niue); .to (Tongo); and .tv (Tuvalu). Some include subdomains dedicated to types of institutions or industries. For example, .co.uk and .ac.uk indicate company and academic institution, respectively, in the United Kingdom.

In general, you can pick your own domain name. It can be any combination of letters and numbers up to 67 characters long (including the top-level domain extension). Case is ignored in domains. Hyphens and underscores may also be used except at the beginning and end. You cannot use, however, spaces and special characters, such as, for example: ! @ # $ % ^ & * ( ) ?".

The use of the @ is reserved for demarcating the division between domain-name and domain-specific portions of an address. Characters on the left-hand side of an @ are subject to whatever interpretation the domain chooses. For example, using the @ in an address like "Michael.Lechter@rich dad.com" makes it clear that some machine in the richdad domain should interpret the string "Michael.Lechter." In the absence of a special divider character (@), such as if the address were "Michael.Lechter.richdad.com," there is an ambiguity, and the DNS software might try to find a machine named "Lechter" or "Michael.Lechter."

Registering a Domain Name

The exclusive right to use a particular term as a domain name on the Internet is acquired through registration; in general, the first to register a term as a domain name gets the exclusive right to that domain name. Only registrars accredited by ICANN are authorized to register .com, .net, and .org names. (Some accredited registrars, however, offer their services through resellers. Nevertheless, the registration contract will be with the accredited registrar, and that registrar will maintain the contact information.) Lists of accredited registrars can be found at http://www.icann.org/registrars/accredited-list.html and http://www.internic.net/alpha.html.

Registering a domain name (assuming that you find one that is not already taken) is relatively straightforward. You simply choose an accredited registrar, go to the registrar's Web site, provide the various contact and technical information, enter a registration contract with the registrar (the terms under which your registration is accepted and will be maintained), and provide a credit card number. Generally, you initially provide the registrar with the name, address, phone, fax, and e-mail address for the registrant (owner of the domain name), a technical contact, an administrative contact, and a billing contact, together with credit card and billing information. Ultimately, the registrar is also provided with actual names and IP addresses for primary and secondary DNS hosts. The cost of registration varies from registrar to registrar, and between top-level domains (presently generally around $30 per year, but ranging anywhere from $15 a year [$150 for 10 years] to upwards of $100 per year). The two-letter country domains tend to be more expensive.

What happens if someone else has already taken the domain name you have chosen? You can check to see if it is available in another top-level domain. (Many entities register their domain names in a number of TLDs, [.com, .net, .org] to avoid the possibility of confusion engendered by someone else having the domain name in other TLDs. However, with the advent of new generic top-level domains, and country code TLDs, it is becoming increasingly expensive to register a domain name in all TLDs.)

If you are interested in finding out who holds the registration to a particular domain name, that information can be obtained through a "whois" query at http://www.internic.net/whois.html.

If someone else has already registered your choice of domain name in the relevant TLDs, your options are somewhat limited. Unless the domain name in question is your trademark, your only choices are to: acquire the domain name from the present registrant; wait in the hope that the registration will expire and not be renewed; or choose a different domain name. On the other hand, if the domain name at issue is your trademark (or otherwise infringes your trademark rights), you may be able to proceed on that basis—either in the federal courts under the federal trademark "cybersquatting" laws,[18] or before an administrative panel under the ICANN "Uniform Domain Name Dispute Resolution Policy" (UDRP). In either case, you are required to show not only a violation of trademark rights, but also that the domain name was registered in "bad faith."

"Cybersquatting"

As previously noted, the federal trademark statute[19] creates a specific civil cause of action for "cybersquatting." To establish a claim of cybersquatting, you must show:

(1) your mark was a distinctive (or famous) mark at the time of the registration of the domain name;

(2) that the defendant "registers, traffics in, or uses a domain name" that is identical or confusingly similar to (and/or, if famous, dilutes) that mark; and

(3) that the defendant has "a bad faith intent to profit from that mark."

How do you determine whether or not there is bad faith? Here again, there is no hard-and-fast rule. The basic issue is whether or not the defendant has a legitimate interest in the domain name, or is merely a cyber pirate. The federal statute[20] provides a (nonexhaustive) list of factors that may be considered:

TRADEMARK OR IP RIGHTS

The existence of legitimate trademark or other IP rights in the domain name tends to show good faith. Conversely, the absence of legitimate trademark or other IP rights in the domain name tends to show bad faith. How can the defendant have legitimate trademark rights? Let's take an example. Assume that your mark does not qualify as famous, and you have been using it in connection with the sale of office supplies. It's possible for the defendant to obtain trademark rights with respect to use of the mark in connection with some other type of unrelated goods—say, dog food. Or assume that you did not have a federal registration on your mark, and the defendant was located outside of your market area and began actually using the mark with goods, before he found out about your earlier use of it. So if the defendant had obtained trademark rights before he registered the mark as a domain name, it would tend to show that the domain name was not adopted in bad faith.

EXISTING RELATIONSHIP TO THE DOMAIN NAME

If the domain name registered by the defendant happens to be his or her legal name or a name that is otherwise commonly used to identify the defendant, or the defendant was actually using the domain name in connection with the bona fide offering of any goods or services prior to registering the name, it would tend to show that the domain name was not adopted in bad faith. Conversely, if the defendant was *not* actually using the domain name in connection with the bona fide offering of goods or services prior to registering the name, it would tend to show bad faith.

MANNER IN WHICH THE DEFENDANT USES THE MARK IN THE WEB SITE

If the only use of your mark in the defendant's Web site corresponding to the domain name is bona fide noncommercial or fair use—in other words, the use is legitimate commentary, parody, or descriptive of the defendants' goods or the defendant's connection to your business—it would tend to show that the domain name was not adopted in bad faith.[21] On the other hand, if the mark is used, say, in metatags in an attempt to draw potential customers away from your Web site to a Web site corresponding to the domain name, for the purpose of commercial gain or with the intent to tarnish or disparage your mark, it would tend to show bad faith.[22]

TRAFFICKING IN DOMAIN NAMES

The ultimate indicator of bad faith is that the defendant is a cyber pirate, and "traffics" in domain names—that is, he registered the domain name with the intent to sell it to someone else (e.g., you) rather than use it in the bona fide offering of any goods or services. Indications that the defendant is a cyber pirate include: providing misleading or false contact information when applying for the registration of the domain name, or intentionally failing to maintain accurate contact information, or the person's prior conduct indicating a pattern of such conduct; and registering or acquiring multiple domain names knowing that they violate your (or others') trademark rights.

THE STRENGTH OF YOUR MARK

The stronger, more distinctive, and more famous your mark, the more likely that the domain name was registered in bad faith. Conversely, if your mark is weak or descriptive, it tends to show an absence of bad faith.

Basically, you would file a cybersquatting action in the federal district court in the same manner as any other trademark infringement action. As previously noted, the statute also deals with the problem of obtaining jurisdiction over foreign nationals who register domain names by providing for in rem jurisdiction to permit civil actions to obtain forfeiture or cancellation of a domain name that violates a trademark right in instances where you otherwise would not be able to obtain jurisdiction over the registrant.[23] A parallel action on the part of a domain name registrant is provided for review of actions by domain name registrars who suspend, disable, or transfer a registered domain name based upon identity or similarity with someone else's mark.[24]

ICANN "Uniform Domain Name Dispute Resolution Policy"

ICANN provides an alternative to litigation in the federal courts. Each ICANN-accredited registrar is required to include, in the registration contract for a domain name, a provision[25] that requires the registrant to submit to a mandatory administrative proceeding before an approved administrative dispute resolution (ADR) service provider.[26] In order to prevail as a "complainant" against a registrant in a proceeding, you must prove each of the following elements:

(i)   the domain name is identical or confusingly similar to your trademark or service mark; and

(ii) the registrant has no rights or legitimate interests in respect of the domain name; and

(iii) the domain name has been registered and is being used in bad faith.

The ICANN UDRP[27] provides a (nonexhaustive) list of things that evidence bad faith:

(i)   circumstances indicating that the domain name was registered or acquired primarily for the purpose of selling, renting, or otherwise transferring the domain name registration to you or to one of your competitors, for valuable consideration; or

(ii) the domain name was registered in order to prevent the owner of the trademark or service mark from reflecting the mark in a corresponding domain name, provided that the registrant has engaged in a pattern of such conduct; or

(iii) the domain name was registered primarily for the purpose of disrupting the business of a competitor; or

(iv) the domain name is used in an intentional attempt to attract, for commercial gain, Internet users to the registrant's Web site or other online location, by creating a likelihood of confusion with your mark as to the source, sponsorship, affiliation, or endorsement of the registrant's Web site or location or of a product or service on the registrant's Web site or location.

It also provides a (nonexhaustive) list of things that evidence good faith and a legitimate interest on the part of the registrant:

(i)   the registrant was using, or had made demonstrable preparations to use, the domain name (or a name corresponding to the domain name) in connection with a bona fide offering of goods or services; or before any notice to the registrant of the dispute;

(ii) the registrant (as an individual, business, or other organization) has been commonly known by the domain name, even if you have acquired no trademark or service mark rights; or

(iii) the registrant is making a legitimate noncommercial or fair use of the domain name, without intent for commercial gain to misleadingly divert consumers or to tarnish the trademark or service mark at issue.

The remedies available to you as a complainant pursuant to any proceeding before an administrative panel are limited to the cancellation of the domain name or the transfer of the domain name registration to you.

Procedures

It is imperative that policies and procedures be implemented to ensure that intellectual property assets are maximized and potential liabilities are minimized. It is desirable for any business to have a written statement of those policies and procedures. Any procedures adopted by a company must be tailored to the particulars of that company. However, the guidelines in the following sections are provided for general reference.

Suggested Procedures for Securing and Maintaining Rights in Technology

Employee Nondisclosure and Non-Use Agreements

In general, an "employee" agreement should be obtained from each employee who may have access to confidential information (e.g., proprietary know-how) or is in a position likely to generate technology. The agreement should impose an obligation of confidentiality (nondisclosure and non-use) on the employee with respect to confidential information, and require the employee to assign to the company rights to any works of authorship and technology developed by the employee that relate to the company's business.

Preliminary State-of-the-Art Investigation

At the beginning of each new project or entry into a new field of endeavor, a preliminary investigation of the state of the art, and, in particular, issued patents should be conducted. This will provide an idea of the patents already held by others in the relevant area of technology, and can help identify potential infringement problems. It can also provide a starting point for research. The preliminary investigation is readily conducted through the Internet. The PTO maintains a publicly available searchable database of the full text of all U.S. patents at www.pto.gov. Other searchable databases of U.S. and foreign patents are also publicly available. "Keyword" searching of the patent databases, and generally of the Web (using available search engines), will typically suffice. In addition to terms relating to the field of interest, the names of known players in the field can be used as search terms. The PTO database includes provisions for searching for patents issued to particular individual inventors (inventor name) and/or owned by a particular entity (assignee name).

The most cost-effective way to perform a preliminary investigation is for you (or your technical people) to do it. You (or your technical people) are the most knowledgeable about your ideas and are best positioned to identify relevant information and to follow up on leads.

Initially Keeping R&D As a Trade Secret

Initially, all R&D should be maintained as a trade secret. Appropriate nondisclosure (confidentiality) agreements should be obtained from all third parties given access to confidential information (vendors and consultants and the like). Preferably, the agreements will also make it clear that all technology that is developed by the consultant or vendor during a project will be assigned to the company.

Maintaining Documentation

Proper records relating to the developmental process should be maintained. The records should establish conception, reduction to practice, and diligence in reducing the invention to practice after conceiving it. The more information and documentation that can be shown, the more likely that the requisite conception, reduction to practice, and diligence for an early date of invention in the United States can be established. Detailed records of the development process can also be critical to defending against third-party claims of trade secret, copyright, and mask work infringement. The necessity of keeping records and more particular suggested procedures will be discussed later in this book.

Timely Consideration of Patent Protection

The prospect of patent protection should be explored for each aspect or feature of a product that provides a competitive advantage in a marketplace. It is important to keep the potential consequences in mind when considering whether to show a product or offer it for sale. A patentability assessment should be performed, and patent applications filed, if appropriate, before any public use or showing, publication, or offer for sale.

A patent disclosure should be generated. In general, the disclosure should be as complete as possible, and it should identify anything that might be relevant to the issue of patentability and any possible public uses or offers for sale. Adopting an appropriate form can facilitate drafting the disclosure. If earlier searches do not make it unnecessary, patentability investigations of particular features of a product should be conducted. Here, again, you or your technical people can take a first cut at the search. Analysis of the results, however, is typically best left to patent counsel.

To ensure timely consideration of patent issues, it is sometimes desirable to establish a systematic procedure involving periodic meetings of a patent committee, or periodic meetings between the engineers and a designated patent liaison or attorney. Any procedure established must be tailored to the particular company.

Infringement Clearance Procedure

Before any product is placed on the market, potentially applicable third-party intellectual property rights should be investigated and analyzed. The various preliminary searches noted above should identify potential infringement problems relatively early on. However, it is sometimes prudent to do additional searching, such as when additional features are added to the product after, or perhaps as a result of, the earlier searches.

If a potential infringement problem is identified, it cannot be ignored. Even if the company's employees are convinced in their own minds that there is in fact no infringement, it still may be necessary to have a formal attorney's invalidity/noninfringement opinion in the file, just in case. If a company is found to infringe a patent of which it is aware, and did not obtain the opinion of a competent patent attorney, the infringement will be considered willful, and the company could be liable for treble damages and the patentee's attorneys' fees. That is what happened to B. Hindthetimes in Horror Story 10 (p. 7).

Keeping Accurate Records of Development

The Need for Keeping Accurate Records

There are a number of instances when it becomes necessary to prove the date and nature of technical activities, and the project with which the activities are associated. For example, such proofs are often determinative in:

- Disputes regarding ownership of technology—whether certain technology was first made under a particular "development" contract or government contract;
- Disputes regarding whether particular technology is covered by a particular license agreement;
- Disputes regarding whether certain technology is subject to a confidentiality or non-use agreement;
- Proving an invention was previously developed, not abandoned, suppressed, or concealed, as a defense to patent infringement under 35 U.S.C., section 102(g); and
- Interference proceedings before the Patent and Trademark Office—contests to determine "priority of invention."

DEVELOPMENT AND GOVERNMENT CONTRACTS

"Development" agreements often specify that a particular party will obtain rights (e.g., title or a license to make, use, and sell) to all technology "arising from work done under the contract" or "first conceived or first made under the contract." Where the company is in the position of a developer under such contracts, it is imperative to be able to show that:

(1) certain technology was created prior to the contract; and
(2) certain technology that was developed on other projects during the term of the agreement was, in fact, developed on those other projects.

Where the preexisting technology can be identified beforehand, such as when there are preexisting patents or patent applications, it is best to expressly except (obtain a waiver with respect to) such technology. However, preexisting technology not anticipated to be relevant to a project frequently turns out to be relevant after the fact. In this case, rights to the technology often turn on the ability to prove that the technology was, in fact, preexisting.

Similar circumstances arise with respect to technology being developed in connection with projects concurrent with, but separate from, work done under the agreement. Rights to technology that would otherwise be held by the company can be lost if records clearly differentiating work done on the respective projects have not been conscientiously and accurately maintained.

LICENSE AGREEMENTS

In general, it is desirable that license agreements clearly and concisely particularize the licensed technology. However, certain license agreements (typically entered into in settlement of a dispute) sometimes relate to all technology "made prior to the date of the agreement." It then becomes imperative to be able to prove, after the fact, when technology was "made" vis-à-vis the date of the agreement. The ability to do this, however, typically turns on the sufficiency of the records that were generated contemporaneously with the technology.

CONFIDENTIALITY AND NON-USE AGREEMENTS

Confidentiality and non-use agreements are often entered into in connection with various business negotiations. Such agreements often include provisions to the effect that technology which:

(a) was already in the possession of the company; or

(b) is independently developed by the company

is *not* subject to the confidentiality and non-use provisions. It is generally incumbent on the recipient of information, however, to prove "prior possession" or "independent development." Thus, records that show the history of the development of the technology (when specific acts occurred and the particular individuals involved in those acts) should be maintained contemporaneously with the development.

PRIOR DEVELOPMENT

As previously discussed, the U.S. patent statute requires that, in order to obtain a patent, an applicant must be the first to have "made" the invention in the United States. The statute states:

§102 A person shall be entitled to a patent unless—

. . . .

(g) before the applicant's invention thereof, the invention was made *in this country* by another who had not abandoned, suppressed, or concealed it. In determining priority of invention, there shall be considered not only the respective dates of conception and reduction to practice of the invention, but also the reasonable diligence of one who was first to conceive and last to reduce to practice, from a time prior to conception by the other.

The situation sometimes arises where two different inventors develop the same invention independently. In such a case, only the first to have "made" the invention in the United States, who did not abandon, suppress, or conceal the invention, is entitled to the patent. If only the second party to "make" the invention files an application that ultimately issues as a patent, and that patent is asserted against the first to have made the invention, "prior development" is a defense against the charge of infringement (assuming no abandonment, suppression, or concealment, that is, assuming the technology was not maintained as a trade secret). If both parties file patent applications, the relative priority of the inventors is determined by an "interference" proceeding conducted by the Patent and Trademark Office, as previously discussed.

THE TWO-STEP PROCESS OF "MAKING AN INVENTION"

As previously discussed, "making" an invention, as that term is used in the statute (and is typically used in the agreements mentioned above), is a two-step process:

(a) *conceiving* the invention (technology); then

(b) reducing the invention to practice.

"Conception" is basically the mental portion of the inventive act. "Reducing the invention to practice" is, in basic terms, building the invention and proving that it works for its intended purpose. The filing of a patent application is considered to be a "constructive" reduction to practice.

With respect to 35 U.S.C., section 102(g), the diligence with which the company works, after the technology has been conceived, to reduce the technology to practice is also a factor. As a general proposition, if inventor A was both the first to conceive and the first to reduce the invention to practice, inventor A will be deemed the first to have "made" the invention. Further, if the first to conceive the invention, but the last to reduce the invention to practice, inventor A will still be deemed first to have made the invention if "diligence" in pursuing the reduction to practice from a time period prior to the conception of the invention by inventor B can be proven. However, if inventor A cannot prove reasonable diligence in pursuing the reduction to practice beginning with a date before inventor B conceived the invention, inventor B will be deemed first to have made the invention.

Record-Keeping Procedures

Record-keeping was discussed briefly in connection with the "first to make the invention" requirement of the patent law. As a general proposition, *each aspect of the two-step process of making an invention must occur (or be transported into) the United States and must be proven by more than just the word of the inventor;* the word of the "inventor" (or even co-inventors) as to when and where an invention was conceived or reduced to practice is essentially worthless without "corroboration." Corroboration can be in the form of dated documents, drawings, time records, and oral testimony by "noninventors."

PRELIMINARY CONCEPT REPORT FORM

Positive proof of a conception date in the United States can be assured by the procedure of filing a preliminary concept report with a designated company official (in the United States) or U.S. attorney when an invention is conceived. The concept report should fully describe the invention, and, to the extent possible, be signed and dated by the inventors, and ultimately be witnessed (read, signed, and dated) by the receiving company official or attorney.

Search request and invention disclosure forms sent to the designated company official or U.S. attorney can also be employed to provide proof of conception in the United States.

NOTEBOOKS

As a practical matter, however, invention disclosure forms typically do not contain the detail necessary to prove "diligence" or actual reduction to practice of an invention. For this reason, *detailed contemporaneous laboratory notebooks should be maintained.* The value of an entry in a laboratory notebook as proof of diligence and/or reduction to practice of an invention is directly proportional to the specificity of the entry and the care that

> **Engineering Notebook**
> - Maintain a *bound* engineering notebook
> - Sign and date every entry
> - Have signed and dated by a "witness"

was taken to date and sign each entry and have each entry read, signed, and dated by a witness. The following guidelines for keeping notebooks are offered:

1. All engineers should maintain a *bound* engineering notebook. The context of the entry in an engineering notebook can sometimes be used to prove a date. For example, if an entry showing conception is found in a *bound* engineering notebook, between entries dated the third of January and the fifth of January, it is relevant proof that the invention was conceived sometime between the third and fifth of January. It would not be so relevant, however, if a loose-leaf engineering notebook had been used. Blank portions of pages should be lined through.

2. Every entry should be signed and dated, indicate the particular project with which the entry is associated, and, if possible, be signed and dated by a "witness." It is often advantageous to include a "header" on each notebook entry:

DATE: _____

PROJECT NO.: _____

SUBJECT: _____

SIGNATURE: _____

WITNESSES: _____

To facilitate such a header, stamps for printing the header can be issued to each person keeping a notebook.

3. All computations, circuit diagrams, test results, etc. should be *contemporaneously* entered *into the notebook.* It is as easy to do calculations, etc., in the notebook as on scratch paper. So long as the entry is legible (and contains sufficient detail), there are no particular format or "neatness" requirements.

4. It is, however, imperative that each notebook entry identify the subject of the work with *particularity* and contains all relevant details. An entry such as "work on new sharpener" sheds little light on whether the "new sharpener" included a specific feature on a particular date.

5. All persons involved in the work should be identified in the corresponding notebook entries. Unless participants are identified, it is often difficult to establish, long after the fact, those involved in particular activities.

6. It is especially important that all loose papers, such as blueprints, schematics, flowcharts, strip charts, oscillographs, photographs of models, etc., be signed and dated, cross-referenced to a particular notebook entry, and, preferably, mounted (taped or stapled) in the body of the appropriate notebook entry. Similarly, physical results of tests, such as samples, models, prototypes, and the like, should be carefully labeled with the date, cross-referenced to notebook entries, and retained.

7. Notebooks and records should be maintained in contemplation of proving not only the dates of conception and reduction to practice, but also diligence in between. To this end, it is desirable to have the

documentary evidence and, in particular, dated note
scribing *all* testing performed, the particular typ
used, and the results of the testing, both good *and*

8. A hard copy, or write-once-read-many-times (wor
eration of computer programs should be generateu, ﹍﹍
and witnessed (or a signed dated log maintained with respect to the
worm copy). Magnetic media or other alterable media provide much
less evidentiary support for establishing a date.

TIME RECORDS

Time records, if carefully and accurately maintained with a sufficiently high
level of discrimination between respective projects, can also be used to
prove, for example, "diligence," "independent development," and that certain technology was not made under a given contract. To make use of time
records to these ends, of course, separate project numbers must be assigned
to specific, relatively narrowly defined tasks.

Conclusion

In all, a documentary record should be maintained that is capable of establishing the dates and activities comprising each of the elements of "making"
an invention, identifying individuals involved in the work who can provide
testimonial proof, and identifying the particular project with which technical
work is associated.

Suggested Procedures for Securing and Maintaining Rights in Trademarks

Choice of a Mark

As previously discussed, a mark is categorized by its primary meaning to an educated consumer—a consumer who is aware of the goods of the type at issue, and is a potential purchaser of the goods. The less descriptive the mark, the more protectable it is. Basically, the strongest and most protectable mark is a simple, arbitrary symbol or design, or a relatively euphonious and easily pronounced coined word. Of course, marketplace considerations may dictate that a term of a more descriptive nature be used.

Use of a Mark As a Source Indicator

The consumer's understanding of a term can be shaped by the manner in which the term is used. The manner in which a mark is used in advertising, promotional materials, and internal and external correspondence can be the determinative factor in this regard. If a perfectly good mark is used as a descriptor or a generic term, it will ultimately come to be understood as a generic or descriptive term and will cease to be protectable.

Consider an accused infringer's argument: "Your Honor, even in their own advertising the word is used as a descriptive, in fact generic, term. Certainly my client is entitled to do the same."

On the other hand, any term, packaging, configuration, or anything that is not clearly generic can be transformed into a protectable trademark through the manner in which it is used in advertising. For example: "Look for the distinctive orange handle!" Or: "If you see the big blue stripe, you know it's from Clientco, and you know it's good."

Using a Trademark

- Use only as indicator of source
- Set off trademarks
- Use only in same form as is registered
- Emphasize mark to customer
- Monitor the use of the mark
- Strict control of use

General Rules

Some general rules for using trademarks in advertising and promotional material are as follows:

1. *Use the mark only as a source indicator.* Except to refer to the company where the trademark is also the company name, the company should take care that neither it, nor others, uses the trademark in other than a trademark sense—that is, other than to designate the company as the source or origin of the goods. A trademark should never be used in a manner that tends to designate (name) or describe the type or characteristics of the goods with which it is used. Except when properly used as a company name, a trademark or service mark should never be used as a shorthand name for the goods, as a noun, hyphenated with another word, as a verb, or in a possessive sense. All too often an aggressive marketer intentionally, through its own advertising and promotional activities, causes a trademark to become synonymous with its goods, and thus unwittingly squanders the sales value of the trademark. To prevent use of the mark as a noun, always follow it with a specific descriptive generic term for the product. The

generic term must provide a satisfactory substitute as the type descriptor for the product. In practice, where the generic term does not adequately indicate the nature of the product, the trademark tends to be employed to serve that function and ultimately becomes genericized. In fact, when a product is the first of its kind, a trademark owner may have to invent not only a source identifier mark, but also a descriptor for the type of product. For example: "The Xerox *photocopier*"; not "the Xerox machine." The term "machine" is, in effect, too generic. It is not sufficiently descriptive to tell the consumer the nature of the product.

2. *The trademark nature of a term or symbol should also be made clear by the manner in which the mark is used.* The mark should always be used in conjunction with a descriptive term or name for the goods. The trademark should, however, be "set off" from the description or name of the goods. This can be done with distinctive fonts, color, quotation marks, capitalization, or the ™ or, if registered, ® symbol. Some form of trademark notice should also be used as appropriate, such as a statement that the mark is a trademark of the company or is registered in the U.S. Patent and Trademark Office. However, it should be noted that setting off a mark or using a registration notice, while a mitigating factor, will not cure an impropriety in the use of the mark.

3. *Do not use the mark in a context that detracts from the trademark significance of the term.* For example, it is typically not appropriate to use a string of consecutive trademarks in relation to a single descriptive term for the goods. In such a case, it could be argued that only one of the terms was being used as a trademark and the others were merely descriptive terms designating a particular type of goods. For the same reason, a mark should not be preceded by the corporate name.

4. *The mark should be used in the same form that it is registered as.*

5. *Emphasize the mark to the consumer.* To the greatest extent possible, advertisements and promotional materials should specifically call the consumer's attention to the mark. This is particularly true if the mark is other than a wordmark. Such emphasis will bolster, if not create, rights in the mark.

6. *Monitor the use of the mark.* Use of the trademark by others, as well as by the company itself, should be monitored to guard against mis-

use. Unauthorized or uncontrolled use of the mark by others can result in its becoming generic or being deemed abandoned. The marketplace should be regularly monitored for the use of a similar mark that is likely to cause confusion among customers, and the Official Gazette of the Patent and Trademark Office should be systematically reviewed against attempts by competitors to register similar marks for use with similar products. Also, publications where the term might appear other than in a context of company-generated text should be reviewed on a systematic basis, and prompt action taken in the event that a misuse is discovered. Typically, the misuse is inadvertent, and publishers tend to cooperate once advised of a misuse.

7. *Maintain strict control of use.* Any authorized use by third parties must be stringently controlled. Quality control must be exercised over all goods or services with which the mark is used, or the mark is at risk of being deemed abandoned.

Procedures for Avoiding Potential Infringement of Third-Party Intellectual Property Rights

In theory, the basic rule with respect to using or copying an aspect of a competitor's product is simple: *Absent an express or implied contractual obligation, a company is at liberty to use and copy any unpatented, uncopyrighted aspect that comes into a company's possession legally, as long as there is no likelihood that the public would be deceived or confused as to the source of a product.*

Practice, however, is another story. The incidence and outcome of intellectual property litigation is often a function of the internal procedures of the contestants.

Avoiding Infringement of Third-Party Trade Secret Rights

An analysis in determining whether any given information or technology constitutes a trade secret or is confidential is inevitably a fact-specific inquiry. Nonetheless, without question, a competitor's trade secret rights cannot prevent a company from independently developing information or technology or, for that matter, using or copying information or technology, if it is obtained legally and the company is not under any express or implied contractual obligation to the contrary.

By way of preventive procedures, any competitor's materials that come into a company's possession should be reviewed for proprietary notices. While in many instances such material is in fact not "confidential" due to lack of controls by the competitor, prudence may dictate discarding it nonetheless. In addition, in an abundance of caution, the following procedures might be adopted:

1. Promulgate a policy statement directing employees not to use any potential trade secret information (or at least to consult counsel prior to using).
2. Any new hire who was formerly an employee of a competitor should be debriefed, and it should be made clear that the company is not interested in using any confidential information regarding the new hire's previous employer that the new hire might have.
3. Detailed records of the development of products should be maintained to prove that any potential trade secret information that might have been acquired from a competitor was not incorporated in a company's products.

Avoiding Infringement of Third-Party Patents

It is also possible that a competitor holds utility patents covering new and unobvious aspects of its products, or design patents covering the appearance of its products. The scope of a utility patent is defined by the patent claims; a patent is infringed if an unlicensed product includes the equivalent of each and every element of any of the patent claims. Infringement exists even if the product has additional features or elements that are not included in the claim and even if those additional elements are themselves patentable. In essence, a design patent is infringed if an unlicensed product is so similar in appearance to the patented design that a consumer, under normal market conditions, is likely to think them the same. Neither a patented invention nor a design need actually be copied from the patent or competitor's product for infringement to exist; independent development is no defense.

Since independent development is no defense to patent infringement, the following preventive procedures are suggested:

1. Prior to entering into any new product area, or initiating the development of significant new features or aspects of a product, have a preliminary investigation performed to collect copies of any relevant patents.
2. Initiate an investigation of all known competitors to obtain copies of any patents they may hold.
3. Examine competitors' products for patent markings or references to pending applications.
4. Maintain a continuing watch for patents issued to major competitors.
5. Consider having an extensive infringement investigation performed prior to introducing a significant new product. (A cost-benefit analysis should be performed in view of previous searching and knowledge of extant patents.)
6. Develop the company's own portfolio of patents for cross-licensing in the event that the claims of a competitor's patent cannot be, or for some reason are not, avoided.

Avoiding Infringement of Third-Party Copyrights

It is prudent to assume that a competitor holds a copyright on all of its "works of authorship," such as booklets, advertising brochures, artistic designs, maps and architectural blueprints, audiotapes and records, and, at least to some extent, computer programs. However, copyright protection is of particularly limited scope: it pertains only to the form of expression and not to substance (ideas, methods, systems, mathematical principles, formulas, and equations are expressly not copyrightable); and actual copying is a requisite element for infringement (independent development *is* a defense).

While independent development is a complete defense to a charge of copyright infringement, copying is presumed from "access" and "substantial similarity." Unfortunately, there is a line of cases that have, through some leap of logic, assumed access merely by virtue of the fact that the copyrighted work was available in the marketplace, where there was substantial similarity. Where software is concerned, this can be problematical. Practical and functional reasons sometimes dictate a particular approach;

indeed, there are optimum ways of programming toward which competent programmers independently gravitate. In addition, various conventions with respect to, for example, labeling instructions and naming variables have been adopted throughout the industry. In view of these circumstances, it is prudent that the development process be documented in depth so that the company will be able to prove that the work was in fact independently developed.

A company must also beware of the use of unauthorized copies of software in the workplace by its employees. The company may be liable for copyright infringement because of its employees' actions. A policy statement forbidding the use of unauthorized copies of software should be issued. It is also prudent to keep records of the acquisition of software on an ongoing basis.

Avoiding Infringement of Third-Party Trademark Rights

A trademark (or service mark) is anything that identifies the source or origin of a product (or service)—that is, anything that distinguishes the goods or services of one company from those of another. It must be appreciated that a competitor can acquire trademark rights not only in logos and brand names, but also in such things as trade dress (package design), arbitrary color schemes, and, in some instances, even the smell of a product. Rights in a trademark can be acquired through actual use of the mark with goods or services in commercial transactions, or by filing an application for trademark registration based upon a bona fide intent to use. (It is as if use of the mark began on the date of the application.) In general, the first to use a given mark in connection with particular goods in a given geographical area obtains the rights to the mark for use with those goods in that area. Federal registration prevents someone in a geographical area where the mark is not currently being used from subsequently obtaining rights in the mark.

In a manner of speaking, a trademark protects the market value of the company's reputation and goodwill, as well as protecting investments in advertising and other promotional activities used to develop goodwill. Under the law, a competitor is prevented from effectively capitalizing on a trademark owner's reputation and goodwill by passing off its goods as those made or sponsored by the trademark owner or otherwise creating, intentionally or unintentionally, a likelihood that consumers might be misled or confused as to sponsorship by, or affiliation with, the trademark owner.

However, a competitor's trademark does not preclude independent development of technology or, for that matter, copying the technology, so long as there is no likelihood that the public will be confused as to the source or origin of the goods or sponsorship or affiliation with the trademark owner. Potential trademark infringements can be avoided by timely investigations prior to adopting a trademark.

Avoiding Infringement of Third-Party Mask Work Registrations

To the extent that any product that a company might ultimately develop includes custom semiconductor chips, third-party "mask work" protection may be applicable. As previously noted, a mask work registration in essence precludes the use of reproductions of the protected mask work to manufacture competing chips. However, the Semiconductor Chip Protection Act protects only against outright copying, and expressly permits reverse-engineering the chip for the purposes of analysis and using any unpatented idea, principle, or technology embodied in the mask work.

Thus, as in the case of copyrights, the independent development of mask work technologies is a complete defense, and, as a matter of procedure, development should be fully documented.

Making Sure You Own What You Pay For

In an ideal world, the respective rights of different entities involved in the creation of intellectual property would be clear and there would be no disagreements or questions as to ownership. This ideal is easily achieved—all that is needed is a written agreement that clearly spells out each entity's rights. All too often, however, intellectual property is created under circumstances where there is no agreement, or, if an agreement exists, it does not clearly specify the rights of those involved with respect to the intellectual property created. If there is no applicable agreement

> **The rules with respect to ownership of IP are often counterintuitive**

regarding the ownership of intellectual property, there are certain default rules that are applied. Unfortunately, the default rules regarding the ownership of intellectual property are far from intuitive.

To put the issue in perspective, recall Horror Story 11 (pp. 7–8). You might think that, since Salco paid for the development Salco would own the software even if there was no written agreement. This, however, is typically not the case. If there was no agreement, then in all likelihood Salco would be considered to have purchased only a license (right) to use the software. The consultant would probably own the software and would probably have the right to license others to use it.

You might also think that, even without a written agreement, intellectual property made on the job by employees would belong to the employer. Not necessarily so. Depending upon the circumstances and the nature of the intellectual property, the employer might own the intellectual property, might have obtained only a limited license to use it, or might have no rights in it at all.

Rights Relating to Know-How of Employees

The knowledge—know-how—of employees can be a significant "intellectual" asset of a company. For example, businesses often invest significant time and capital in training employees. This typically results in the creation of "know-how." There is clearly an investment by the company in training the employee; it costs time and money to train an employee, and the knowledge of the employee is an intellectual asset of the company. If the use of that know-how was lost to the company, it would cost time and money to replace and reestablish.

Depending upon the nature and subject matter of the know-how, it is "nonproprietary" (i.e., generally known in an industry, or basic skills or practices employed in an industry), or "proprietary" (a trade secret). A typical example of training that results in nonproprietary know-how is teaching employees how to operate a commercially available machine. An example of proprietary know-how is learning a trade secret process.

In the absence of an agreement, the relative rights of the employer and employee in the know-how depend in large part on whether the know-how qualifies as a trade secret and, if so, whether or not the trade secret originated with the employee. Ownership of know-how, in essence, has three components: (a) the right and ability to use and exploit the know-how "in-house," (b) the right to disclose the know-how to others, (c) the right to permit others to use and exploit the know-how. With respect to nonproprietary know-how, the primary concern of the company is to be able to retain the ability to continue to use and exploit the know-how in-house. On the other hand, where proprietary know-how is involved, the company must be concerned with all aspects of ownership.

NONPROPRIETARY KNOW-HOW

How can a company be assured that it will continue to be able to use and exploit its investment in nonproprietary know-how, such as the time and money spent training employees? What can a company do to minimize the consequences of the departure of a skilled employee? There are basically three mechanisms: employee retention, institutionalization, and memorialization.

The most straightforward approach is employee retention, retaining the repository of the know-how—keeping the employees on the job after they have been trained. The issue of a departing employee leaving with the know-how is simply avoided. However, relying on retaining employees is a risky proposition. Indentured servitude is a thing of the past. Today's workplace is highly mobile, and employees leave for many reasons.

How can employees be induced to stay on the job? An obvious, but brute force, approach is to offer better than competitive salary and standard benefits packages. Specially crafted incentive packages for highly skilled or critical employees provide a more strategic protection. For example, an employee can be paid a royalty for inventions embodied in company products, or for increased productivity as a result of employee suggestions, but only as long as the employee is with the company. Longevity bonuses (payment of a bonus at the end of a certain number of years of employment) or delayed vesting of benefits can be used to encourage continued employment. Conditional benefits can also be a tool. For example, the employer can agree to pay for an employee's training, such as by sending the employee to a course or seminar, only if the employee agrees beforehand to repay the company if he or she does not stay with the company for at least a specified time after attending the course. (Of course, the employer can always forgive repayment if the circumstances of the employee's departure warrant it.) As will be discussed, noncompetition provisions in employee agreements can also sometimes be used to prevent competitors from appropriating a company's investment in employee training or other know-how. However, such agreements with employees are often difficult to enforce.

Institutionalizing know-how means making sure that no single employee is the sole repository of particular know-how—that it is possessed by a number of people within the company. This can be facilitated by procedures to establish redundancy, and cross-training to make sure know-how is shared.

Such procedures include: sending more than one employee to training courses; holding a group "debriefing" each time an employee returns from a seminar or course; having skilled employees hold training sessions on a periodic basis; employee teams; and establishing formalized "apprenticeship" or other training programs to make sure that more than one employee is trained on each process, software program, and piece of equipment used in the business.

Both retention (by definition) and institutionalization ultimately rely upon the stability of the workforce. The only way to ensure that know-how will be retained irrespective of employee departures is to memorialize the know-how. Procedures can be established for recording the details of processes, methods, techniques, and data used by skilled employees, for particularized and detailed documentation of software, and for retaining possession of, and retrieving, those records.

Institutionalization and memorialization of know-how are not a panacea, but they do provide a modicum of protection; at least the know-how is not entirely lost if an employee leaves.

PROPRIETARY KNOW-HOW

As noted above, where your ownership of proprietary know-how is at issue, you need to be concerned with both: (a) the right and ability to use and exploit the know-how, and (b) the right to control the disclosure of the know-how to others. If know-how qualifies as a trade secret, the relative rights of the employer and employee in the know-how in the absence of an agreement depend in large part on whether or not the trade secret originated with the employee. Unless the trade secret originated with the employee, the employee cannot legally affect your right to use and exploit it, and the employee has no right to use or exploit it outside the scope of employment and is precluded from disclosing it to others. On the other hand, if the employee is an originator/creator of the trade secret, it is in effect an "invention" for the purposes of determining the relative rights of employer and employee.

Ownership of an Invention

In general, "inventions" are new technological developments or discoveries produced or created through the exercise of independent creative thought, investigation, or experimentation. Inventions may constitute know-how (typically trade secrets) and be protected as such, or may be the subject of patents granted by the governments of various countries. As a basic proposition, absent some express or implied contractual agreement to the contrary, the ownership of a patent belongs to the inventor. Where there are joint inventors, each owns an equal undivided interest in the whole of the patent. Absent an agreement to the contrary, all joint inventors are entitled to make, use, and sell (and license others to make, use, and sell) the invention, without accounting to the other co-inventors.[1]

Under certain circumstances, rights in an invention are held by an employer. For example, where an employee is specifically hired to develop a particular product, or is specifically directed to direct efforts to solve a particular problem, there is an implied agreement that the employer will own all rights to that product.[2] Similarly, where an invention is made on company time and/or using company facilities, the company may acquire "shop rights" (in essence a royalty-free license) to the invention.[3] However, disputes often arise as to whether an employee was hired to make a given invention (was the invention within the scope of employment?) or whether the employer consented to the use of facilities or otherwise released its rights in a development. Accordingly, companies typically require each employee to execute an "employee's invention agreement" as a condition of employment, which obligates the employee to assign all rights in inventions to the company. However, a number of states[4] have enacted statutes that limit the permissible scope of such agreements and place certain restrictions on an employer's ability to require employees to assign all inventions made during the term of their employment. These statutes in effect preclude an employer from compelling assignments of inventions that fall outside of the field of the company business, were developed by the employee outside of their scope of employment, and were developed without the use of company time or resources.

RECORDING OF ASSIGNMENTS, GRANTS, AND CONVEYANCES

Any transfer of ownership (assignment) of a patent must be in writing. It must also be recorded with the Patent and Trademark Office (PTO) in order to be effective against any subsequent purchaser for value without knowledge.[5] Security interests in patents must also be recorded with the PTO in order to be effective against any subsequent purchaser who "pays" value for the security interest (i.e., the security interest is not a gift) and without knowledge of the prior purchase.

It may also be prudent to file financing statements with respect to the security interest under the Uniform Commercial Code (UCC).[6] The UCC treats patents (as well as the other forms of intellectual property) as "general intangibles." Security interests in general intangibles are perfected by filing a financing statement with a state government agency (typically the secretary of state). The holder of a perfected UCC security interest has priority over unperfected security interests, subsequent purchasers, and holders of subsequently perfected security interests. The holder of a perfected security interest has priority over most lien creditors, and over the rights of the trustee or debtor-in-possession in bankruptcy.

Ownership of a Copyright

Typically, the author (creator, originator) of a work owns the copyright.[7] However, if the work qualifies as a "work for hire," then the employer of the creator, or the entity that commissioned the work, is considered to be the author and holder of the copyright.[8] To be a work for hire the work must either: (1)have been prepared by an employee within the scope of the employee's duties; or (2) fall within one of certain specified categories of works, be especially ordered or commissioned, and be the subject of an express written agreement specifying that it will be a work for hire.[9] The specified categories include: collective works (a work including a number of contributions each constituting a separate and independent work that is assembled into a collective whole); audiovisual works, such as motion pictures and phonorecords; compilation works (a work formed by the collection and assembly of preexisting materials or of data that are selected, coordinated, or arranged in such a way that the resulting work as a whole constitutes an original work); supplementary works (works prepared as a secondary adjunct to another work, such as illustrations, forewords, or afterwords); instructional text, tests, and test answers; translations; and atlases. The requirements to qualify as a work for hire are very strictly construed. Unless the creator qualifies as an employee, and the work is created within the scope of employment, the existence of an express written agreement specifying that the work is a work for hire is imperative.[10] Employee status is determined under the law of agency and is based upon such factors as: the skill required to do the work; where the work is done (for example, at the facility of the entity that commissioned the work?); who supplies the facilities and tools; the right to assign additional work; discretion over when and how long to work; who hires and pays the creator's assistants; whether the creator is a separate business entity; the provision of employee benefits; and tax treatment (are Social Security and income tax withheld?).[11] While no single factor is determinative, as a practical matter, unless the creator is treated as an employee for tax and Social Security purposes, the person is likely to be deemed an independent contractor and the owner of the copyright in the absence of a written agreement.

As discussed below, even if a work does not qualify as a work for hire, a party commissioning a work can still obtain ownership of the copyright by assignment. There is, however, a practical difference between obtaining the copyright by assignment and being the author by virtue of work for hire; assignments by individual authors are subject to a right of termination.[12]

It should also be noted that, with respect to a periodical or other "collective work," the copyright to the compilation of works is separate and distinct from the copyright in each separate contribution. The copyright in the separate contribution is thus initially with the originator of the contribution (unless it is a work for hire, in which case the person commissioning the work is considered the author).

Absent agreement to the contrary, authors of a joint work (a work prepared by two or more authors with the intention that the respective contributions be merged into inseparable or interdependent parts of a unitary work) are co-owners of the copyright. Each co-author owns a proportionate share of the copyright, and, in the absence of an agreement, is entitled to contribution, that is, a share of any royalties received from licensing. A joint owner may generally use or license the use of the work without the consent of co-owners, but must account to them for their shares of profits derived from any license to a third party. Potentially, contribution to other co-owners may be required for use of the copyrighted work by a particular co-owner.[13]

Assignment of Copyrights

The author of a work can assign a copyright to another. However, the assignment requires a written agreement[14] that must be recorded in the Copyright Office in order to be effective against a subsequent recorded transfer to a party who did not have notice of the earlier transfer and who paid a valuable consideration for the copyright.[15]

However, under the statute,[16] any license or transfer of right in a copyright in other than a work made for hire may be subject to a right of termination that cannot be assigned; during a five-year period beginning thirty-five years after the transfer, the author, or the author's heir, may terminate the rights granted. Termination does not require the grantee to cease the use of derivative works that were prepared under the authority of the grant before it was terminated,[17] but the preparation of further derivative works is not permitted.

Ownership of Rights in Trademarks

In general, the standard test of ownership of trademark rights in the United States is priority of use. To acquire ownership of a trademark it is not enough to have invented the mark first or even to have registered it first; the mark belongs to the first to actually (or constructively through a perfected intent-to-use application) use the mark in the sale of goods or services.[18] A federal registration of the mark is prima facie evidence that the registrant is the owner of the mark.[19]

As noted above, "invention of" or conceiving the idea for the trademark is not a basis for claiming rights in the mark. Since a trademark is typically used in connection with the goods or services of a business as opposed to those of an employee or a "trademark consultant," issues as to rights in the trademark rarely occur in those contexts. However, trademark ownership issues more commonly arise between manufacturer and distributor. In situations where either (1) the manufacturer licenses the distributor to use a trademark already being used by the manufacturer, or (2) the distributor is already using its own mark, sometimes called a "private label," which it affixes to the manufacturer's product before delivery to an end user, ownership of the mark is determined by which party was the initial owner. When the mark was not clearly in use by one party or the other prior to the initiation of the distribution relationship, courts will look first to any agreement between the parties regarding trademark rights.[20] If there is no agreement between the parties, the manufacturer is presumed to own the trademark.[21] This presumption, however, is rebuttable[22] based on the following factors:

(1) which party invented and first affixed the mark onto the product;

(2) which party's name appeared with the trademark;

(3) which party maintained the quality and uniformity of the product;

(4) with which party the public identified the product and to whom purchasers made complaints; and

(5) which party possesses the goodwill associated with the product, or which party the public believes stands behind the product.

The moral of the story is that whether you are the distributor or the manufacturer, be sure that you have an agreement in place that very explicitly lays out the intent of the parties.

Agreements Are the Best Defense

Agreements are often essential to obtaining and maintaining rights in intellectual property. At the very least, having a definitive (written) agreement in place will avoid issues down the line. As will be discussed in more detail, an agreement should be obtained from anyone (employee, contractor, consultant, vendor) who may have access to confidential information (such as proprietary know-how) or is in a position likely to create technology or other intellectual property relating to your business. The agreement should impose an obligation of confidentiality (nondisclosure and non-use) with respect to confidential information, and require the assignment to you of rights to any works of authorship, technology, and other intellectual property that relate to your business developed in the course of the business relationship. Where particularly critical confidential information is involved, or the person is in a crucial position or involved in a crucial project, noncompetition provisions may be appropriately included.

Putting It in Perspective (An All-Too-Real Hypothetical)

It was Friday afternoon, and I had finally signed off on the last document that had to get out that day. For a change, it seemed like I would be able to get out of the office before the sun went down. Then the telephone rang, and, against my better judgment, I answered.

I heard an all-too-familiar voice. "Hey, Mike. It's Joe from TSI. Your favorite client."

Joe Theoretico was the president and majority stockholder of Theoretico Software Inc., an up-and-coming player in the personal computer industry. TSI hit the big time with a product called Hi-Bird, a system for generating 3-D images on a conventional color monitor, using conventional hardware and proprietary software. Joe had come to me a couple of months ago when he ran into some difficulties with one of his distributors, appropriately named Piraco. The distributor had been provided a master disk and given extensive training by Theoretico, then decided to come out with its own competing product. Of course, they infringed a few of Theoretico's intellectual property rights along the way.[23] I'm not sure I would call Joe my "favorite client," but he was good about paying his bills.

"Hi, Joe. I've been hoping to hear back from you. You were going to let me know when it would be convenient to get together to do that IP audit we were talking about. I think you understand the trouble that inadequate agreements can cause from the dispute with Piraco. I am a little concerned that there may be a few more snakes out there. Let's not wait until they raise their ugly heads."

There was a brief moment of silence. "Yeah, I know we really do need to do that, but that is not why I was calling . . . Did you ever meet John Markett and Tran Prom?"

"No, I don't think so. Markett is your marketing guy, right?"

"Yeah. He *was* my vice president of marketing and sales. Prom *was* the programmer in charge of the new High-Fly product—you remember, the new 3-D display software we are supposed to introduce next month." From the emphasis Joe put on "was," I sensed something was going on. "Well, the sons of a gun just resigned. They are going to work for Piraco!" As he talked, the decibel level kept rising. At this point, he was literally shouting into the phone. He continued:

"You know what really frosts me? When that damn Prom first started working for me, he knew nothing. In fact, he just barely spoke English. I sent him to school. I trained him. I paid to send him to all those seminars. I figure I've got a good solid fifty grand invested just in his education and training. Now, he's going to use all that training for Piraco! On top of that, he has stolen the work that was done on High-Fly. He downloaded everything to his home computer, then wiped the disks on the TSI server. He took everything related to the project, all the documentation, all the files—everything. It's all gone. When I asked him about it, he said that High-Fly was his work—so he owned it and was taking it with him!

"And Markett! That scumbag has been with me since the beginning. He knows everything there is to know about the company. All the marketing plans. All our suppliers. All our accounts. He says that he made all the contacts and there is no reason why he can't contact them on behalf of Piraco. He also says that he can use the marketing plan that we had worked out for High-Fly, because High-Fly belongs to Prom anyway."

Joe was really beginning to get wound up. It was time to interrupt. "Okay, Joe, let's talk this through. Can you fax over copies of the employee agreements with these two?"

There was an embarrassed silence over the telephone. I had a premonition of what was coming, even before Joe finally muttered, "There are no employee agreements."

"Joe, this is the sort of thing that we were talking about before." The professor in me was starting to take over. I unconsciously shifted into lecture mode. "Generally, companies use written agreements with their employees to avoid these types of 'misunderstandings.' These agreements generally do a number of things. First of all, the agreement obligates the employee to assign all intellectual property to the company, although some states have laws that limit the scope of what the company can require be assigned to inventions relating to company business. The agreement also makes it very clear that the employee has an obligation of confidentiality to the company and lays out the uses an employee can and cannot make of the company's confidential information."

"Well, I didn't get agreements from the employees when they first started, and somebody told me that unless you got the agreement when they start, it's no good."

"Not necessarily so, particularly in Arizona. Generally, in order for there to be an enforceable contract, there has to be some 'give' in return for the 'take.' In legalese it's called 'consideration.' In some states, if an employee is forced to sign an agreement and does not get anything that he or she doesn't already have in return, then there is no consideration and the contract is not valid. In other states, like Arizona, where there isn't an employment contract for a definite duration, then *continued employment* is considered to be enough consideration to support an agreement to assign inventions and maintain confidentiality. One of the other things that written employee agreements tend to do is to establish the law that would be applied when interpreting the contract. On issues like the sufficiency of continued employment as consideration, this can be important."

"Well," Joe snapped, "there isn't any agreement, so I guess I'm dead in the water, huh?"

"Not necessarily. Things would have been much simpler if you had a written agreement, but there are certain basic rights that you have as an employer under the common law based upon the employer-employee relationship. First of all, employees do have an obligation of confidentiality. To the extent that you have things that qualify as trade secrets—that is, things that have added value because they are not readily ascertainable by the public, and reasonable efforts have been taken to keep them confidential—an employee has an obligation to keep them secret. What are reasonable efforts to keep them confidential? Well, generally they include having confidentiality agreements with everyone who has access to the information, including employees, use of proprietary legends, restricting access to the information, and things like that. The fact that you don't have confidentiality agreements with your employees doesn't help, but it is not determinative since there is an obligation of confidentiality imposed on the employee by law. This is particularly true where you are talking about someone in a fiduciary relationship—an officer of the corporation."

"Like Markett? He is an officer."

"Probably."

"So can I stop them from going to work for Piraco?"

"To the extent that they have things rising to the level of trade secrets, you can stop them from disclosing the information to Piraco. And if it is absolutely inevitable that they would disclose trade secret information to Piraco if they are employed in a particular position, then you may be able to stop them from taking that position. But, as a general proposition, unless you have a enforceable noncompetition agreement—and to be enforceable, it has to be reasonable as to duration, scope of precluded activities, and geographical area—you won't be able to stop a former employee from competing."

"'Scope of precluded activities' . . . You sound like a lawyer."

"Sorry, I have a tendency to do that. The particular things that they can't do. Anyway, one thing that you generally cannot do is take away a former employee's means of livelihood. You can't stop the employee from using information that is generally known in the trade, or basic skills or practices. I know that there is a major investment by the company in training an employee and that the knowledge and skills accumulated by the employee—I call this 'nonproprietary know-how'—can be a significant asset of the company. But there is little that can be done to protect it. It generally is lost when an employee leaves. Sometimes a company can use written noncompetition agreements to keep nonproprietary know-how from being used to compete against it, but noncompetition agreements with employees are often difficult to enforce. Some companies also will require repayment of money paid out for employee education if the employee leaves within a certain time of the expenditure—but there has to be an agreement to that effect beforehand. One thing that the company definitely should do is to establish procedures for recording the details of processes and techniques and so forth used by the employees, and for retaining possession of those records. At least the know-how won't be entirely lost if the employee leaves."

"Okay, what about the rights to High-Fly? They claim that it belongs to Prom."

"All right, let's look at that issue. First of all, we need to recognize that High-Fly has a number of separate aspects; we need to look at each one individually. Let's start with inventions embodied—used—in the product. The general rule is that in the absence of an agreement to the contrary, the actual inventor—the employee—owns the rights to the invention, and any patent obtained on the invention."

I heard Joe gasp over the phone, so I hurried on. "But there are exceptions to that. The primary exception is where the employee was 'hired to invent.' If an employee is in a position in which he or she is expected to develop technology, or if the employee is assigned the task of solving a particular problem and the invention was conceived or developed while solving that problem, then the employer would own the invention. My guess is that Prom was hired to create, and his work on High-Fly probably falls into that exception."

Joe's sigh of relief was audible, even through the phone. I went on.

"Let's talk for a moment about filing patent applications. The law in the U.S. requires that patent applications be in the name of the actual inventor—and that the applicant sign a declaration in connection with the application. If Hi-Fly includes Prom's inventions, any patent applications would have to name him as the applicant. Of course that doesn't mean that the company wouldn't own the patents—Prom would be required to assign them to the company. There are also provisions for filing a patent application even if Prom refuses to sign, but you will have to prove to the patent office that you have sufficient proprietary interest—that you really are the owner.

"Even if an employer is not entitled to an assignment—ownership—of the invention, there may still be something referred to as 'shop rights' that would provide limited rights to use the invention. If the employee makes the invention using the employer's facilities, equipment, or materials, the employer gets a nonexclusive, nontransferable, royalty-free license to use the invention. This does not, however, stop the employee from using the invention elsewhere.

"The copyrightable aspects of High-Fly are easier. As a general proposition, the creator of a work is considered the author under the copyright law, and in the absence of a written agreement, the author owns the copyright. However, the copyright law makes an exception where the copyrighted work—the program code—is created by an employee within the scope of employment. Then the employer is considered the author—and owner of the copyright."

I realized I was making an assumption. It's always dangerous to make any assumptions where Theoretico was concerned. "Prom is an employee, right? As opposed to an independent contractor. I mean, you are withholding taxes and paying Social Security for him, right?"

"Yeah, and the same for Markett."

It was my turn to sigh in relief. "Good." I continued:

"There are also a number of other things that we should take a look at. There are certain things that an employee simply cannot do while still employed by a company. They can't divert corporate opportunities—send potential customers to their prospective new employer. This is particularly true for fiduciaries—officers. We also need to look at whether or not Prom or Markett have taken tangible property belonging to the company—listings, or magnetic media. It is also possible that Prom's access to the computer system through the telephone line was a computer crime under Arizona law. Here, let me see . . ." I paused for a moment while I consulted my copy of the statute. "Okay, it is A.R.S., section 13-2316—

> a person commits computer fraud in the second degree by inten-
> tionally and without authorization accessing, altering, damaging or
> destroying any computer, computer system or computer network or
> any computer software program or data contained in such computer,
> computer system or computer network.

"It seems to me Prom blasted your data intentionally and without autho-rization.

"Look, we're going to need to take a real hard look at what exactly the facts are, and what we can prove. Tell you what, why don't I come on over, and you can pull together whatever records you have while I'm on my way."

Once more, Theoretico's sigh of relief was clearly audible over the phone. "Thanks. I'll see you in a little while."

Oh well, so much for getting home before the sun went down.

Overview and Comparison of Agreements Affecting Intellectual Property Rights and Liabilities

Rights in intellectual property are often affected, and liabilities created, by various types of agreements. Obviously, this includes agreements specifically related to the transfer of rights (assignment, licenses, franchises, and technical assistance). However, certain other types of agreements, while not intended for the specific purpose of affecting intellectual property rights,

> **The only way to be sure of your rights is to have a clear, unequivocal, and complete written agreement**

> **With agreements, the devil is in the details**

may well affect intellectual property rights or create potential liabilities. Those agreements tend to relate to three broad categories of subject matter: internal relationships (employee and noncompetition); third-party business relationships (confidentiality, consulting, development, maintenance and support, manufacturing, and joint venture); and sales and market relationships (purchase, distribution, VAR, and OEM).

In the sections that follow, brief descriptions of the more common examples of such agreements and the intellectual property issues most often encountered in such agreements are provided.

Agreements Regarding Transfers of Rights

Assignments, licenses, and technical assistance agreements (and sometimes joint ventures) directly affect rights in intellectual property; all are vehicles for transferring or granting rights in intellectual property to an entity.

Assignments

An assignment is a document that effects a present transfer of title to, for example, various intellectual property rights. In most instances, to be effective with respect to a patent, copyright, or trademark, an assignment must be recorded with the Patent and Trademark or Copyright Office. In general, there should be a recorded assignment with respect to each patent owned by the company, and with respect to each copyright or trademark acquired from outside of the company.

Where the assignment pertains to an invention, the document typically should cover rights both in the United States and throughout the world, including any rights or priorities under international treaties. The assignment should also cover any continuing applications. The document should also include a provision requiring the assignee to execute any papers necessary to perfect the assignor's rights.

License Agreements: In General

A license agreement is, in general terms, an agreement whereby the "licensor," for an agreed-upon consideration, grants to the "licensee" certain rights with respect to intellectual property of the licensor. A license is to be distinguished from a sale or an assignment. A sale or assignment transfers substantially all commercial rights and title to the intellectual property to the assignee. In the case of a license, the licensor retains title to the intellectual property.

There are a number of reasons why a company would be willing to permit others to use its intellectual property. Some of these, such as obtaining a royalty income in consideration for the use of the intellectual property, are obvious. This is particularly so where the licensor does not itself use the technology, or the licensor is unable or unwilling to meet the demand for products that use its intellectual property. For example, the licensor may not have the capital to expand its production facilities. Or it may have other product lines to which it must devote all of its resources. For a company to export product into a particular geographic area, or to establish its own manufacturing facilities in that area, may, for various reasons, be impractical or uneconomical. In some cases, the licensor does not have the resources or contacts to develop a necessary distribution system in the area.

There are additional reasons for licensing intellectual property, however, that are not necessarily obvious. For example, having an additional source for a given product may increase the market acceptance of the product. In other instances, the licensor itself might use the licensed product as a part in another product, or sell the licensed product as part of an overall line of products, but find it uneconomical or impractical to manufacture the licensed product itself. By licensing another party that can economically manufacture the product, the licensor can ensure a source of supply. That the product may also be available to the licensor's competitors is offset by the compensation paid to the licensor by the licensee. In other instances, licensing a local entity in a given geographic area to manufacture one product may create a market in that geographical area (or at least increase market acceptance) for other products of the licensor.

All license agreements should include certain basic elements. In the most general of terms, for a license agreement to be enforceable, the agreement must: somehow identify, or be attributable to, respective legal entities with the capacity to enter the agreement; include some manifestation of assent by the parties; reflect some manner of consideration between the parties (in some cases a specific recitation of consideration is required); and include terms that are not illegal or otherwise unenforceable under the applicable law.

The typical license agreement includes a number of major sections:

1. A preamble that identifies the parties;
2. A set of recitals that, in effect, describe the background understandings of the agreement of the parties;
3. A recital of consideration, where necessary;
4. Provisions relating to the grant of rights and ownership to intellectual property and confidentiality;
5. Provisions relating to performance by the parties;
6. Provisions relating to the consideration to be paid;
7. Provisions relating to representations and warranties by the parties;
8. Provisions relating to the term and termination of the agreement;
9. Various miscellaneous provisions; and
10. Signatures and acknowledgments.

If the agreement is well written, it will also include definitions for every significant term in the agreement that could conceivably be misunderstood. The definitions are typically included as a separate section at the beginning of the agreement. However, the definitions are also sometimes provided in the body of the agreement as the terms are introduced in context.

Patent Licenses

A patent license is an agreement under which the "licensor," for an agreed-upon consideration, agrees not to interfere with the performance of some act by the "licensee" that the licensee would otherwise be precluded from doing by the licensor's patent. In the broadest sense, the licensor agrees not to enforce the patent against the licensee with respect to certain acts by the licensee, typically making, using, or selling processes or products covered by the patent. The patent license typically permits the licensee to use, or manufacture and sell, the patented product while at the same time protecting the licensee from competition. Nonlicensed third parties are not permitted to manufacture the product.

A patent license may be no more than a covenant not to enforce the patent, or may be coupled with an agreement providing the transfer of know-how or technical assistance. Essentially all countries that have patent systems in place recognize patent licenses.

Know-How Licenses

A know-how license is an agreement whereby the licensor, for an agreed-upon consideration, permits the licensee to have access to, and use, the licensor's know-how. The know-how may be proprietary or nonproprietary. If proprietary know-how is involved, significant features of the license agreement are provisions requiring the licensee to maintain the know-how in confidence (nondisclosure provisions), and, typically, provisions restricting the manner in which the know-how can be used. Such provisions are necessary to protect the licensor's proprietary interest in the know-how.

Trademark Licenses

A trademark license is an agreement under which the owner of a trademark, for an agreed-upon consideration, permits another entity to employ the trademark in connection with the other entity's goods or services. In practice, a trademark license permits the licensee to take advantage of the goodwill associated with the trademark. At the same time, the licensor is able to expand its goodwill through, and, of course, make money from, the licensee's efforts. Trademark licensing is recognized under the laws of most but not all countries. In most instances, however, in order for the trademark owner to retain rights in the mark, the trademark owner must maintain careful quality control over the products of the licensee.

When is a trademark license necessary to maintain the trademark owner's rights in a mark? As a general proposition, a merchant or dealer who merely resells bona fide goods bearing a trademark, without changing those goods, does not require a trademark license, as long as the dealer is not holding itself to be authorized or otherwise sponsored by or associated with the trademark owner. A trademark license is necessary when an entity other than the trademark owner is manufacturing goods and using the trademark in connection with those goods.

Franchise Agreements

A franchise agreement can be considered a species of license agreement that grants particularly significant rights and establishes a close, ongoing relationship between the transferor and transferee. Very often the franchise agreement involves a trademark license, together with agreements as to know-how and technical assistance, as well as a license under any applicable patents. Franchise agreements are closely regulated throughout the United States and in many countries.

Technical Services and Assistance Agreements

There are no standard definitions for the terms "technical assistance agreement" or "technical services agreement." In general, however, these are hybrid consulting/know-how agreements relating to provisions of know-how, instruction, and training to the receiving party. Proprietary or nonproprietary know-how, or both, may be involved. For example, an entity with special expertise may be engaged to assist in implementing or installing an equipment plant or process, and to instruct and train the contracting party in the operation and management of the plant or process. The plant, process, or equipment may have been acquired from a consultant, or may have been acquired from a third party, and the consultant is merely engaged to install the equipment and train the other party in its use.

Hybrid License Agreements

A given licensing agreement can pertain to any number of types of intellectual property. For example, a single agreement can grant rights with respect to patents, existing proprietary know-how (trade secret) rights, existing nonproprietary know-how, rights to use certain trademarks and/or trade dress, and the rights to future intellectual property acquired by the licensor.

Where patents covering the subject matter of a license agreement exist, the agreement normally will include a grant of some manner of rights under the patent; rights to use know-how may be worthless if the only practical use to which the know-how can be put is precluded by an applicable patent.

A know-how or technical assistance or service agreement is typically employed when there are no applicable patents, and may sometimes be used in conjunction with a trademark license or franchising agreement.

Where both patents and know-how are involved in a transaction, the grants with respect to both patents and know-how are typically included in a single agreement. The typical practice with respect to trademarks, however, is to have a separate trademark license agreement, even if patents or know-how are also being licensed as part of the overall arrangement. The exception to this practice is where know-how is transferred to facilitate the quality control provisions of the trademark license agreement.

Agreements Regarding Internal Relationships

Agreements with employees are often essential to obtaining and maintaining rights in intellectual property.

Employee Agreements As to Confidentiality and Ownership of Intellectual Property

In general, from a company's perspective, each employee who may have access to confidential information (such as proprietary know-how) should be the signatory of an agreement imposing an obligation of confidentiality (nondisclosure and non-use) on the employee with respect to confidential information. The agreement should also require the employee to assign to the company all rights to any works of authorship and technology developed by the employee that relate to the company's business.

One issue that tends to arise in employee agreements relates to the invalidity of the agreements for lack of consideration. In general, employee agreements are valid if signed prior to or contemporaneously with initial employment. Some states, however, have held agreements to be invalid in the absence of some additional consideration to the employee, if entered into after the commencement of employment. This problem is avoided by conditioning a raise or benefit to the employee upon their entering into the agreement.

Noncompetition Agreements

Where particularly critical confidential information is involved, or the employee is in a crucial position, noncompetition provisions may be appropriately included. Various states impose restrictions upon the scope of such employee agreements. Noncompetition provisions tend to be very strictly construed, and are typically unenforceable if not reasonable in scope as to geography, time, and precluded employment.

Agreements Regarding Third-Party Business Relationships

Agreements creating or relating to business relationships with third parties beyond the marketing of products often include provisions that can affect rights in intellectual property or create potential liabilities.

Confidentiality Agreements

A confidentiality agreement is a general term used to describe an agreement drafted solely to impose an obligation of confidentiality on a party who has access to confidential information (such as proprietary know-how).

If the agreement is well written it will preclude disclosure of the information and will *also* limit the use of the information by the recipient to a specific purpose, for instance, in connection with the business relationship between the parties. Such an agreement should be in place anytime a third party is given access to proprietary know-how, outside of the context of a broader agreement including provisions to impose such a confidentiality obligation.

Consulting and Development Agreements

A consulting agreement may be broadly defined as an agreement under which a third party (individual or business entity) having a particular expertise is engaged to apply that expertise on behalf of the hiring company. The consulting agreement may relate to a particular project of the hiring company or may be more open-ended, with the consultant available for any issue involving his or her area of expertise.

A development agreement is sometimes considered a species of consulting agreement where it is specifically contemplated that the consultant (developer) will generate technology. In many cases, the developer is not intimately involved with the operation of the hiring company, and may work on a largely independent basis. There are a number of different approaches to defining the subject matter and administration of development agreements. If a company has sufficient in-house expertise respecting the subject matter of the development, it may itself generate a detailed specification for the item to be developed. Alternatively, a consultant (other than the entity ultimately engaged to do the development work) may be engaged to develop or assist in developing a detailed specification. Or a detailed specification can be developed by the developer, as an initial phase of the development agreement. Still another approach is to issue a more general request for proposals, eliciting proposed specifications from prospective developers. Each of these approaches presents different issues with respect to confidentiality and the ownership of rights in technology resulting from the work. Compliance issues also often arise with respect to the developer's meeting specified milestones; the provision of data, documentation, and reports called for under the contract; and the testing and acceptance of items delivered under the contract.

If well written, the consulting or development agreement will include provisions that, as pertaining to intellectual property:

- Impose confidentiality (nondisclosure, non-use) obligations;
- Clearly define the scope of the engagement, and all tangible items and documentation to be delivered;
- Define the respective rights of the parties as to ownership of any technology that might be developed during the course of the relationship and rights to preexisting technology incorporated into the developed product; and

- Allocate the risk of infringement of third-party intellectual property rights.

In the absence of a written agreement to the contrary, the copyright to any writings or software authored by the consultant or developer will belong to the developer. Likewise, the rights to any inventions made during the course of the engagement will likely belong to the developer, unless the agreement specifies otherwise.

Depending upon the nature and subject matter of the engagement, the agreement may also include provisions precluding the consultant from providing similar services to competitors during the term of the engagement, and for a reasonable period after the termination of the agreement.

Maintenance and Support Agreements

Maintenance and support agreements cover a wide variety of circumstances, but are most commonly encountered in connection with software products. The agreements often involve the provision of updates and error correction of licensed software.

Intellectual property issues tend to arise with respect to ownership and the rights of the licensee to new developments. There can also be problems concerning statements by the service persons pertaining to the software and availability of updates or error corrections.

Manufacturing Agreements

A manufacturing agreement is a general term used to describe an agreement under which a company hires a third party (vendor, supplier) to manufacture goods (typically a part or component to be used in a company's product) according to specifications provided by the company. The arrangement very often involves the communication of confidential information (e.g., the specification). Appropriate confidentiality provisions and, in some cases, restricted licenses under other types of intellectual property (such as patents) should be included in the agreement.

Joint Ventures

A joint venture is a form of alliance of two separate companies; the companies agree to act together, typically forming a separate legal entity, for a particular purpose. In the context of technology transfer, a joint venture can be distinguished from a license in that the owner of the intellectual property actively participates in the enterprise licensed to use the technology. The formation of a joint venture can sometimes provide security to the licensor of intellectual property. Since the licensor is involved in the management of the licensee, the use of the licensed intellectual property can be controlled. This is particularly important in countries that do not have strong intellectual property laws.

Agreements Regarding Sales and Market Relationships

Agreements relating to transactions in the marketplace or creating marketing relationships often include provisions that can affect rights in intellectual property or create potential liabilities.

Purchase Agreements

In general, a purchase agreement is an agreement under which a vendor (supplier) transfers the title to a product to a purchaser (customer). The terms of the purchase agreement are often established by preprinted forms—purchase order, and order acknowledgment or confirmation forms. Issues tend to arise as to the precise terms of the agreement when the terms in the purchase order conflict with those of the confirmation or acknowledgment form. Generally, the contract will be based upon the terms of the order acknowledgment/confirmation form unless the new terms materially alter the crucial terms of the agreement, the terms of the purchase order form expressly preclude formation of a contract under the current terms, or the vendor makes a timely written objection.

In many instances, however, a purchase order will expressly preclude changes in terms, while the responsive order acknowledgment/confirmation form provides for differing terms, and states that a contract would be formed only upon acceptance of the new terms. Often the individual employees of the parties overlook or ignore the inconsistent positions and proceed in any event with the delivery and acceptance of the goods. Under the Uniform Commercial Code (UCC), that course of dealing does create a contract, based upon the terms that are common to the respective forms, and various other terms supplied by the UCC. Very often, the variant terms relate to warranties (and disclaimer of warranties) and assignment of risks with respect to, among other things, intellectual property right infringement. When this is the case, the UCC implied warranties of noninfringement, merchantability, and fitness for a particular purpose may be deemed applicable.

Distribution Agreements

A distribution agreement can be broadly defined as an agreement under which the owner of a product (manufacturer, developer) engages a distributor to market a product in substantially unmodified form. In some instances, the distributor may install, service, or customize the product for an end user.

Intellectual property issues typically arise with respect to the extent to which, if at all, the distributor is licensed to use the intellectual property of the manufacturing/developing company. This will be specified with particularity in the agreement, if it is well drafted. Where the agreement calls for the distributor to sell the product alone and in unmodified form, intellectual property issues tend to relate to the extent to which, if at all, the distributor is permitted to use the manufacturer/developer's trademarks, and the allocation of risk of liability for the infringement of third-party intellectual property rights.

Other intellectual property issues concern distribution agreements involving products that include a software component. For example, where the product is predominantly software, the distributor agreement typically specifies the manner in which the software is to be marketed by the distributor to the end user. Alternative manners of marketing include selling a copy of the software to the end user, acting as an agent for the developer company, acting as a broker for an end-user license agreement between the developer company and the end user, or entering into a sublicense agreement with the end user. The substance of a sublicense is typically specified to ensure that the developer company's rights are adequately protected.

Software distribution agreements also tend to present different types of administration/compliance issues. The agreement typically specifies how to generate copies of software that will be delivered to the end user. The copies may be provided by the developer company on an as-ordered basis, provided from an inventory maintained by the distributor, or made by the distributor on an as-needed basis from a "master copy" provided by the developer company. There are also a number of alternative approaches to providing remuneration to the developer company: a distributor may pay the developer company a preset discounted fee (keeping the difference from fees obtained from the end user) for each copy of the software; the developer company may receive a specified percentage of fees received by the distributor; or the distributor can receive a commission on each transaction, with the fees from the end user going directly to the developer company.

VAR and OEM Agreements

Value added remarketer (VAR) and original equipment manufacturer (OEM) agreements are agreements wherein the owner of technology or a product licenses the VAR or OEM to market the technology/product as part of an overall system or product. While there is no standard definition of OEM and VAR agreements, the distinction between the two is often drawn based upon the extent to which the supplied technology/product retains its separate identity. Where the supplied product is a separate module identified to, or identifiable by, the end user, the agreement is typically characterized as a VAR agreement. Conversely, under an OEM agreement, the supplied technology/product tends to lose its separate identity, becoming an integral part of a product marketed under the OEM's name.

Many of the same intellectual property and compliance issues arise with OEM and VAR agreements as do with distribution agreements. However, significant intellectual property issues relating to technology tend to occur more often with OEM and VAR agreements; compared to a distributor, the OEM or VAR typically has greater access to, and more latitude with respect to the use of, the proprietor company's technology.

The agreement, if competently drafted, also will include provisions allocating risks of liability with respect to defects in the products, and provisions relating to the infringement of third-party intellectual property rights. It is particularly important to include such provisions, as well as provisions providing for indemnification against liability based on the acts of the other party, in VAR and OEM agreements. This is especially true if the VAR or OEM is permitted to modify the supplied product. Indemnity provisions in the agreement often create potential liability on the part of the manufacturer/developer with respect to infringement claims as to unmodified product. On the other hand, to the extent that infringement claims relate to modifications of the product by the VAR or OEM, the provisions protect the manufacturer/developer.

Compliance issues can be substantial, and tend to arise not only with respect to the payment of fees, the administration of orders, and the completion of deliveries under the agreement, but also concerning various intellectual property–related provisions, such as the use of trademarks, and the extent to which technology is used or modified. Where the product includes a significant software component, the mechanism by which it is marketed (such as in the sale of copies, the brokering of licenses directly between the proprietor company and end user, or sublicenses between the VAR/OEM and end user) is also an important aspect of the agreement that often gives rise to compliance issues.

Some Basic Considerations in Negotiating Agreements

Certain basic principles or philosophies are common to the success of any type of agreement.

The Principle of Reasonableness

To be successful, a long-term agreement must be fair to both parties. Both must benefit from the agreement. If the agreement is unfair to one of the parties, that party will tend to spend all of its energy in looking for some way to escape the agreement, rather than in performance. Never negotiate a license with the idea of "pulling the wool over the other party's eyes." One partner's unhappiness in a marriage leads to the unhappiness of both.

The Principle of Definiteness

To ensure that there is no possible misunderstanding between the parties as to their respective expectations from the agreement, it is imperative that care be taken to carefully and precisely define all terms. This is particularly true where there are cultural or language differences between the parties.

Very often a word that is commonplace to one party, which that party thinks is clear and concise, will not have a precise and definite meaning to the other party. Take, for example, the term "exclusive." To a licensor from the United States, an "exclusive" license has a particular meaning. This may not be the case elsewhere in the world. Rather than chance any misconception, it is better to explicitly define all critical terms in the agreement.

The Principle of Completeness

The agreement should attempt to contemplate all contingencies and circumstances and clearly set forth the rights and obligations of the parties in the event that those circumstances arise. Specifically dealing with potential problems that may arise in the future does not imply any particular expectation that those problems will in fact arise, or any lack of trust or unwillingness to cooperate between the parties. It merely assures that the parties have a complete understanding of each other's expectations and the manner in which foreseeable issues will be dealt with if they occur. This is particularly important where the parties come from different cultures and may have very different expectations and approaches to dealing with problems.

Also, particularly with respect to long-term agreements, the individuals negotiating the agreement, or initially performing under the agreement, may not always be available—those individuals may retire, transfer, or otherwise leave the company. The replacements for the original individuals, who were not a party to the negotiations, may not have the same understandings and may come to different conclusions on the terms or administration of the agreement. To provide consistency of interpretation and order, it is particularly important that the written agreement be complete and include all understandings.

The Periodic Intellectual Property Audit

This book has attempted to familiarize the reader with various types of intellectual property, the common types of agreements concerning or giving rise to intellectual property rights and potential liabilities, and some of the situations where intellectual property issues tend to occur. Various procedures have also been suggested to prevent the inadvertent loss of intellectual property rights.

Intellectual property is becoming increasingly important to the typical successful company. Often a company's intellectual property is very valuable; in fact, it may be the *most* valuable asset of a company. Yet while audits of tangible assets and liabilities are commonplace, focused audits of the intellectual property assets and liabilities of a company extending beyond royalty payment compliance are still a relative rarity.

An intellectual property audit involves more than just compiling an inventory of a company's intellectual property assets. It also involves determining potential liabilities that may be incurred from the use of technology and other items that might be the subject of third-party intellectual property rights. An audit must also consider the development of systems and procedures for ensuring that a company's intellectual property is appropriately protected, and that the infringement of third-party intellectual property rights is avoided. Unless appropriate procedures are implemented, loss of rights and third-party intellectual property claims can adversely affect the company.

A formal intellectual property audit can be an important managerial tool; up-to-date information on a company's intellectual property assets and potential liabilities can be invaluable to proper management. Such an audit can identify potentially licensable intellectual property of which the company was previously unaware, and this could have the result in an increase in the company's licensing revenues. It can also identify potential infringement of third-party intellectual property rights before the company incurs any liability or, if liability cannot be avoided, in time to control or minimize the liability and perhaps avoid costly litigation. Additionally, contractual obligations can be systematically identified to ensure compliance, and potential disputes and liabilities can be minimized. Perhaps most importantly, an intellectual property audit can serve as a vehicle for establishing procedures to make certain that intellectual property assets are protected and exploited to the fullest extent, and that costly intellectual property liabilities and contractual disputes are avoided or minimized. Thus, if properly employed, an intellectual property audit can significantly and positively impact the company balance sheet.

Conclusion

In conclusion, it should again be stressed that this handbook is not intended to be a definitive text on the various mechanisms for protecting intellectual property. Volumes have been written on aspects and concepts of intellectual property law that have here been allotted only a sentence or two. In many cases, concepts are described here in very simplistic terms, and many of the ramifications and subtleties involved in the issues are left unexplored. Basically, this book is no more than an attempt to alert the reader to various problem areas and to provide a basic understanding of the types of protection available and the procedures by which these protections are obtained.

It is vitally important for a business to be sensitive to intellectual property issues. A few relatively painless and simple procedures and precautions can make all the difference in protecting a company's investment in R&D, new products, and the nurturing of goodwill and reputation.

Appendix
Comparison of U.S. Intellectual Property Protection Mechanisms

Protection mechanism	Term	Scope of protection	Compatible concurrent forms of protection
Trade secret	Potentially infinite	Protects anything that can be kept secret No protection against independent development	Trademark
Trademark	Potentially infinite	Protects against others trading on TM owner's reputation—against confusion as to origins of products or affiliation	Trade Secret Design patent Utility patent Copyright
Design patent	14 years from issue date	Protects ornamental features only	Utility patent Copyright Trademark
Utility patent	20 years from filing date of application	Protects concept of invention as set forth in claims	Copyright Design patent Mask work Trademark
Copyright	Life of last surviving author and 70 years or work for hire; shortest of 75 years from publication or 100 years from creation	Protects only the form of expression—not substance or content	Trademark Design patent Utility patent
Mask work	Until end of 10th calendar year after registration or first commercial exploitation, whichever is first	Protects against use of reproductions of masks in production of competing chips	Trade secret Trademark Utility patent

Notes

TRADE SECRET PROTECTION

1. The Economic Espionage Act of 1996, 18 U.S.C. § 1831 et seq., authorizes the government to take legal (criminal and civil) actions for economic espionage and theft of trade secrets

2. See *Bonito Boats Inc. v. Thunder Craft Boats,* 489 U.S. 141, 152 (1989); *Sears, Roebuck & Co. v. Stiffel Co.,* 376 U.S. 225 (1964); *Compco Corp. v. DayBrite Lighting Inc.,* 376 U.S. 234 (1964); *Roboserve Ltd. v. Tom's Foods Inc.,* 20 U.S.P.Q.2d 1321 (11th Cir. 1991); *Gates Rubber Co. v. Bando American Inc.,* 798 F. Supp. 1489 (D. Colo. 1992); *Cuisinarts Corp. v. Appliance Science Corp.,* 21 U.S.P.Q.2d 1318 (D. Conn. 1991); *Darling v. Standard Alaska Products Co.,* 20 U.S.P.Q.2d 1688, 1691 (Alaska 1991); see also *infra* note 6. There is no issue of preemption by the Economic Espionage Act of 1996; it expressly states that there is no preemption, 18 U.S.C. § 1838.

3. These states are: Alaska, Arkansas, California, Connecticut, Illinois, Indiana, Louisiana, Rhode Island, Washington, Alabama, Arizona, Colorado, Delaware, District of Columbia, Florida, Georgia, Hawaii, Idaho, Iowa, Kansas, Kentucky, Maine, Maryland, Michigan, Minnesota, Mississippi, Missouri, Montana, Nebraska, Nevada, New Hampshire, New Mexico, North Dakota, Ohio, Oklahoma, Oregon, South Carolina, South Dakota, Tennessee, Utah, Vermont, Virginia, West Virginia, and Wisconsin.

4. The patent law (35 U.S.C. § 273) does, however, include a limited personal "prior inventor" defense with respect to use of a business method and/or the sale or disposition of a "useful end product" made by the method, if the accused infringer can prove, clearly and convincingly, that, among other things,

the business method was actually reduced to practice, independently from the patent owner, at least one year prior to the effective filing date of the patent, and was commercially used (whether or not accessible or known to the public) before the effective filing date of the patent.

5. For example, in Arizona, continued employment is presently sufficient consideration for an employee to enter into such an agreement.

6. See, e.g., *Scott v. Snelling & Snelling Inc.*, 732 F. Supp. 1034, 1043 (N.D. Cal. 1990); *Telxon Corp. v. Hoffman*, 13 U.S.P.Q.2d 1577 (N.D. Ill. 1989); *Cambridge Filter Corp. v. International Filter Co.*, 548 F. Supp. 1301 (D. Nev. 1982); *Al S. Chomers v. Continental Aviation & Engineering Corp.*, 255 F. Supp. 645 (E.D. Mich. 1966); *American Broadcasting Companies Inc. v. Wolf*, 438 N.Y.S.2d 482, 420 N.E.2d 363 (Ct. App. 1981).

7. For a more complete discussion of license agreements see "License Agreements: In General," p. 317.

8. See *ProCD Inc. v. Zeidenberg*, 86 F.3d 1447, 39 U.S.P.Q.2d 1161 (7th Cir. 1996); *Morgan Laboratories Inc. v. Micro Data Base Systems Inc.*, 41 U.S.P.Q.2d 1850 (N.D. Cal. Jan. 21, 1997).

9. See, e.g., *DSC Communications Corp. v. Pulse Communications Inc.*,__ F.3d__, 50 U.S.P.Q.2d 1001 (Fed. Cir. 1999); *Technicon Medical Information Sys. Corp. v. Green Bay Packaging Inc.*, 687 F.2d 1032, 215 U.S.P.Q. 1001 (7th Cir. 1982); *Gates Rubber Co. v. Bando American Inc.*, 798 F. Supp. 1499 (D. Colo. 1992); *Warrington Assoc. Inc. v. Real-Time Eng'g Sys. Inc.*, 522 F. Supp. 367, 216 U.S.P.Q. 1024 (N.D. Ill. 1981); *Avdo Corp. v Precision Air Parts Inc.*, 210 U.S.P.Q. 894 (M.D. Ala. 1980); *Synercom Technology Inc. v. University Computing Co.*, 474 F. Supp. 37, 204 U.S.P.Q. 29 (N.D. Tex. 1979); *M. Bryce & Assoc. Inc. v. Gladstone*, 107 Wis. 2d 241, 319 N.W.2d 907, 215 U.S.P.Q. 81 (App. 1982).

10. See, e.g., *Gates Rubber Co. v. Bando American Inc.*, 798 F. Supp. at 1522.

UTILITY PATENT PROTECTION

1. 35 U.S.C. § 101.
2. 35 U.S.C. § 102.
3. 35 U.S.C. § 103.
4. 35 U.S.C. § 102.
5. *Pfaff v. Wells Elecs. Inc.*, 124 F.3d 1429, 43 U.S.P.Q.2d 1928, 1933 (Fed. Cir. 1997), affirmed, 525 U.S. 55, (1998); *UMC Elec. Co. v. United States*, 816 F.2d 647, 656, 2 U.S.P.Q.2d 1465, 1472 (Fed. Cir. 1987).
6. *Vaupel Textilmaschinen RG v. Meccanica Euro Italia S.P.A.*, 944 F.2d 870 (Fed. Cir. 1991).
7. 35 U.S.C. § 101. See *Diamond v. Chakrabarty*, 447 U.S. 303, 309 (1980).
8. 35 U.S.C. § 102.
9. 35 U.S.C. § 103.

10. Since most (albeit not all) of the business method inventions involve Internet communication, and/or the use of databases, I tend to continue to think of the patenting of software and business method inventions as related subjects.

11. *Diamond v. Diehr*, 450 U.S. 175, 101 S. Ct. 1048, 209 U.S.P.Q. 1 (1981); *State Street Bank & Trust Co. v. Signature Financial Group Inc.*, 149 F.3d 1368, 47 U.S.P.Q.2d 1596, 1600 (Fed. Cir. 1998).

12. See U.S. Patent No. 4,614,364, issued September 30, 1986, relating to an advertising insert.

13. *Diamond v. Diehr*, 450 U.S. 175, 101 S. Ct. 1048 (1981).

14. *Diamond v. Bradley*, 450 U.S. 381, 101 S. Ct. 1495 (1981).

15. *South Corp. & Seal Fleet Inc. v. United States*, 690 F.2d 1368 (Fed. Cir. 1982).

16. *In re Freeman*, 573 F.2d 1237, 197 U.S.P.Q. 464 (C.C.P.A. 1978), as modified by *In re Walter*, 618 F.2d 758 (C.C.P.A. 1980); see also *In re Meyer*, 688 F.2d 789 (C.C.P.A. 1982); *In re Maucorps*, 609 F.2d 481 (C.C.P.A. 1979); *In re Gelnovatch*, 594 F.2d 32 (C.C.P.A. 1979); *In re Johnson*, 589 F.2d 1070 (C.C.P.A. 1978); *In re Sarkar*, 588 F.2d 1330 (C.C.P.A. 1978); *In re Waldbaum*, 559 F.2d 611 (C.C.P.A. 1977); *In re Deutsch*, 553 F.2d 689 (C.C.P.A. 1977); *In re Chetfield*, 545 F2d 152 (C.C.P.A. 1976); cert. denied, 434 U.S. 875 (1977).

17. *In re Pardo and Landau*, 684 F.2d 912, 214 U.S.P.Q. 673, 676 (C.C.P.A. 1982).

18. Id. at 677.

19. *In re Taner*, 681 F.2d 787, 214 U.S.P.Q. 678 (C.C.P.A. 1982); *In re Abele*, 684 F.2d 902, 214 U.S.P.Q. 682 (C.C.P.A. 1982).

20. *Manual of Patent Examining Procedure* § 2106, 7th ed., 1999.

21. *State Street Bank & Trust Co. v. Signature Financial Group Inc.*, 149 F.3d 1368, 47 U.S.P.Q.2d 1596, 1600–1602 (Fed. Cir. 1998); *AT&T Corp v. Excel Communications Inc.*, 50 U.S.P.Q.2d 1447, 1452–1453 (Fed. Cir. 1999).

22. *State Street Bank & Trust Co. v. Signature Financial Group Inc.*, 149 F.3d 1368, 47 U.S.P.Q.2d 1596, 1600–02 (Fed. Cir. 1998).

23. *In re Alappat*, 33 F.3d 1526, 1540–41, 31 U.S.P.Q.2d 1545, 1554 (Fed. Cir. 1994) (in banc).

24. *Arrhythmia Research Technology v. Corazonix Corp.*, 958 F.2d 1053 (Fed. Cir. 1992).

25. *State Street*, 149 F.3d at 1373, 47 U.S.P.Q.2d at 1600–01.

26. Id., 47 U.S.P.Q.2d at 1601.

27. *Manual of Patent Examining Procedure* § 2106, 7th ed., rev. 1, Feb. 2000.

28. *Manual of Patent Examining Procedure* § 2106, 7th ed., rev. 1, Feb. 2000, P2100-5-6.

29. *Manual of Patent Examining Procedure* § 2106, 7th ed., rev. 1, Feb. 2000, P2100-5-6; Examination Guidelines for Computer-Related Inventions (Final Version), February 28, 1996, Federal Register (61 Fed. Reg. 7478), as modified May 3, 1999.

30. See *In re Warmerdam*, 33 F.3d 1360, 1361, 31 U.S.P.Q.2d 1754, 1760 (Fed. Cir. 1994) (claim to a data structure per se held nonstatutory); *In re Schrader*, 22

F.3d 290, 297–98, 30 U.S.P.Q.2d 1455, 1461–62 (Fed. Cir. 1994) (claims directed to a method for competitively bidding on plurality of related items held nonstatutory). See also *In re Grams*, 888 F.2d 835 (Fed. Cir. 1989); *Ex parte Akamatsu*, 22 U.S.P.Q. 2d 1915, 1918 (PTO Board of Appeals 1992); *Ex parte Logan*, 20 U.S.P.Q.2d 1465 (PTO Board of Appeals 1991); see also *In re Zeltz*, 892 F.2d 319 (Fed. Cir. 1989); *In re Priest*, 582 F.2d 33, 37 (C.C.P.A. 1978).

31. See Patents classified in PTO Classes: 705 (Automated Business Data Processing Technologies) 701 (Data Processing: Vehicles, Navigation, and Relative Location); 702 (Data Processing: Measuring, Calibrating, or Testing); 704 (Data Processing: Speech Signal Processing, Linguistics, Language Translation, and Audio Compression/Decompression); Class 705 (Data Processing: Financial, Business Practice, Management, or Cost/Price Determination); 706 (Data Processing: Artificial Intelligence); 707 (Data Processing: Financial, Business Practice, Management, or Cost/Price Determination); 708 (Electrical Computers: Arithmetic Processing and Calculating); 709 (Electrical Computers and Digital Processing Systems: Multiple Computer or Process Coordinating); 710 (Electrical Computers and Digital Data Processing Systems: Input/Output); Class 711 (Electrical Computers and Digital Processing Systems: Memory); 712 (Electrical Computers and Digital Processing Systems: Processing Architectures and Instruction Processing [e.g., Processors]); 713 (Electrical Computers and Digital Processing Systems: Support); 714 (Error Detection/Correction and Fault Detection/Recovery); and 364 (Electronic Computer and Data Processors).

32. U.S. PTO White Paper on Business Method Patents, March 2000.

33. *AT&T Corp v. Excel Communications Inc.*, 50 U.S.P.Q.2d 1447, 1452–1453 (Fed. Cir. 1999); *State Street Bank & Trust Co. v. Signature Financial Group Inc.*, 149 F.3d 1368, 47 U.S.P.Q.2d 1596, 1600–1602 (Fed. Cir. 1998); *Amazon.com Inc. v. Barnesandnoble.com Inc.*, 53 U.S.P.Q.2d 1115 (D. WWash. 1999); *Paine, Webber, Jackson & Curtis Inc. v. Merrill Lynch, Pierce, Fenner & Smith Inc.*, 564 F. Supp. 1358, 218 U.S.P.Q. 212 (D. Del. 1983); *Stac Electronics v. Microsoft Corp.*, Case No. CV 93–0413-ER (BX) (C.D. Cal. 1994).

34. 35 U.S.C. § 101.

35. 35 U.S.C. § 102.

36. 35 U.S.C. § 103.

37. *Pfaff v. Wells Elecs. Inc.*, 124 F.3d 1429, 43 U.S.P.Q.2d 1928, 1933 (Fed. Cir. 1997), affirmed, 525 U.S. 55. . . . (1998); *UMC Elec. Co. v. United States*, 816 F.2d 647, 656, 2 U.S.P.Q.2d 1465, 1472 (Fed. Cir. 1987).

38. 35 U.S.C. § 102.

39. *Helifix Ltd. v. Blok-Lok Ltd.*, 54 U.S.P.Q.2d 1299, 1303 (Fed. Cir. 2000).

40. 35 U.S.C. § 103.

41. *Pfaff v. Wells Elecs. Inc.*, 124 F.3d 1429, 43 U.S.P.Q.2d 1928, 1933 (Fed. Cir. 1997), affirmed, 525 U.S. 55. . . . (1998); *UMC Elec. Co. v. United States*, 816 F.2d 647, 656, 2 U.S.P.Q.2d 1465, 1472 (Fed. Cir. 1987).

42. See *J.A. LaPorte Inc. v. Norfolk Dredging Co.*, 787 F.2d 1577 (Fed. Cir. 1986); *W.L. Gore & Associates Inc. v. Garlock Inc.* 721 F.2d 1540 (Fed. Cir. 1983). See also *Lockwood v. American Airlines Inc*, 107 F.3d 1565, 41 U.S.P.Q.2d 1961 (Fed. Cir. 1997). See also 35 U.S.C. § 273.

43. See *Northern Telecom Inc. v. Datapoint Corp.,* 908 F.2d 931, 935, 15 U.S.P.Q.2d 1321 (Fed. Cir.), cert. denied, 498 U.S. 920 (1990); *Massachusetts Institute of Technology v. AB Fortia*, 774 F.2d 1104, 1109, 227 U.S.P.Q. 428, 432 (Fed. Cir. 1985).

44. See *Constant v. Advance Micro Devices Inc.*, 848 F.2d 1560 (Fed. Cir. 1988); *In re Hall*, 781 F.2d 897 (Fed. Cir. 1986); *Massachusetts Institute of Technology v. A.B. Fortia*, 777 F.2d 1104 (Fed. Cir. 1985); see also *Northern Telcom Inc. v. Datapoint Corp.,* 908 F.2d 931 (Fed. Cir. 1990); *In re Cronyn*, 890 F.2d 1158 (Fed. Cir. 1989); *Preemption Devices Inc. v. Minnesota Mining & Manufacturing Co.*, 732 F.2d 903 (Fed. Cir. 1984).

45. See *In re Hall*, 781 F.2d 897 (Fed. Cir. 1986).

46. See, e.g., *In re Mann*, 861 F.2d 1581 (Fed. Cir. 1988); *Harrington Manufacturing Co. v. Powell Manufacturing Co.*, 815 F.2d 1478 (Fed. Cir. 1986).

47. See *Baxter Int'l. Inc. v. COBE Laboratories Inc.*, 88 F.3d 1054, 1058–59, 39 U.S.P.Q.2d 1437, 1440 (Fed. Cir. 1996) (third-party prior use accessible to the public is a section 102[b] bar); *Lockwood v. American Airlines Inc*, 107 F.3d 1565, 41 U.S.P.Q.2d 1961 (Fed. Cir. 1997).

48. See *W.L. Gore & Associates Inc. v. Garlock Inc.*, 721 F.2d 1540 (Fed. Cir. 1983); see also *J.A. LaPorte Inc. v. Norfolk Dredging Co.*, 787 F.2d 1577 (Fed. Cir. 1986). See also 35 U.S.C. § 273 ("prior inventor" defense to business method patent is not a bar).

49. See *Kinzenbaw v. Deere & Co.*, 741 F.2d 383 (Fed. Cir. 1984); *D.L. Auld Co. v. Chroma Graphics Corp.*, 714 F.2d 1144, 1150, 219 U.S.P.Q. 13, 17 (Fed. Cir. 1983).

50. See, e.g., *Kinzenbaw v. Deere & Co.*, 741 F.2d 383 (Fed. Cir. 1984), *D.L. Auld Co. v. Chroma Graphics Corp.*, 714 F.2d 1144, 1150, 219 U.S.P.Q. 13, 17 (Fed. Cir. 1983); *W. L. Gore & Associates v. Garlock Inc.*, 721 F.2d 1540, 220 U.S.P.Q. 303 (Fed. Cir. 1983); *Grain Processing Corp. v. American Maize Products Corp.*, 840 F.2d 902 (Fed. Cir. 1988).

51. See *LaBounty Manufacturing Inc. v. U.S. ITC,* 958 F.2d 1066 (Fed. Cir. 1992); *Manville Sales Corp. v. Paramount Systems Inc.,* 917 F.2d 544 (Fed. Cir. 1990); *Grain Processing Corp. v. American Maize Products Corp.,* 840 F.2d 902 (Fed. Cir. 1988); *In re Brigance*, 792 F.2d 1103 (Fed. Cir. 1986).

52. See *U.S. Environmental Products Inc. v. Westall,* 911 F.2d 713 (Fed. Cir. 1990); *In re Hamilton*, 882 F.2d 1576 (Fed. Cir. 1989); *Baker Oil Tools Inc. v. Geo Vann Inc.,* 828 F.2d 1588 (Fed. Cir. 1987); *Western Marine Electronics Inc. v. Furuno Electric Co.*, 764 F.2d 840 (Fed. Cir. 1985).

53. *U.S. Environmental Products Inc. v. Westall,* 911 F.2d 713 (Fed. Cir. 1990).

54. See, e.g., *RCA Corp. v. Data General Corp.,* 887 F.2d 1056 (Fed. Cir. 1989); *In*

re Mann, 861 F.2d 1581 (Fed. Cir. 1988); *In re Brigance*, 792 F.2d 1103 (Fed. Cir. 1986); *Pennwalt Corp. v. Akzona Inc.*, 740 F.2d 1573 (Fed. Cir. 1984); *In re Smith*, 714 F.2d 1127 (Fed. Cir. 1983).

55. *Pfaff v. Wells Elecs. Inc.*, 525 U.S. 55, 119 S.Ct. 304, 311, 48 U.S.P.Q.2d 1641, 1646 (1998).

56. *Pfaff v. Wells Elecs. Inc.*, 124 F.3d 1429, 43 U.S.P.Q.2d 1928, 1933 (Fed. Cir. 1997), affirmed, 525 U.S. 55, (1998), citing *Baker Oil Tools v. Geo Vann Inc.*, 828 F.2d 1558, 1563, 4 U.S.P.Q.2d 1210, 1213 (Fed. Cir. 1987).

57. *UMC Elec. Co. v. United States*, 816 F.2d 647, 656, 2 U.S.P.Q.2d 1465, 1472 (Fed. Cir. 1987).

58. *Buildex Inc. v. Kason Indus.*, 849 F.2d 1461, 1464, 7 U.S.P.Q.2d 1325, 1327–28 (Fed. Cir. 1988).

59. See e.g., *Kinzenbaw v. Deere & Co.*, 741 F.2d 383 (Fed. Cir. 1984), *D.L. Auld Co. v. Chroma Graphics Corp.*, 714 F.2d 1144, 1150, 219 U.S.P.Q. 13, 17 (Fed. Cir. 1983); *W. L. Gore & Associates v. Garlock Inc.*, 721 F.2d 1540, 220 U.S.P.Q. 303 (Fed. Cir. 1983).

60. *Moleculon Research Corp. v. CBS Inc.*, 793 F.2d 1261, 1267, 229 U.S.P.Q. 805, 809 (Fed. Cir. 1986) (holding that "[a]n assignment or sale of rights in the invention and potential patent rights is not a sale of the invention within the meaning of section 102[b]").

61. See *Robotic Vision Sys. Inc. v. View Eng'g. Inc.*, 112 F.3d 1163, 42 U.S.P.Q.2d 1619, 1624 (Fed. Cir. 1997) ("Completion of the invention prior to the critical date, pursuant to an offer to sell that invention, would validate what had been theretofore an inchoate, but not yet established, bar. It would validate it, however, as of the date of that completion, not the date of the original offer. Completion after the critical date, even if pursuant to the offer, would not create a bar.")

62. See *STX LLC v. Brine Inc.*, 54 U.S.P.Q.2d 1347, 1350 (Fed. Cir. 2000); *Weatherchem Corp. v. J.L. Clark Inc.*, 163 F.3d 1326, 1333–4, 49 U.S.P.Q.2d 1001, 1007 (Fed. Cir. 1998).

63. See *Weatherchem Corp. v. J.L. Clark Inc.*, 163 F.3d 1326, 1333–4, 49 U.S.P.Q.2d 1001, 1007 (Fed. Cir. 1998).

64. U.S. patent applications filed prior to November 29, 2000, are maintained in secrecy until the application issues as a patent, or is abandoned and referred to in an issued (published) patent. However, in an attempt to harmonize the U.S. law with that of other countries, applications filed after November 29, 2000, will be published 18 months after filing, unless a request not to publish is filed with the U.S. application, certifying that the invention disclosed in the application will not be published in another jurisdiction (i.e., is not the subject of an application filed in a publishing jurisdiction) or is abandoned within 18 months of filing. See 35 U.S.C. § 122.

65. See *Paulik v. Rizkalla*, 760 F.2d 1270 (Fed. Cir. 1985).

66. 35 U.S.C. §§ 184, 185.

67. See, e.g., *PerSeptive Biosystems Inc. v. Pharmacia Biotech Inc.*, 56 U.S.P.Q.2d 1001 (Fed. Cir. 2000); *New England Braiding Co. Inc. v. A.W. Chesterton Co.*, 970 F.2d 878 (Fed. Cir. 1992); *MCV Inc. v. King-Seeley Thermos Co.*, 870 F.2d 1568 (Fed. Cir. 1989); *Transworld Mfg. Corp. v. Al Nyman & Sons Inc.*, 750 F.2d 1552 (Fed. Cir. 1984).

68. 35 U.S.C. §§ 116, 256; 37 C.F.R. § 1.48. See *Stark v. Advanced Magnetics Inc.*, 119 F.3d 1551, 43 U.S.P.Q.2d 1321 (Fed. Cir. 1997).

69. 35 U.S.C. §§ 116, 262. See *Kimberly Clark Corp. v. Proctor & Gamble Distributing Co. Inc.*, 973 F.2d 911 (Fed. Cir. 1992); *In re Kaplan*, 789 F.2d 1574 (Fed. Cir. 1986).

70. 35 U.S.C. § 120.

71. 35 U.S.C. § 103.

72. If the invention concerned is a method of doing or conducting business there is a limited personal "prior inventor" defense applicable even if the invention was maintained as a secret. This prior inventor defense, however, does not bar obtaining a patent enforceable against anyone who is not a "prior inventor." 35 U.S.C. § 273.

73. See, e.g., *New Idea Farm Equip. Corp. v. Sperry Corp.*, 916 F.2d 1561 (Fed. Cir. 1990).

74. See, e.g., *Cooper v. Goldfarb*, 154 F.3d 1321, 1327, 47 U.S.P.Q.2d 1896, 1901 (Fed. Cir. 1998); *Hybritech Inc. v. Monoclonal Antibodies Inc.*, 802 F.2d 1367 (Fed. Cir. 1986); *Coleman v. Dines*, 754 F.2d 353 (Fed. Cir. 1985); *Morgan v. Hirsch*, 728 F.2d 1449 (Fed. Cir. 1984).

75. See, e.g., *Coleman v. Dines*, 754 F.2d 353.

76. See *DSL Dynamic Sciences Ltd. v. Union Switch & Signal Inc.*, 928 F.2d 1122 (Fed. Cir. 1991); *UMC Electronics Co. v. United States*, 816 F.2d 647 (Fed. Cir. 1987); *Newkirk v. Lulejian*, 825 F.2d 1581 (Fed. Cir. 1987).

77. See, e.g., *Hazeltine Corp. v. United States*, 820 F.2d 1190 (Fed. Cir. 1987).

78. *Holmwood v. Balasubramanyan Sugavanam*, 948 F.2d 1236 (Fed. Cir. 1991); *New Idea Farm Equip. Corp. v. Sperry Corp.*, 916 F.2d 1561 (Fed. Cir. 1990); *Hahn v. Wong*, 892 F.2d 1028 (Fed. Cir. 1989).

79. 35 U.S.C. § 103.

80. See, e.g., *Ryko Manufacturing Co. v. Hu-Star Inc.*, 950 F.2d 714 (Fed. Cir. 1991); *Custom Accessories Inc. v. Jeffrey-Allen Industries Inc.*, 807 F.2d 955 (Fed. Cir. 1986); *Vandenberg v. Dairy Equip. Co., Div. of DEC Int'l. Inc.*, 740 F.2d 1560, 224 U.S.P.Q. 195 (Fed. Cir. 1984); *Orthopedic Equip. Co. v. United States*, 702 F.2d 1005, 217 U.S.P.Q 193 (Fed. Cir. 1983); *Stratoflex Inc. v. Aeroquip Corp.*, 713 F.2d 1530, 218 U.S.P.Q. 871 (Fed. Cir. 1983); *Chore-Time Equip. Inc. v. Cumberland Corp.*, 713 F.2d 774, 218 U.S.P.Q. 673 (Fed. Cir. 1983).

81. *Heidelberger Druckmoschinen AG v. Hantscho Commercial Products Inc.*, 30 U.S.P.Q. 2d 1377 (Fed. Cir. 1994); *In re Fritch*, 972 F.2d 1200 (Fed. Cir. 1992); *Uniroyal Inc. v. Rudkin-Wiley Corp.*, 837 F.2d 1044 (Fed. Cir. 1988).

82. *Eibel Process Co. v. Minnesota & Ontario Paper Co.*, 261 U.S. 45, 43. S.Ct. 322 (1923); *In re Wright,* 848 F.2d 1216 (Fed. Cir. 1988).

83. See, e.g., *In re Jones,* 958 F.2d 347 (Fed. Cir. 1992); *In re Vaeck,* 947 F.2d 488 (Fed. Cir. 1991); *Northern Telecom Inc. v. Datapoint Corp.,* 908 F.2d 931 (Fed. Cir. 1990); *In re Laskowski,* 871 F.2d 115 (Fed. Cir. 1989); *Diversitech Corp. v. Century Steps Inc.*, 850 F.2d 675 (Fed. Cir. 1988); *Smith Kline Diagnostics Inc. v. Helena Laboratories Corp.*, 859 F.2d 878 (Fed. Cir. 1988); *Vandenberg,* 740 F.2d 1560; *ACS Hosp. Sys. Inc. v. Montefiore Hosp.*, 732 F.2d 1572, 221 U.S.P.Q. 929 (Fed. Cir. 1984); *In re Piasecki,* 745 F.2d 1468, 223 U.S.P.Q. 785 (Fed. Cir. 1984); *Lear Siegler Inc. v. Aeroquip Corp.*, 733 F.2d 881, 221 U.S.P.Q. 1025 (Fed. Cir. 1984); *In re Sernaker,* 702 F.2d 989, 217 U.S.P.Q. 1 (Fed. Cir. 1983).

84. 35 U.S.C. § 273.

85. 35 U.S.C. §§ 273(a)(3), 273(b)3(A).

86. 35 U.S.C. § 273(b)(3)(B).

87. 35 U.S.C. § 273(b)(1).

88. 35 U.S.C. §§ 273(a)(1), 273(b)(1).

89. 35 U.S.C. § 273(b)(6).

90. 35 U.S.C. §§ 273(a)(3), 273(b)3(A).

91. 35 U.S.C. § 273(b)3(B).

92. 35 U.S.C. § 273(b)2.

93. 35 U.S.C. § 273(b)3(C).

94. 35 U.S.C. § 273(b)6.

95. 35 U.S.C. § 273(b)7.

96. 35 U.S.C. § 273(b)8.

97. 35 U.S.C. § 120.

98. 35 U.S.C. § 154(a)(2).

99. 37 C.F.R. § 1.114.

100. 35 U.S.C. § 121.

101. 35 U.S.C. § 154(a)(2).

102. 35 U.S.C. § 111.

103. 37 C.F.R. § 154(f).

104. 35 U.S.C. § 111(b).

105. 35 U.S.C. § 111(b).

106. 37 C.F.R. § 153(i).

107. 37 C.F.R. § 178(a)(3)–(4).

108. 35 U.S.C. §§ 111(b), 287(a).

109. 35 U.S.C. § 119.

110. 35 U.S.C. §§ 111(b), 119(e).

111. 35 U.S.C. § 154(a)(2).

112. 35 U.S.C. § 111(b)(1)(A), 37 C.F.R. §§ 1.51(c), 1.53(c), 1.71.

113. MPEP § 601.

114. 35 U.S.C. §§ 111, 112, 113, 115; 37 C.F.R. § 1.51.
115. 37 C.F.R. § 154(f).
116. See 37 C.F.R. § 1.77; Manual of Patent Examining Procedure § 608.01(a).
117. 35 U.S.C. § 113; 37 C.F.R. §§ 1.81–1.88; see also *Manual of Patent Examining Procedure* § 608.2.
118. 37 C.F.R. § 1.63.
119. 37 C.F.R. § 1.53.
120. See 37 C.F.R. §§ 1.97, 1.98.
121. 37 C.F.R. § 1.10.
122. *Hazeltine Corp. v. United States*, 820 F.2d 1190 (Fed. Cir. 1987).
123. 37 C.F.R. § 1.53.
124. 37 C.F.R. § 1.53(d).
125. The amount of the surcharge is set forth in 37 C.F.R. § 1.16(e).
126. 37 C.F.R. § 1.136.
127. 35 U.S.C. § 287(a).
128. 35 U.S.C. § 292.
129. 35 U.S.C. §§ 271, 284.
130. See *CR Bard Inc. v. Advanced Cardiovascular Systems Inc.*, 911 F.2d 670 (Fed. Cir. 1990); *Hewlett-Packard Co. v. Bausch & Lomb Inc.*, 909 F.2d 1464 (Fed. Cir. 1990); *Lumnis Industries Inc. v. DM&E Corp.*, 862 F.2d 267 (Fed. Cir. 1988); *Hodosh v. Block Drug Co.*, 833 F.2d 1575 (Fed. Cir. 1987); *Dana Corp. v. American Precision Co.*, 827 F.2d 755 (Fed. Cir. 1987).
131. See, e.g., *Hewlett-Packard v. Bausch & Lomb*, 909 F.2d 1464 (Fed. Cir. 1990); *Water Technologies Corp. v. Calco Ltd.*, 850 F.2d 660 (Fed. Cir. 1988); *Orthokinetics, Inc. v. Safety Travel Chairs Inc.*, 806 F.2d 1565 (Fed. Cir. 1986); *Powerlift Inc. v. Lang Pools Inc.*, 774 F.2d 478 (Fed. Cir. 1985).
132. 35 U.S.C. § 271(f).
133. 28 U.S.C. § 1338.
134. 28 U.S.C. §§ 1391(c), 1400, 1694; *In re the Regents of the Univ. of Cal.*, 964 F.2d 1128, 1132 (Fed. Cir. 1992); *V.E. Holding Corp. v. Johnson Gas Appliance Co.*, 917 F.2d 1574, 1584, 16 U.S.P.Q.2d 1614 (Fed. Cir. 1990); cert. denied, 111 S. Ct. 1315 (1991).
135. 35 U.S.C. § 284.
136. 35 U.S.C. § 283.
137. 35 U.S.C. § 285
138. 35 U.S.C. § 284.
139. *Beatrice Foods Co. v. New England Printing & Lithographing Co.*, 899 F.2d 1171 (Fed. Cir. 1990); *Smithkline Diagnostics Inc. v. Helena Laboratories Corp.*, 926 F.2d 1161 (Fed. Cir. 1991); *Minnesota Mining & Manufacturing Co. v. Johnson & Johnson Orthopaedics Inc.*, 976 F.2d 1559 (Fed. Cir. 1992).
140. *Smithkline Diagnostics Inc. v. Helena Laboratories Corp.*, 926 F.2d 1161

(Fed. Cir. 1991); *Minnesota Mining & Manufacturing Co. v. Johnson & John-son Orthopaedics Inc.,* 976 F.2d 1559 (Fed. Cir. 1992).

141. Pursuant to 35 U.S.C. § 122.

142. 35 U.S.C. § 154(d).

143. *Radio Stell & Mfg. Co. v. MTD Products Inc.,* 788 F.2d 1554 (Fed. Cir. 1986).

144. 35 U.S.C. § 284.

145. *Read Corp. v. Portec Inc.,* 970 F.2d 816 (Fed. Cir. 1992); *Braun Inc. v. Dynamics Corporation of America,* 975 F.2d 815 (Fed. Cir. 1992); *Minnesota Mining & Manufacturing Co. v. Johnson & Johnson Orthopaedics Inc.,* 976 F.2d 1559 (Fed. Cir. 1992).

146. 35 U.S.C. § 284.

147. 35 U.S.C. § 286. However, an action for "provisional rights damages" must be brought within six years of the patent issue date. 35 U.S.C. § 154(d)(3).

148. 35 U.S.C. § 287; see also, e.g., Devices for Medicine Inc. v. Boehl, 822 F.2d 1062 (Fed. Cir. 1987).

149. 19 U.S.C. § 1337.

150. 19 U.S.C. § 1337(a).

151. 35 U.S.C. § 41(c).

152. 35 U.S.C. § 301; 37 C.F.R. § 1.501.

153. The prosecution history of a patent is not generally available to the public during the pendency of the application (except for publication of the application at 18 months under 35 U.S.C. § 122). It is, however, accessible to the public after the patent is granted.

154. 35 U.S.C. §§ 301–307; 35 U.S.C. §§ 311–318; 37 C.F.R. §§ 1.510, 1.525–1.565.

155. 35 U.S.C. §§ 301–307.

156. 35 U.S.C. § 305.

157. 35 U.S.C. § 306.

158. 35 U.S.C. § 314.

159. 35 U.S.C. § 314(b)(3).

160. 35 U.S.C. § 315(b).

161. 35 U.S.C. § 315(c).

162. See 35 U.S.C. § 262; *Willingham v. Star Cutter Co.,* 555 F.2d 1340, 1344 (6th Cir. 1977); *Lemelson v. Synergistics Res. Co.,* 669 F.Supp. 642, 645 (S.D.N.Y. 1987); *Intel Corp. v. ULSI System Technology Inc.,* 27 U.S.P.Q.2d 1136 (Fed. Cir. 1993); *Schering Corp. v. Roussel-UCLAF SA* 41 U.S.P.Q.2d 1359 (Fed. Cir. 1997); *Ethicon Inc. v. United States Surgical Corp.* 45 U.S.P.Q.2d 1545 (Fed. Cir. 1998).

163. *Teets v. Chromalloy Gas Turbine Corp.,* 38 U.S.P.Q.2d 1695 ● (Fed. Cir. 1996).

164. See *United States v. Dubliler Condenser Corp.,* 289 U.S. 178 (1938); *McElmurry v. Arkansas Power & Light Co.* 27 U.S.P.Q.2d 1129 (Fed. Cir. 1993); *Marshall v. Colgate Palmolive-Peet Co.,* 175 F.2d 215 (3d Cir. 1949); *Wellington Print Works v. Magid,* 242 F. Supp. 614 (E.D. Pa. 1965); *Simms v. Mac Truck Corp.,* 488 F. Supp. 592 (E.D. Pa. 1980).

DESIGN PATENT PROTECTION

1. See *Ex parte Strijland*, 26 U.S.P.Q.2d 1259 (PTO Board of Appeals and Interferences, 1992).
2. 35 U.S.C. § 171.
3. See *Lee v. Dayton-Hudson Corp.*, 838 F.2d 1186 (Fed. Cir. 1988).
4. *Gorham v. White*, 81 U.S. 511, 528 (1971); *Goodyear Tire & Rubber Co. v. Hercules Tire and Rubber Co.*, 48 U.S.P.Q.2d 1767 (Fed. Cir. 1998); *Elmer v. ICC Fabricating Inc.*, 67 F.3d 1571, 1577, 36 U.S.P.Q.2d 1417, 1420 (Fed. Cir. 1995); *Sun Hill Industries Inc. v. Easter Unlimited Inc.*, 33 U.S.P.Q.2d 1925 (Fed. Cir., 1995); *Braun Inc. v. Dynamics Corporation of America*, 975 F.2d 815 (Fed. Cir. 1992); *Oakley Inc. v. International Tropic-Cal Inc.*, 923 F.2d 167 (Fed. Cir. 1991); *Avia Group International Inc. v. L.A. Gear California Inc.*, 853 F.2d 1557 (Fed. Cir. 1988); *FMC Corp. v. Hennessey Industries Inc.*, 836 F.2d 521 (Fed. Cir. 1987); *Litton Systems Inc. v. Whirlpool Corp.*, 728 F.2d 1423 (Fed. Cir. 1984).
5. 35 U.S.C. § 289.

COPYRIGHT PROTECTION

1. *Harper & Row Publishers Inc. v. Nation Enterprises*, 471 U.S. 539, 546 (1985) ("The rights conferred by copyright are designed to assure contributors to the store to knowledge a fair return for their labors.")
2. 17 U.S.C. § 106.
3. 17 U.S.C. § 101 (definition of work of visual art); 17 U.S.C. § 106A.
4. 17 U.S.C. §§ 1201 et. seq.
5. 17 U.S.C. § 1201(a)(1)(A).
6. 17 U.S.C. § 1201(a)(2).
7. 17 U.S.C. § 1202.
8. 17 U.S.C. § 512.
9. 17 U.S.C. § 102(a).
10. 17 U.S.C. § 101 (a "computer program" is a set of statements or instructions to be used directly or indirectly computer in order to bring about a certain result; "Literary works" are works . . . expressed in words, numbers, or other verbal or numerical symbols or indicia, regardless of the nature of the material objects, such as . . . film, tapes, disks, or cards, in which they are embodied); 17 U.S.C. § 117; *Gates Rubber Co. v. Bando Chemical Indus. Ltd*, 9 F.3d 823, 28 U.S.P.Q.2d 1503, 1513 (10th Cir. 1993).
11. 17 U.S.C. § 101 (a "compilation" is a work formed by the collection and assembling of pre-existing materials or of data that are selected, coordinated, or arranged in such a way that the resulting work as a whole constitutes an original work of authorship); 17 U.S.C. § 103.

12. 17 U.S.C. § 102(b).

13. *Feist Publications Inc. v. Rural Telephone Services Co.*, 111 S. Ct. 1282, 1296, 18 U.S.P.Q.2d 1275 (1991).

14. *Feist*, 111 S. Ct. at 1288.

15. *Feist Publications Inc. v. Rural Telephone Services Co.*, 111 S. Ct. 1282, 18 U.S.P.Q.2d 1275 (1991); *CMM Cable Rep. Inc. v. Ocean Coast Properties Inc.*, 97 F.3d 1504, U.S.P.Q.2d 1065, 1077–78 (1st Cir. 1996).

16. *Toro Co. v. R & R Products Co.*, 787 F.2d 1208, 1213, 229 U.S.P.Q. 282 (8th Cir. 1986).

17. *Mitel Inc. v. Iqtel Inc.*, 124 F.3d 1366, 44 U.S.P.Q.2d 1172, 1178 (10th Cir. 1997).

18. *CMM Cable Rep Inc. v. Ocean Coast Properties Inc.*, 97 F.3d 1504, U.S.P.Q.2d 1065, 1077–78 (1st Cir. 1996) (copyright law denies protection to "fragmentary words and phrases" . . . on the grounds that these materials do not exhibit the minimal level of creativity necessary to warrant copyright protection). See also *Arica Inst. Inc. v. Palmer,* 970 F.2d 1067, 1072–73, 23 U.S.P.Q.2d 1593 (2d Cir. 1992) (noting that single words and short phrases in copyrighted text are not copyrightable); *Alberto-Culver Co. v. Andrea Dumon Inc.*, 466 F.2d 705, 711, 175 U.S.P.Q. 194 (7th Cir. 1972) (holding that "most personal sort of deodorant" is short phrase or expression, not an "appreciable amount of text," and thus not protectable); *Perma Greetings Inc. v. Russ Berrie & Co. Inc.*, 598 F. Supp. 445, 448 223 U.S.P.Q. 670 (E.D.Mo. 1984) ("Cliched language, phrases and expressions conveying an idea that is typically expressed in a limited number of stereotypic fashions, [*sic*] are not subject to copyright protection.")

19. See *West Publ'g. Co. v. Mead Data Central Inc.*, 799 F.2d 1219, 230 U.S.P.Q. 801 (8th Cir. 1986).

20. For the sake of simplicity, I have adopted certain shorthand conventions. I use the term "idea" to include not only "ideas," but also "concepts," "principles," and "discoveries." I use the terms "functional element," "utilitarian element," and/or "useful article" to mean anything that has an intrinsic function other than just portraying appearance or conveying information (such as a procedure, process, system, or method of operation) or which is required to be in a particular form because of some external factor.

21. *Baker v. Selden*, 101 U.S. 99 (1979).

22. *CMM Cable Rep Inc. v. Ocean Coast Properties Inc.,* 97 F.3d 1504, 1516 41 U.S.P.Q.2d 1065 (1st Cir. 1996).

23. *Gates Rubber Co. v. Bando Chemical Indus. Ltd.*, 9 F.3d 823, 28 U.S.P.Q.2d 1503 (10th Cir. 1993).

24. *Feist*, 111 S. Ct. at 1289; *Applied Innovations Inc. v. Regents of the Univ. of Minnesota,* 876 F.2d 626, 636, 11 U.S.P.Q.2d 1041 (8th Cir. 1989).

25. *Feist*, 111 S. Ct. at 1290.

26. *Feist*, 111 S. Ct. 1288.

27. If the elements that are copied (e.g., the characters) create a likelihood that consumers would think that there is an association between the respective authors, there may be unfair competition—trademark infringement.

28. See *Warner Bros. Inc. v. American Broadcasting Co. Inc.*, 720 F.2d 231, 241, 222 U.S.P.Q. 101 (2d Cir. 1983); *Burroughs v. Metro-Goldwyn-Mayer Inc.*, 683 F.2d 610, 621, 215 U.S.P.Q. 495, 504 (2d Cir. 1982).

29. *Reyher v. Children's Television Workshop*, 533 F.2d 87, 90–91, 190 U.S.P.Q. 387, 390 (2d Cir.), cert. denied, 429 U.S. 980, 192 U.S.P.Q. 64 (1976).

30. *Warner Bros. Pictures Inc. v. Columbia Broadcasting System Inc.*, 216 F.2d 945, 104 U.S.P.Q. 103 (9th Cir. 1954), cert. denied, 348 U.S. 971, 105 U.S.P.Q. 518 (1955). (It is conceivable that the character really constitutes the story being told, but if the character is only the chessman in the game of telling the story he is not within the area of the protection afforded by the copyright.) But see *Ideal Toy Corp. v. Kenner Products Division of General Mills Fun Group Inc.*, 443 F.Supp. 291, 305, 197 U.S.P.Q. 738, 749 (S.D. N.Y. 1977).

31. *Attia v. Society of the New York Hospital*, 201 F.3d 50, 59, 53 U.S.P.Q.2d 1253 (2d Cir. 1999).

32. *CMM Cable Rep Inc. v. Ocean Coast Properties Inc.*, 97 F.3d 1504, 1516, 41 U.S.P.Q.2d 1065 (1st Cir. 1996) (copyright law denies protection to "forms of expression dictated solely at functional considerations"); *Kregos v. Associated Press*, 937 F.2d 700, 705, 19 U.S.P.Q.2d 1161 (2d Cir. 1991) (in those instances where there is only one or so few ways of expressing an idea that protection of the expression would effectively accord protection to the idea itself).

33. *Feist Publications v. Rural Telephone Service Co.*, 111 U.S. 1282 (1991); *Atari Games Corp. v. Nintendo of America*, 975 F.2d 832, 837 (Fed. Cir. 1992); *Brown Bag Software v. Symantec Corp.*, 960 F.2d 1465 (9th Cir. 1992); *SOS Inc. v. Payday Inc.*, 886 F.2d 1081, 1085 (9th Cir. 1989).

34. *Atari Inc. v. North Am. Philips Consumer Elec. Corp.*, 672 F.2d 607 (7th Cir. 1982), cert. denied, 103 S.Ct. 176 (1982).

35. The statute of limitations with respect to copyright actions is three years from the date the claim accrued (typically interpreted to be when the copyright holder should have become aware of the purported infringement). See 17 U.S.C. § 507(b).

36. 17 U.S.C. §§ 107–112.

37. 17 U.S.C. § 117.

38. 17 U.S.C. § 107.

39. See, e.g., *Harper & Row Publishers v. Nation Enter.*, 471 U.S. 539 (1985); *20th Century Music v. Aiken*, 422 U.S. 151 (1975); *Sega Enterprises Ltd. v. Accolade Inc.*, 977 F.2d 1510 (9th Cir. 1993); *Atari Games Corp. v. Nintendo of America Inc.*, 975 F.2d 832 (Fed. Cir. 1992); *New Kids on the Block v. News AM Publishing*, 971 F.2d 302 (9th Cir. 1992); *Lewis Galoob Toys Inc. v. Nintendo of America Inc.*, 22 U.S.P.Q.2d 1857 (9th Cir. 1992); *Narell v. Freeman*,

872 F.2d 907 (9th Cir. 1989); *Fisher v. Dees,* 794 F.2d 432 (9th Cir. 1986); *American Geophysical Union v. Texaco Inc.,* 24 U.S.P.Q.2d 1796 (S.D. N.Y. 1992).

40. *Campbell v. Acuff-Rose Music Inc.*, 510 U.S. 569, 586, 29 U.S.P.Q.2d 1961 (1994).

41. *Campbell v. Acuff-Rose Music Inc.*, 510 U.S. 569, 586, 29 U.S.P.Q.2d 1961 (1994).

42. *Sony Computer Entertainment Inc. v. Connectix Corp.,* 203 F.3d 596, 606, 53 U.S.P.Q.2d 1705 (9th Cir. 2000); *Sega Enters. Ltd. v. Accolade Inc.*, 977 F.2d 1510, 1520, 24 U.S.P.Q.2d 1561 (9th Cir. 1993).

43. 17 U.S.C. § 110.

44. 17 U.S.C. § 110(1).

45. 17 U.S.C. § 110(2).

46. 17 U.S.C. §§ 110(2), (8)–(10).

47. 17 U.S.C. § 110(3).

48. 17 U.S.C. §§ 110(4), (10).

49. 17 U.S.C. § 110(5).

50. The copyright statute (17 U.S.C. § 101), defines an "establishment" as "a store, shop, or any similar place of business open to the general public for the primary purpose of selling goods or services in which the majority of the gross square feet of space that is nonresidential is used for that purpose, and in which nondramatic musical works are performed publicly."

51. 17 U.S.C. § 110(5).

52. 17 U.S.C. § 110(5)(B)(i), (B)(ii).

53. A "food service or drinking establishment" is defined (17 U.S.C. § 101) as "a restaurant, inn, bar, tavern, or any other similar place of business in which the public or patrons assemble for the primary purpose of being served food or drink, in which the majority of the gross square feet of space that is nonresidential is used for that purpose, and in which nondramatic musical works are performed publicly."

54. The copyright statute (17 U.S.C. § 101) defines the "gross square feet of space of an establishment" as "the entire interior space of that establishment, and any adjoining outdoor space used to serve patrons, whether on a seasonal basis or otherwise."

55. "Phonorecords," including audiotapes and records, are covered by special provisions of the copyright law, but will not be dealt with in this handbook.

56. 17 U.S.C. § 101 (a "computer program" is a set of statements or instructions to be used directly or indirectly computer in order to bring about a certain result; "literary works" are works . . . expressed in words, numbers, or other verbal or numerical symbols or indicia, regardless of the nature of the material objects, such as . . . film, tapes, disks, or cards, in which they are embodied); 17 U.S.C. § 117; *Gates Rubber Co. v. Bando Chemical Indus. Ltd.*, 9 F.3d 823, 28 U.S.P.Q.2d 1503, 1513 (10th Cir. 1993).

57. *Midway Mfg. Co. v. Dirkschneider,* 543 F.Supp. 466, 214 U.S.P.Q. 417 (D. Neb.

1981); *Atari Inc. v. Amusement World Inc.*, 547 F.Supp. 222, 215 U.S.P.Q. 929 (D. Md. 1981); *Stern Elec. Inc. v. Kaufman*, 523 F. Supp. 635, 213 U.S.P.Q. 75 (E.D. N.Y. 1981), *affirmed*, 669 F.2d 852, 213 U.S.P.Q. 443 (2d Cir. 1982).

58. *Manufactures Technologies Inc. v. Cams Inc.*, 706 F.Supp. 984, 10 U.S.P.Q. 1321 (D. Conn. 1989); *Broderbund Software Inc. v. Unison World Inc.*, 648 F. Supp. 1127, 231 U.S.P.Q. 700 (N.D. Cal. 1986).

59. *Digital Communications Assoc. v. Softklone Distrib. Corp.*, 659 F.Supp. 499, 2 U.S.P.Q. 1385 (N.D. Ga.1987).

60. *Data Cash Sys. Inc. v. JS&A Group Inc.*, 480 F.Supp. 1063, 203 U.S.P.Q. 735 (N.D. Ill. 1979) aff'd. on other grounds, 628 F.2d 1038, 208 U.S.P.Q. 197 (7th Cir. 1980).

61. *Apple Computer Inc. v. Formula Int'l Inc.*, 725 F.2d 521, 221 U.S.P.Q. 762 (9th Cir. 1984); *Apple Computer Inc. v. Franklin Computer Corp.*, 714 F.2d 1240, 219 U.S.P.Q. 113 (3d Cir. 1983); *Williams Elec. Inc. v. Artic Int'l. Inc.*, 685 F.2d 870, 215 U.S.P.Q. 405 (3d Cir. 1982); *GCA Corp. v. Chance*, 217 U.S.P.Q. 718 (N.D. Cal. 1982); *Midway Mfg. Co. v. Artic Int'l. Inc.*, 547 F.Supp. 999 (N.D. Ill. 1982); *Tandy Corp. v. Personal Micro Computers Inc.*, 524 F.Supp. 171 214 U.S.P.Q. 178 (N.D. Cal. 1981).

62. *GCA v. Chance*, 217 U.S.P.Q. 718; *Data Cash*, 480 F. Supp. 1063; *Apple v. Franklin*, 714 F.2d 1240.

63. *Apple v. Franklin*, 714 F.2d 1240; *Williams*, 685 F.2d 870; *NEC Corp. v. Intel Corp.*, 645 F. Supp. 590, 1 U.S.P.Q.2d 1492 (N.D. Cal. 1986); *GCA v. Chance*, 217 U.S.P.Q. 718; *Tandy*, 524 F.Supp. 171; *Data Cash*, 480 F.Supp. 1063.

64. See, e.g., *Sega Enterprises Ltd. v. Accolade Inc.*, 977 F.2d 1510 (9th Cir. 1993); *Atari Games Corp. v. Nintendo of America Inc.*, 975 F.2d 832 (Fed. Cir. 1992); *Computer Associates, Int'l. Inc. v. Altai Inc.*, 23 U.S.P.Q.2d 1241 (2d Cir. 1992); *Johnson Controls v. Phoenix Control Sys. Inc.*, 886 F.2d 1173 (9th Cir. 1989).

65. *Stenograph L.L.C. v. Bossard Assocs. Inc.*, 144 F.3d 96, 100, 46 U.S.P.Q.2d 1936 (D.C. Cir. 1998). See also *Triad Systems Corp. v. Southeastern Express Co.*, 64 F.3d 1330, 1335, 36 U.S.P.Q.2d 1028 (9th Cir. 1995) (where defendant's conduct "involved copying entire programs, there is no doubt that protected elements of the software were copied").

66. See, e.g., *Closed Development Corp. v. Paperback Software Int'l.*, 740 F. Supp. 37 (D. Mass. 1990).

67. *MiTek Holdings Inc. v. Arce Eng'g. Co.*, 89 F.3d 1548, 39 U.S.P.Q.2d 1609, 1617 (11th Cir. 1996); *Digital Communications Assocs. Inc. v. Softklone Distrib. Corp.*, 659 F. Supp. 449, 463, 2 U.S.P.Q.2d 1385 (N.D. Ga. 1987).

68. *Digital Communications Assoc. v. Softklone Distrib. Corp.*, 659 F. Supp. 449 (N.D. Ga. 1987).

69. 17 U.S.C. § 102(b).

70. *Eckes v. Card Prices Update*, 736 F.2d 859, 222 U.S.P.Q. 762 (2d Cir. 1984); *Atari Inc. v. North Am. Philips Consumer Elec. Corp.*, 672 F.2d 607, 214

U.S.P.Q. 33 (7th Cir. 1982); *Atari Inc. v. Williams*, 217 U.S.P.Q. 746 (E.D. Cal. 1981).

71. *GCA Corp. v. Chance,* 217 U.S.P.Q. 718 (N.D. Cal. 1982); *Synercom Technologies Inc. v. University Computing Co.,* 462 F. Supp. 1003, 1013, 199 U.S.P.Q. 537 (N.D. Tex 1978).

72. *Johnson Controls Inc. v. Phoenix Control Sys. Inc.,* 886 F.2d 1173 (9th Cir. 1989); *Whelan Associates Inc. v. Jaslow Dental Laboratory Inc.,* 797 F.2d 122 (3d Cir. 1986); cert. denied, 479 U.S. 1031 (1987); *Broderbund Software Inc. v. Unison World Inc.,* 687 F. Supp. 1127 (N.D. Cal. 1986); *SAS Institute Inc. v. S&H Computer Systems Inc.,* 605 F. Supp. 816 (M.D. Tenn. 1985).

73. *Computer Management Assistance Co. v. Robert F. DeCastro Inc.,* 55 U.S.P.Q.2d 1643 (5th Cir. 2000); *Softel v. Dragon Med. & Scientific Communications,* 118 F.3d 955, 969, 43 U.S.P.Q.2d 1385 (2d Cir. 1997); *MiTek Holdings Inc. v. Arce Eng'g. Co.,* 89 F.3d 1548, 39 U.S.P.Q.2d 1609 (11th Cir. 1996); *Bateman v. Mnemonics Inc.,* 79 F.3d 1532, 38 U.S.P.Q.2d 1225 (11th Cir. 1996); *Lotus Develop. Corp. v. Borland Int'l.,* 49 F.3d 807, 815 34 U.S.P.Q.2d 1014 (1st Cir. 1995); *Gates Rubber Co. v. Bando Chemical Indus. Ltd.,* 9 F.3d 823, 28 U.S.P.Q.2d 1503 (10th Cir. 1993); *Computer Associates Int'l. Inc. v. Altai Inc.,* 982 F.2d 693, 23 U.S.P.Q.2d 1241 (2d Cir. 1992); *Atari Games Corp. v. Nintendo of America Inc.,* 975 F.2d 832 (Fed. Cir. 1992); *Brown Bag Software v. Symantec Inc.,* 22 U.S.P.Q.2d 1429 (9th Cir. 1992); *Johnson Controls Inc. v. Phoenix Control Sys. Inc.,* 886 F.2d 1173 (9th Cir. 1989); *Plains Cotton Coop Ass'n. v. Goodpasture Computer Service Inc.,* 807 F.2d 1256, 1 U.S.P.Q.2d 1635 (5th Cir. 1987); cert. denied, 108 S. Ct. 80 (1987); *Manufacturers Technologies Inc. v. KAMS Inc.,* 706 F. Supp. 984 (D. Conn. 1989); *Telemarketing Resources v. Symantec Corp.,* 12 U.S.P.Q. 2d 1991 (N.D. Cal. 1989); *Digital Communications Assoc. v. Softklone Distrib. Corp.,* 659 F. Supp. 499, 2 U.S.P.Q. 1385 (N.D. Ga. 1987); *Broderbund Software Inc. v. Unison World Inc.,* 64 F. Supp. 1127 (N.D. Cal. 1986); *Q-Co Industries v. Hoffman,* 625 F. Supp. 608 (S.D. N.Y. 1985).

74. *Gates Rubber Co. v. Bando Chemical Indus., Ltd.,* 9 F.3d 823, 28 U.S.P.Q.2d 1503, 1509 (10th Cir. 1993).

75. See *Manufacturer's Technologies Inc. v. Cams Inc.,* 706 F. Supp. 984, 995, 10 U.S.P.Q.2d 1321 (D. Conn. 1989).

76. *Sega Enterprises Ltd. v. Accolade Inc.,* 977 F.2d 1510, 1525–27 24 U.S.P.Q.2d 1561 (9th Cir. 1993).

77. See *Plains Cotton Co-op Ass'n. v. Goodpasture Computer Serv. Inc.,* 807 F.2d 1256, 1262, 1 U.S.P.Q.2d 1635 (5th Cir.), cert. denied, 484 U.S. 821 (1987).

78. See *Apple Computer Inc. v. Microsoft Corp.,* 799 F. Supp. 1006, 1033, 24 U.S.P.Q.2d 1081 (N.D. Cal. 1992), order clarified, 821 F. Supp. 616, 27 U.S.P.Q.2d 1081 (1993).

79. *Gates Rubber Co. v. Bando Chemical Indus. Ltd.,* 9 F.3d 823, 28 U.S.P.Q.2d 1503, 1512-13 (10th Cir. 1993).

80. *MiTek Holdings Inc. v. Arce Eng'g. Co.,* 89 F.3d 1548, 39 U.S.P.Q.2d 1609,

1616–17 (11th Cir. 1996). See *Apple Computer Inc. v. Microsoft Corp.,* 35 F.3d 1435, 1446, 32 U.S.P.Q.2d 1086 (9th Cir. 1994) (as to a work as a whole [i.e., a compilation], "there can be no infringement unless the works are virtually identical"), cert. denied, U.S. 115 S.Ct. 1176, 130 L.Ed.2d 1129 (1995); *Harper House Inc. v. Thomas Nelson Inc.,* 889 F.2d 197, 205 12 U.S.P.Q.2d 1779 (9th Cir. 1989) (as with factual compilations, copyright infringement of compilations consisting of largely uncopyrightable elements should not be found in the absence of "bodily appropriation of expression").

81. 17 U.S.C. § 117.

82. *Micro-Sparc Inc. v. Amtype Corp.,* 592 F. Supp. 33, 223 U.S.P.Q. 1210 (D. Mass 1984).

83. *Vault Corp. v. Quaid Software Ltd.,* 847 F.2d 255 (5th Cir. 1988).

84. *MAI Systems Corp. v. Peak Computer,* 991 F.2d. 511, 26 U.S.P.Q.2d 1458 (9th Cir. 1993).

85. *Sony Computer Entertainment Inc. v. Connectix Corp.,* 203 F.3d 596, 606, 53 U.S.P.Q.2d 1705 (9th Cir. 2000); *Sega Enterprises Ltd. v. Accolade Inc.,* 977 F.2d 1510 (9th Cir. 1993); *Atari Games Corp. v. Nintendo of America Inc.,* 975 F.2d 834 (Fed. Cir. 1992); *Lewis Galoob Toys Inc. v. Nintendo of America Inc.,* 22 U.S.P.Q.2d 1857 (9th Cir. 1992).

86. 17 U.S.C. § 401(d) (1988).

87. 37 C.F.R. § 201.20.

88. 17 U.S.C. §§ 302(a)–(b).

89. 17 U.S.C. §§ 302(c).

90. 37 C.F.R. § 202.19(d)(2)(vii).

91. 37 C.F.R. § 202.19(e).

92. 17 U.S.C. § 411.

93. 17 U.S.C. § 410.

94. 17 U.S.C. § 504.

95. 17 U.S.C. § 505.

96. 17 U.S.C. § 412.

97. 37 C.F.R. § 202.20–21.

98. See *Fonar Corp. v. Magnetic Resonance Plus Inc.,* 920 F. Supp. 508, 39 U.S.P.Q.2d 1294 (S.D.N.Y. 1996), vacated 105 F.3d 99, 41 U.S.P.Q.2d 1496 (2d Cir.), cert. denied, 118 S. Ct. 265 (1997). Although ultimately vacated, the case illustrates the potential problems that can be avoided by taking care in the selection of "identifying portions."

99. 17 U.S.C. § 501.

100. 17 U.S.C. § 106.

101. A "work of visual art" is a painting, drawing, sculpture, or still photograph which is (a) a limited edition (there is only a single copy or less than 200 copies, which are signed, and consecutively numbered), (b) not a "work for hire, and (c) not commercial art such as posters, advertising, or merchandising items, etc. 17 U.S.C. § 101.

102. 17 U.S.C. § 106A.

103. *Intellectual Reserve Inc. v. Utah Lighthouse Ministry Inc.*, 75 F. Supp. 2d 1290 (D. Utah 1999) (providing links to other sites that were known to contain infringing copies of a work and encouraging the use of the links to obtain unauthorized copies constituted contributory copyright infringement).

104. 17 U.S.C. § 512.

105. 17 U.S.C. § 512(k)(1)(B).

106. *Feist Publications v. Rural Telephone Service Co.*, 111 U.S. 1282 (1991); *Atari Games Corp. v. Nintendo of America*, 975 F.2d 832, 837 (Fed. Cir. 1992); *Brown Bag Software v. Symantec Corp.*, 960 F.2d 1465 (9th Cir. 1992); *SOS Inc. v. Payday Inc.*, 886 F.2d 1081, 1085 (9th Cir. 1989).

107. *Atari Inc. v. North Am. Philips Consumer Elec. Corp*, 672 F.2d 607 (7th Cir. 1982), cert. denied, 103 S.Ct. 176 (1982).

108. 28 U.S.C. § 1338.

109. 17 U.S.C. § 411.

110. 28 U.S.C. §§ 1391(c), 1400, 1694.

111. 17 U.S.C. § 504.

112. 17 U.S.C. § 502.

113. 17 U.S.C. §§ 503, 509.

114. 17 U.S.C. § 505.

115. 17 U.S.C. § 505.

116. 17 U.S.C. § 504.

117. 17 U.S.C. § 412.

118. See 17 U.S.C. §101.

119. 17 U.S.C. §§ 101, 201(b).

120. U.S.C. § 101.

121. See, e.g., *Community for Creative Nonviolence v. Reid*, 490 U.S. 730 (1989).

122. See *Community for Creative Nonviolence v. Reid*, 490 U.S. at 51–752; *MacLean Assoc. Inc. v. Mercer-Meidinger Hanson Inc.*, 21 U.S.P.Q.2d 1345 (3d Cir. 1991).

123. 17 U.S.C. § 203.

124. See *Weissman v. Freeman*, 684 F. Supp. 1248, 1259–60 (S.D. N.Y. 1988); *Crosney v. Edward Small Productions Inc.*, 52 F. Supp. 559 (S.D. N.Y. 1942); *Jerry Vogel Music Co. Inc. v. Miller Music Inc.*, 74 N.Y.S.2d 425 (N.Y. App. Div. 1947); aff'd, 299 N.Y. 782, 82 U.S.P.Q. 458 (1949).

125. 17 U.S.C. § 204.

126. 17 U.S.C. §205(d).

127. 17 U.S.C. §203.

128. *Burroughs v. Metro-Goldwyn-Mayer Inc.*, 683 F.2d 610, 621, 215 U.S.P.Q. 495, 504 (2d Cir. 1982).

129. 17 U.S.C. § 203(b)(1).

TRADEMARK PROTECTION

1. 15 U.S.C. § 1127 (definition of "use in commerce").
2. 15 U.S.C. § 1057(c).
3. 15 U.S.C. § 1051(b) (1988).
4. 15 U.S.C. § 1051(d) (1988).
5. 15 U.S.C. § 1126 (1988).
6. Lanham Act, 15 U.S.C. § 1051 et seq.
7. 15 U.S.C. § 1125(c).
8. 15 U.S.C. § 1127.
9. 15 U.S.C. § 1125(c)(4).
10. *Panavision Int'l. L.P. v. Toeppen,* 141 F.3d 1316, 46 U.S.P.Q.2d 1511, 1520 (9th Cir. 1998); *Eli Lilly & Co. v. Natural Answers Inc.*, 56 U.S.P.Q.2d 1942, 1949 (7th Cir. 2000).
11. 15 U.S.C. § 1125(c)(1).
12. *Panavision Int'l. L.P. v. Toeppen,* 141 F.3d 1316, 46 U.S.P.Q.2d 1511, 1518 (9th Cir. 1998); *I.P. Lund Trading ApS v. Kohler Co.,* 163 F.3d 27, 49 U.S.P.Q.2d 1225 (1st Cir. 1998).
13. *I.P. Lund Trading ApS v. Kohler Co.,* 163 F.3d 27, 49 U.S.P.Q.2d 1225, 1240 (1st Cir. 1998).
14. *Hasbro Inc. v. Clue Computing Inc.*, 66 F. Supp.2d 117, 119, 52 U.S.P.Q.2d 1402 (D. Mass. 1999), affirmed 56 U.S.P.Q.2d 1766 (1st Cir. 2000).
15. *I.P. Lund Trading ApS v. Kohler Co.,* 163 F.3d 27, 49 U.S.P.Q.2d 1225, 1239 (1st Cir. 1998); *Hasbro Inc. v. Clue Computing Inc.*, 66 F. Supp.2d 117, 119, 52 U.S.P.Q.2d 1402, 1412–13 (D. Mass. 1999), affirmed 56 U.S.P.Q.2d 1766 (1st Cir 2000).
16. *Westchester Media v. PRL USA Holdings Inc.,* 214 F.3d 658, 671, 55 U.S.P.Q.2d 1225 (requiring proof of actual harm), and *Ringling Bros. Barnum & Bailey Combined Shows, Inc. v. Utah Div. of Travel Dev.*, 170 F.3d 449, 461, 50 U.S.P.Q.2d 1065 (4th Cir.) (same), cert. denied, 120 S. Ct. 286 (1999).
17. *Eli Lilly & Co. v. Natural Answers Inc.*, 56 U.S.P.Q.2d 1942 (7th Cir. 2000), *Nabisco Inc. v. PF Brands Inc.,* 191 F.3d 208, 224–25, 51 U.S.P.Q.2d 1882 (2d Cir. 1999) (likelihood of dilution sufficient). See also *Times Mirror Magazines Inc. v. Las Vegas Sports News L.L.C.*, 212 F.3d 157, 179 n.11, 54 U.S.P.Q.2d 1577 (3d Cir. 2000) (dissenting judge agreeing with majority's implicit holding "that the District Court did not err in finding that irreparable injury may be shown even in the absence of actual economic harm").
18. See, e.g., A.R.S. § 44–1448.01.
19. A person shall be liable in a civil action by the owner of a mark, including a personal name which is protected as a mark under this section, if, without regard to the goods or services of the parties, that person—
    (i) has a bad faith intent to profit from that mark, including a personal name which is protected as a mark under this section; and

     (ii) registers, traffics in, or uses a domain name that—

          (I) in the case of a mark that is distinctive at the time of registration of the domain name, is identical or confusingly similar to that mark;

          (II) in the case of a famous mark that is famous at the time of registration of the domain name, is identical or confusingly similar to or dilutive of that mark; . . . (15 U.S.C. § 1125[d][1]).

20. 15 U.S.C. § 1114(v).
21. 15 U.S.C. § 1125(d)(2).
22. 15 U.S.C. § 1072.
23. 15 U.S.C. § 1057(a), (b).
24. 15 U.S.C. § 1065.
25. 15 U.S.C. § 1115(b).
26. 15 U.S.C. §§ 1124, 1125(b), 19 C.F.R. § 133.
27. 15 U.S.C. § 1052.
28. 15 U.S.C. § 1091.
29. 15 U.S.C. § 1072.
30. 15 U.S.C. § 1057(a), (b).
31. 15 U.S.C. § 1096.
32. 15 U.S.C. § 1095.
33. 15 U.S.C. § 1052.
34. 15 U.S.C. § 1052.
35. 15 U.S.C. § 1062(a).
36. 15 U.S.C. § 1063.
37. 15 U.S.C. § 1051(b), (c), (d).
38. 15 U.S.C. § 1057(c).
39. 15 U.S.C. § 1063; 37 C.F.R. §§ 2.101–2.106, 2.116–2.135.
40. 15 U.S.C. § 1064; 37 C.F.R. §§ 2.111–2.115, 2.116–2.135.
41. 15 U.S.C. § 1064.
42. 15 U.S.C. § 1111.
43. 15 U.S.C. § 1058(a).
44. 15 U.S.C. § 1065.
45. A.R.S. § 44–1441 et seq. (Title 44, chapter 10, article 3—Registration and Protection of Trademarks), and specifically A.R.S. § 44–1451(A)(3), (B)(3)–(4),(6).
46. 28 U.S.C. § 1338(a), 15 U.S.C. §§ 1121, 1114(1).
47. 15 U.S.C. §§ 1121(b).
48. 15 U.S.C. §§ 1114(l), 1125(a)(1)(A).
49. 15 U.S.C. § 1125(c).
50. 15 U.S.C. § 1125(d).
51. 15 U.S.C. § 1125(a)(1)(B).
52. 28 U.S.C. §§ 1391(b).
53. 28 U.S.C. §§ 1391(c).

54. 15 U.S.C. § 1116.
55. 15 U.S.C. § 1117(a).
56. 15 U.S.C. § 1117.
57. 15 U.S.C. § 1118.
58. 15 U.S.C. § 1117(a).
59. 15 U.S.C. § 1116 (d)(1)(B); 15 U.S.C. § 1127 (definition of "counterfeit").
60. 15 U.S.C. § 1116 (d).

MASK WORK PROTECTION

1. 35 U.S.C. §§ 102, 103.
2. 17 U.S.C. § 101 et seq.
3. Semiconductor Chip Protection Act of 1984, 17 U.S.C. § 901(a)(2).
4. 17 U.S.C. § 902(b).
5. 17 U.S.C. § 908(a).
6. 17 U.S.C. § 902(a).
7. Generally, analogous laws have been enacted in, for example, Australia, Belgium, Canada, Denmark, Finland, France, Germany, Greece, Ireland, Italy, Japan, Korea, Luxembourg, Netherlands, Norway, Portugal, Spain, Sweden, and the United Kingdom.
8. 17 U.S.C. § 901(a)(6).
9. 17 U.S.C. § 913.
10. 17 U.S.C. § 914.
11. 1094 Off. Gaz. Pat. Office 30.
12. 17 U.S.C. § 906(a)(1).
13. 17 U.S.C. §§ 902(c), 906(a)(2).
14. 17 U.S.C. § 905.
15. 17 U.S.C. § 906(a).
16. 17 U.S.C. § 901(a)(7), (8).
17. 17 U.S.C. § 907(a), (d).
18. 17 U.S.C. § 907(b).
19. 17 U.S.C. § 906(b).
20. 17 U.S.C. § 909.
21. 17 U.S.C. § 904.
22. 17 U.S.C. § 908(a).
23. 17 U.S.C. § 901(a); See also *Brooktree Corp. v. Advanced Micro Devices Inc.*, 10 U.S.P.Q.2d 1374 (S.D.Cal. 1988), aff'd, 24 U.S.P.Q.2d 1401 (Fed. Cir. 1992).
24. 17 U.S.C. § 911(a), (b).
25. 17 U.S.C. § 911(f).
26. 17 U.S.C. § 911(c).
27. 17 U.S.C. § 911(e).

COMPARISON OF THE PROTECTION MECHANISMS

1. 35 U.S.C. § 122.

THE INTERNET AND YOUR INTELLECTUAL PROPERTY

1. *Mink v. AAAA Development Inc.*, 190 F.3d 333, 336 52 U.S.P.Q.2d 1218 (5th Cir. 1999). (For interactive sites, an exercise of personal jurisdiction is always appropriate, whereas for passive sites, personal jurisdiction is never appropriate. Semi-interactive sites fall somewhere in the middle of the spectrum, and the exercise of personal jurisdiction is determined by the degree of interactivity and the commercial nature of the site. Action dismissed for lack of personal jurisdiction because the site merely provided its users with nothing more than product and contact information.) *Cybersell Inc. v. Cybersell Inc.*, 130 F.3d 414, 418–419, 44 U.S.P.Q.2d 1928 (9th Cir. 1997). (When making an interactivity determination, the court must find "something more" than an advertisement or solicitation for sale of goods to indicate that the defendant purposefully [albeit electronically] directed his activity in a substantial way to the forum state.) *Amberson Holdings L.L.C. v. Westside Story Newspaper*, 56 U.S.P.Q.2d 1847 (D.C. N.J. 2000) (insufficient contacts for personal jurisdiction based on passive site [not possible to exchange information with the host computer] being hosted on Internet server within jurisdiction). See also *Panavision Int'l. L.P. v. Toeppen*, 141 F.3d 1316, 1321, 46 U.S.P.Q.2d 1511 (9th Cir. 1998); *CompuServe Inc. v. Patterson*, 89 F.3d 1257, 39 U.S.P.Q.2d 1502 (6th Cir. 1996).

2. *A&M Records Inc. v. Napster Inc.* 55 U.S.P.Q.2d 1780 (N.D. Cal. 2000).

3. *UMG Recordings Inc. v. MP3.com Inc.*, 92 F. Supp.2d 349, 351, 54 U.S.P.Q.2d 1668 (S.D. N.Y. 2000) (concluding that repackaging copyrighted recordings in MP3 format suitable for downloading "adds no 'new aesthetics, new insights and understandings' to the original" and usurps a further market that directly derives from reproduction of the plaintiffs' copyrighted works).

4. *Brookfield Communications Inc. v. West Coast Entertainment Corp.*, 174 F.3d 1036, 50 U.S.P.Q.2d 1545 (9th Cir. 1999); *Niton Corp. v. Radiation Monitoring Devices Inc.*, 27 F. Supp.2d 102, 52 U.S.P.Q.2d 1380 (D. Mass. 1998); *Oppedahl & Larson v. Advanced Concepts*, Civ. No. 97-Z-1592 (D.C. Colo. July 23, 1997); *Insituform Technologies Inc. v. National Envirotech Group, L.L.C.*, Civ. No. 97-2064 (E.D. La., final consent judgment entered Aug. 27, 1997); *Playboy Enters. Inc. v. Calvin Designer Label*, 985 F. Supp. 1220, 1221, 44 U.S.P.Q.2d 1156 (N.D. Cal. 1997) (preliminarily enjoining defendant's Web site, "www.playboyxxx.com" and repeated use of the "Playboy" trademark in defendant's metatags); *Playboy Enters. Inc. v. Asiafocus Int'l. Inc.*, No. Civ. A. 97-734-A, 1998 WL 724000, at *3, *6–*7 (E.D. Va. Apr. 10,

1998) (use of the marks in the domain name and metatags of defendant's Web site enjoined where trademarks used as the metatags such that a search for "Playboy" Web site would produce a list that included defendant's site); *New York State Society of Certified Public Accountants v. Eric Louis Assocs.,* 79 F. Supp.2d 331, 340 (S.D. N.Y. 1999), 79 F. Supp.2d at 341; *OBH Inc. v. Spotlight Magazine Inc.,* 86 F. Supp.2d 176, 190, 54 U.S.P.Q.2d 1383 (W.D. N.Y. 2000); *Bihari v. Gross,* 56 U.S.P.Q.2d 1489 (D.C. S.N.Y. 2000) (fair use as comentary); *Terri Welles vs. Playboy,* 47 U.S.P.Q.2d 1186 (S.D. Cal. 1999) (found to be fair use of mark in descriptive sense); *Bally Total Fitness Holding Corp. v. Faber,* 29 F. Supp.2d 1161, 1165, 50 U.S.P.Q.2d 1840 (C.D. Cal. 1998) (fair use as commentary).

5. *Ticketmaster Corp. v. Tickets.Com Inc.,* 54 U.S.P.Q.2d 1344, 1346 (C.D. Cal, 2000).

6. *Playboy Enterprises Inc. v. Universal Tel-A-Talk Inc.,* 48 U.S.P.Q.2d 1779 (E.D. Pa. 1998); *Ticketmaster Corp. v. Tickets.Com Inc.,* 54 U.S.P.Q.2d 1344, 1346 (C.D. Cal. 2000).

7. *Intellectual Reserve Inc. v. Utah Lighthouse Ministry Inc.,* 75 F. Supp. 2d 1290, 53 U.S.P.Q.2d 1425 (D. Utah 1999).

8. *Futuredontics Inc. v. Applied Anagramics Inc.,* 45 U.S.P.Q.2d 2005 (C.D. Cal. 1997).

9. 15 U.S.C. §§ 1114, 1125.

10. 15 U.S.C. § 1114 (2)(D)(i)–(iv).

11. 15 U.S.C. § 1125(d)(1).

12. 15 U.S.C. § 1114 (v).

13. One of the primary protocols adopted for the Internet is the "transmission control protocol/Internet protocol" (TCP/IP). In essence, the TCP/IP protocol breaks information into small packets, puts the IP address of the target computer at the front of the packet, and transmits the packet through the Internet. The packets are routed to the target computer, where they are reassembled. Since every computer in the Internet follows the rules of TCP/IP, the packets are reassembled in the same order in which they were sent.

  A number of different schemes have been adopted to identify the type of resource to be reached and/or what mechanism to use to obtain that resource. These schemes include the "hypertext transfer protocol" (HTTP), file transfer protocol (FTP), gopher protocol (gopher), Usenet news (news), and electronic mail (mailto). For example, the HTTP protocol, specifically designed for use with the World Wide Web, establishes a common scheme for identification of different types of information (e.g., text, graphics, music, movies, and other information), the way in which information is formatted, and the actions that computers should take in response to various commands.

14. There are four original NAPs: New York (operated by Sprint); Washington, D.C. (operated by MCIWorldCom); Chicago (operated by Ameritech); and San Francisco (operated by PacBell).

15. Examples include networks provided by MCIWorldCom, Sprint, SAVVIS, AGIS, and Intermedia Solutions. More complete lists of Internet backbone networks can be found at http://www.ispworld.com/isp/bb/Backbone_Profiles.htm and http://navigators.com/isp.html.

16. An extensive list of providers (searchable by country, state, or area code) can be accessed at http://thelist.iworld.com/.

17. See footnote 4.

18. 15 U.S.C. § 1125(d).

19. A person shall be liable in a civil action by the owner of a mark, including a personal name which is protected as a mark under this section, if, without regard to the goods or services of the parties, that person—

    (i) has a bad faith intent to profit from that mark, including a personal name which is protected as a mark under this section; and

    (ii) registers, traffics in, or uses a domain name that—

        (I) in the case of a mark that is distinctive at the time of registration of the domain name, is identical or confusingly similar to that mark;

        (II) in the case of a famous mark that is famous at the time of registration of the domain name, is identical or confusingly similar to or dilutive of that mark;

    ... (15 U.S.C. § 1125[d][1])

20. 15 U.S.C. § 1125(d)(1)(B).

21. See *Bihari v. Gross*, 56 U.S.P.Q.2d 1489, 1499 (S.D. N.Y. 2000).

22. *Eli Lilly & Co. v. Natural Answers Inc.*, 56 U.S.P.Q.2d 1942 (7th Cir 2000).

23. 15 U.S.C. § 1125(d)(2).

24. 15 U.S.C. § 1114(v).

25. ICANN UDRP ¶4(a).

26. Approved ADR service providers presently include: the CPR Institute for Dispute Resolution (CPR); eResolution (eRes); the National Arbitration Forum (NAF); and the World Intellectual Property Organization (WIPO). A complete list of approved ADR service providers can be found at http://www.icann.org/udrp/approved-providers.htm.

27. ICANN UDRP ¶4(b).

MAKING SURE YOU OWN WHAT YOU PAY FOR

1. See 35 U.S.C. § 262; *Willingham v. Star Cutter Co.*, 555 F.2d 1340, 1344 (6th Cir. 1977); *Lemelson v. Synergistics Res. Co.*, 669 F. Supp. 642, 645 (S.D. N.Y. 1987); *Intel Corp. v. ULSI System Technology Inc.*, 27 U.S.P.Q.2d 1136 (Fed. Cir. 1993); *Schering Corp. v. Roussel-UCLAF SA*, 41 U.S.P.Q.2d 1359 (Fed. Cir.1997); *Ethicon Inc. v. United States Surgical Corp.*, 45 U.S.P.Q.2d 1545 (Fed. Cir. 1998).

2. *Teets v. Chromalloy Gas Turbine Corp.,* 38 U.S.P.Q.2d 1695 (Fed. Cir. 1996).

3. See *United States v. Dubliler Condenser Corp.,* 289 U.S. 178 (1938); *McElmurry v. Arkansas Power & Light Co.,* 27 U.S.P.Q.2d 1129 (Fed. Cir. 1993); *Marshall v. Colgate Palmolive-Peet Co.,* 175 F.2d 215 (3d Cir. 1949); *Wellington Print Works v. Magid,* 242 F. Supp. 614 (E.D. Pa. 1965); *Simms v. Mac Truck Corp.,* 488 F. Supp. 592 (E.D. Pa. 1980).

4. For example, Minnesota, Washington, California, Utah, North Carolina, and Illinois.

5. 35 U.S.C. § 261.

6. While the federal statutes make recording with the PTO requisite, and may make a UCC filing unnecessary, it is clearly permissible. It is recommended that mortgages, collateral assignments, and other security interests be recorded both in the PTO and perfected under the UCC.

7. See 17 U.S.C. § 101.

8. 17 U.S.C. §§ 101, 201(b).

9. U.S.C. § 101.

10. See, e.g., *Community for Creative Nonviolence v. Reid,* 490 U.S. 730 (1989).

11. See *Community for Creative Nonviolence v. Reid,* 490 U.S. at 51–752; *MacLean Assoc. Inc. v. Mercer-Meidinger Hanson Inc.,* 21 U.S.P.Q.2d 1345 (3d Cir. 1991).

12. 17 U.S.C. § 203.

13. See *Weissman v. Freeman,* 684 F. Supp. 1248, 1259–60 (S.D. N.Y. 1988); *Crosney v. Edward Small Productions Inc.,* 52 F. Supp 559 (S.D. N.Y. 1942); *Jerry Vogel Music Co. Inc. v. Miller Music Inc.,* 74 N.Y.S.2d 425 (N.Y. App. Div. 1947); aff'd, 299 N.Y. 782, 82 U.S.P.Q. 458 (1949).

14. 17 U.S.C. § 204.

15. 17 U.S.C. § 205(d).

16. 17 U.S.C. § 203.

17. 17 U.S.C. § 203(b)(1).

18. *Sengoku Works Ltd. v. RMC International Ltd.,* 96 F.3d 1217, 40 U.S.P.Q.2d 1149 (9th Cir. 1996), cert. denied, 117 S.Ct. 2478 (1997); *Omega Nutrition v. Spectrum Marketing,* 756 F. Supp. 435, 18 U.S.P.Q.2d 1373 (N.D. Cal. 1991); *Aveda Corp. v. Evita Marketing Inc.,* 706 F. Supp. 1419, 12 U.S.P.Q.2d 1091 (D. Minn. 1989).

19. 15 U.S.C. §§ 1057(b), 1115(a).

20. *Sengoku,* 40 U.S.P.Q.2d at 1151; *Premier Dental Products v. Darby Dental Supply Co.,* 794 F.2d 850, 854, 230 U.S.P.Q. 233 (3d Cir.), cert. denied, 479 U.S. 950 (1986).

21. *Sengoku,* 40 U.S.P.Q.2d at 1151–52; *Energy Jet, Inc. v. Forex Corp.,* 589 F. Supp. 1110, 1116, 223 U.S.P.Q. 643 (E.D. Mich. 1984); *Wrist-Rocket Mfr. Co. v. Saunders,* 379 F. Supp. 902, 909, 183 U.S.P.Q. 17 (D. Neb. 1974), affirmed in part and revised in part on other grounds, 516 F.2d 846, 186 U.S.P.Q. 5 (8th Cir.), cert. denied, 423 U.S. 870 (1975); *Automated Productions Inc. v.*

FMB Maschinenbaugesellschaft mbH & Co., 36 U.S.P.Q.2d 1714, 1716 (N.D. Ill. 1995).

22. *Sengoku,* 40 U.S.P.Q.2d at 1152; *Omega Nutrition v. Spectrum Marketing,* 756 F. Supp. 435, 18 U.S.P.Q.2d 1373 (N.D. Cal. 1991); *Premier Dental,* 794 F.2d at 854.

23. We discussed that situation earlier in the book.

About the Author

MICHAEL A. LECHTER, esq., author of *Protecting Your #1 Asset: Creating Fortunes from Your Ideas—An Intellectual Property Handbook* in the Rich Dad's Advisors series, is counsel to the international law firm of Squire, Sanders & Dempsey, LLP, and an adjunct professor at Arizona State University. When asked what he does for a living, he typically replies, "I build forts and fight pirates." He has specialized in intellectual property law since the early 1970s. He is a patent attorney who has been admitted to practice in a number of states as well as to the patent bar. Michael is also the coordinating editor of *Successful Patents and Patenting for Engineers and Scientists*, and contributing author to the *Encyclopedia of Electrical and Electronics Engineering.* He has lectured extensively throughout the world on intellectual property law. Upon request of the House Judiciary Committee, he has submitted testimony to the Congress of the United States and has participated in various United Nations and foreign government proceedings on intellectual property law and technology transfer.

When not writing, speaking, or practicing law, Michael spends his time studying martial arts (he has black belts in tae kwon do and hop ki do) and trying to keep up with his wife, Sharon, and their three grown children. You can contact Michael Lechter at mlechter@richdad.com.

More Tools

Protecting Your #1 Asset will alert you to the pitfalls that can strip your rights or create liability. It is not, however, intended to be an exhaustive treatise on the subject of intellectual property (IP) and will not turn you into an instant attorney. An additional set of documentary IP tools to aid you in turning your ideas into assets, protecting your intellectual property, and avoiding liability to third parties is available from Michael Lechter:

- An **intellectual property self-audit checklist** to help you inventory your intellectual property and identify areas that need attention.
- A **patent disclosure form** (with instructions and examples) to help organize materials and information regarding an invention for presentation to a patent attorney in connection with the preparation of a patent application.
- A sample of a **basic confidentiality agreement** used in situations where circumstances dictate disclosing your confidential information to third parties such as potential investors, suppliers, or customers.
- A sample of a **basic mutual confidentiality agreement** used in situations where there is an exchange of proprietary information.
- A sample of a **basic employee agreement** relating to confidentiality and ownership of intellectual property.
- A sample of a **basic alpha/beta testing agreement** used to prevent inadvertent triggering of statutory bar time periods that would preclude obtaining a patent on an invention.

A sample **intellectual property policy statement** (for a large multinational corporation).

While, like this book, these additional tools will not take the place of advice from good intellectual property counsel, they can be of great assistance to you with respect to your intellectual property. For further information about these and other tools, visit Michael Lechter's Web site at MLechter.com.

CASHFLOW® TECHNOLOGIES, INC.

CASHFLOW® Technologies, Inc., and richdad.com, the collaborative efforts of Robert and Kim Kiyosaki and Sharon Lechter, produce innovative financial education products.

The Company's mission statement is
"To elevate the financial well-being of humanity."

CASHFLOW® Technologies, Inc., presents Robert's teaching through books: *Rich Dad Poor Dad™, Rich Dad's CASHFLOW® Quadrant™, Rich Dad's Guide to Investing™,* and *Rich Kid Smart Kid™*; board games *CASHFLOW® 101, CASHFLOW® 202,* and *CASHFLOW for Kids®*; and tape sets. Additional products are available and under development for people searching for financial education to guide them on their path to financial freedom. For updated information, see richdad.com or contact info@richdad.com.

Rich Dad's
ADVISORS™

Rich Dad's Advisors is a collection of books and educational products reflecting the expertise of the professional advisors that *CASHFLOW®* Technologies, Inc., and its principals, Robert and Kim Kiyosaki and Sharon Lechter, use to build their financial freedom. Each advisor is a specialist in their respective areas of the B-I Triangle, the business foundation taught by *CASHFLOW®* Technologies, Inc.

Robert Kiyosaki's Edumercial
An Educational Commercial

The Three Incomes

In the world of accounting, there are three different types of income: earned, passive, and portfolio. When my real dad said to me, "Go to school, get good grades, and find a safe secure job," he was recommending I work for earned income. When my rich dad said, "The rich don't work for money, they have their money work for them," he was talking about passive income and portfolio income. Passive income, in most cases, is derived from real estate investments. Portfolio income is income derived from paper assets such as stocks, bonds, and mutual funds.

Rich dad used to say, "The key to becoming wealthy is the ability to convert earned income into passive income and/or portfolio income as quickly as possible." He would say, "The taxes are highest on earned income. The least taxed income is passive income. That is another reason why you want your money working hard for you. The government taxes the income you work hard for more than the income your money works hard for."

The Key to Financial Freedom

The key to financial freedom and great wealth is a person's ability or skill to convert earned income into passive income and/or portfolio income. That is the skill that my rich dad spent a lot of time teaching Mike and me. Having that skill is the reason my wife, Kim, and I are financially free, never needing to work again. We continue to work because we choose to. Today we own a real estate investment company for passive income and participate in private placements and initial public offerings of stock for portfolio income.

Investing to become rich requires a different set of personal skills, skills essential for financial success as well as low-risk and high-investment returns. In other words, the knowledge to create assets that buy other assets. The problem is that gaining the basic education and experience required is often time consuming, frightening, and expensive, especially when you make mistakes with your own money. That is why I created my patented educational board games, trademarked as CASHFLOW.

Three Different Games
CASHFLOW, Investing 101®:

CASHFLOW® 101 teaches you the basics of fundamental investing, but it also does much more. *CASHFLOW® 101* teaches you how to take control of your personal finances, build a business through proper cash flow management, and learn how to invest with greater confidence in real estate and other businesses.

This educational product is for you if you want to improve your business and investing skills by learning how to take your ideas and turn them into assets such as your own business. Many small businesses fail because the owner lacks capital, real-life experience, and basic accounting skills. Many people think investing is risky simply because they cannot read financial statements. *CASHFLOW® 101* teaches the fundamental skills of financial literacy and investing. This educational product includes the board game, a video, and audiotapes. It takes approximately two complete times playing the game to understand it. Then we recommend that you play the game at least six times to begin to master the fundamentals of cash flow management and investing. **Price $195 U.S.**

CASHFLOW, Investing 202®:

CASHFLOW® 202 teaches you the advanced skills of technical investing. After you are comfortable with the fundamentals of *CASHFLOW® 101*, the next educational challenge is learning how to manage the ups and downs of the market, often called volatility. *CASHFLOW® 202* uses the same board game as *101*, but it comes with a completely different set of cards and score sheets and more advanced audiotapes. *CASHFLOW® 202* teaches you to use the investment techniques of qualified investors—techniques such as short selling, call options, put options, and straddles—that can be very expensive to learn in the real market. Most investors are afraid of a market crash. A qualified investor uses the tools taught in *CASHFLOW® 202* to make money when the markets go up and when the markets come down.

After you have mastered *101*, *CASHFLOW® 202* becomes very exciting because you learn to react to the highs and lows of the market, and you make a lot of paper money. Again, it is a lot less expensive to learn these advanced trading techniques on a board game using paper money than trading in the market with real money. While these games cannot guarantee your investment success, they will improve your financial vocabulary and knowledge of these advanced investing techniques.

Price $95 U.S.

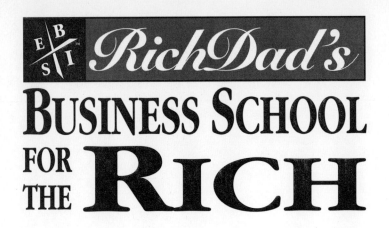

Please visit our Web site,
www.richdad.com
to review:

- Additional Information About Our Financial Education Products
- Frequently Asked Questions (FAQs) About Our Products
- Seminars, Events, and Appearances with Robert Kiyosaki

Thank You,